SUMMA PUBLICATIONS, INC.

Thomas M. Hines
Publisher

William C. Carter
Editor in chief

Editorial Board

William Berg
University of Wisconsin

Germaine Brée
Wake Forest University

Michael Cartwright
McGill University

Hugh M. Davidson
University of Virginia

Elyane Dezon-Jones
Washington University

John D. Erickson
University of Kentucky

James Hamilton
University of Cincinnati

Freeman G. Henry
University of South Carolina

Norris J. Lacy
Pennsylvania State University

Jerry C. Nash
University of North Texas

Allan Pasco
University of Kansas

Albert Sonnenfeld
University of Southern California

Orders:
P.O. Box 660725
Birmingham, AL 35266-0725

Editorial Address:
306 Morningside Circle
Birmingham, AL 35213

of Self**

Colette and the Conquest of Self

Laurel Cummins

SUMMA PUBLICATIONS, INC.
Birmingham, Alabama
2005

Copyright 2005
Summa Publications, Inc.
ISBN 1-88479-46-0

Library of Congress Control Number 2004113408

Printed in the United States of America

All rights reserved.

To the memory of my parents,
Kathleen Jeannero and Robert Adair Cummins

Contents

Note on Translations	ix
Acknowledgments	xi
List of Abbreviations	xiii
Introduction:	1
1 Reading: Domination, Resistance, Autonomy	23
2 Writing as Other	51
3 Writing through the Mother	75
4 Love and Self: *Chéri*	121
5 Androgynous Selfhood as Resistance	147
Conclusion	179
Notes	181
Works Cited	205
Index	213

Note on Translations

In translating Colette's works, I have relied for the most part on published translations. I have on occasion modified these translations in order to stay closer to the original text, and in these cases I indicate this in the citation. In some instances, where it was simpler, I provided my own translation, and this is also indicated in the citations. For longer passages from Colette, I have also retained the French original. As regards secondary sources, when a published translation of the work exists, I have used that, and the translator is indicated in the full reference in the bibliography at the end of this study. In the case of secondary sources for which no published translation exists, all translations are my own.

Acknowledgments

An earlier version of chapter 1 appeared in *Studies in Twentieth Century Literature* vol. 20, no. 2 (summer 1996): 451-65.

I would also like to make some personal acknowledgments. Many people have helped bring this project to completion, and it is a pleasure to thank them here.

Virginia Pichietti, Ronald Dunbar, N. Ann Rider, Rosetta Haynes, Sheila Cummins, Brigitte Hamon-Porter, and Dave Astor, for critiquing parts of the manuscript, and helping to shape its final form.

Laura Salsini, for her readings, criticism, encouragement, and support over the years.

The Department of Languages, Literatures and Linguistics at Indiana State University for funding granted in the summer of 2001 in aid of my research, and Ronald Dunbar particularly for all his support.

Gilbert Chaitin and Rosemary Lloyd, for their guidance and helpful suggestions.

My especial thanks go to Margaret Gray, for her guidance, and for her warm, enthusiastic, and unfailing encouragement and support over the last fifteen years.

The students in my Colette seminars at Victoria University of Wellington, for their enthusiasm and dedication, and for experiences that taught me so much.

Thanks also to Arvana Edwards and Oriana Kopec, for their invaluable practical help.

My gratitude is extended to Lynn Carter, my editor, and Summa publisher Thomas Hines for their help.

Thanks go as well to Diana, Elizabeth, Angelo, Nan, and others, for their friendship.

Finally, I give my love and thanks to my family, for their help and support, and to Dave, for his love, encouragement and faith in me.

—L. C.

List of Abbreviations

I have chosen to cite works by Colette parenthetically in the text, as these references are numerous. Following is a list of the abbreviations used to identify works by Colette in English. See the bibliography at the end of this study for the complete reference for each of these texts.

C at S:	*Claudine at School*
CM:	*Claudine Married*
RL:	*Retreat from Love*
Vagabond:	*The Vagabond*
Chéri:	*Chéri*
MMH:	*My Mother's House*
L of Ch:	*The Last of Chéri*
BD:	*Break of Day*
Other:	*The Other One*
Sido:	*Sido*
PI:	*The Pure and the Impure*
Cat:	*The Cat*
MA:	*My Apprenticeships*

Introduction

> *Occasionally, in my extreme youth, I found myself sighing to "be somebody." If I had had the courage to express my wish fully, I should have said "somebody else." But I soon gave it up. I have never succeeded in becoming somebody else.*
> —Colette, *My Apprenticeships*

> *. . . a woman who was called upon more than once to rise from her ashes . . .*
> —Colette, *My Apprenticeships*

Dualities, dichotomies, paradoxes. Colette's formulation of selfhood as inscribed in *My Apprenticeships* is one—she both affirms the narrator's presence in the world as unique, yet characterizes it through the phoenix image as everchanging. In looking closely at Colette's writing and at what has been written about her, we encounter such paradoxes, it seems, at every turn. Both "free and fettered," in Michèle Sarde's formulation, long held in esteem by the literary establishment yet at the same time consistently trivialized, a feminist to some and the antithesis of one to others, Colette has given rise to perhaps more double talk than any other literary figure of comparable stature. In the chapters that follow, it is my project to explore the untamable nature of Colette's writing, which has so often led to dualistic reactions to her work. It is also my project to trace dualities and paradoxes in Colette's work itself—their development and their undoing—, in pursuit of what has been for me the object of an endlessly fascinating quest—the inscription of a female 'I'; or the construction, deconstruction, and reconstruction of "self" in Colette.

To this purpose, I will examine several facets of Colette's work. The semiautobiographical works reveal the narrator's coming to selfhood, although they do not actually trace the factual history of Colette's life, and these works will be of primary concern. The theme of accession to selfhood in Colette's strictly fictional works, from the beginning of her career to her maturity, adds another dimension to our understanding of this question, and so I will also examine some of Colette's key novels. In fact, the "conquest of self"—I borrow the phrase from Elaine Marks[1]—is both a literary theme in Colette's work, both fictional and semiautobiographical, and also the end result, for the narrator, of the writing project itself. The conquest of self is crucial to understanding Colette's work and is the central focus of the study I undertake here. In order to gain a clearer understanding of this question, let us take a moment to define the terms "selfhood" and "self."

Webster's Third New International Dictionary gives two main definitions of selfhood: "the state of possessing an individual identity or the individuality so possessed," and "one's own character or personality." Thus on an initial level, "selfhood" and hence "self" can be understood as having to do with personal identity, and linked with such general psychological notions as maturity, individuality, and independence. I will at times use these terms in this general sense. However, a more profound and specific meaning of the term "self" will also come into play in my arguments, and it is this meaning that I outline here.

Charles Taylor, in his work *Sources of the Self: The Making of the Modern Identity,* has traced the many strands in the history of thought that make up the "modern notion of what it is to be a human agent, a person, or a self."[2] The strands that make up this notion are numerous, often contradictory, and at the same time coexistent. One of the most salient features of this notion, and one particularly important for understanding Colette, is that of moral autonomy.

Taylor notes that the notion of selfhood is inextricably linked with the question of the good, thus of morality. He therefore begins with a central concern of what he terms the first axis of moral thought, that involving our obligations to others. This central concern is that of respect for the human being, and he asserts that this is a "moral universal" across time and place. However, what is peculiar to the modern West, his argument continues, is that this moral universal has come to be defined in terms of rights (11). This is not without consequences for the notion of the self, as he points out.

> To talk of universal, natural, or human rights is to connect respect for human life and integrity with the notion of autonomy. It is to conceive people as active cooperators in establishing and ensuring the respect which is due them. (12)

So, he summarizes, in the modern Western conception of selfhood, "autonomy has a central place in our understanding of respect" (12). This central feature is complemented by another, which is linked but is not identical—the notion that the source of our moral direction is properly within.

In this area, Taylor traces the tremendously important influence of Rousseau. In opposition to a "naturalist" Enlightenment, Rousseau's thinking restores a moral dimension to human existence. And this takes place within the conflict he establishes between nature and culture. Taylor quotes the following words from Rousseau's *Emile:* "Let us lay it down as an incontrovertible rule that the first impulses of nature are always right; there is no original sin in the human heart." Taylor then continues in his commentary on Rousseau:

> But there has been a Fall; perversity has come upon us. Humans have done this to themselves. [. . .] The original impulse of nature is right, but the effect of a depraved culture is that we lose contact with it. (357)

Taylor takes exception with the popular notion of Rousseau as primitivist. Rousseau does not argue for a return to a presocietal stage of human existence, he contends. "Rather," he writes,

> the recovery of contact with nature was seen more as an escape from calculating other-dependence, from the force of opinion and the ambitions it engendered, through a kind of alignment or fusion [. . .] of culture/society on one hand, and the true élan of nature on the other.

> Conscience is the voice of nature as it emerges in a being who has entered society and is endowed with language and hence reason. (359)

Despite Rousseau's obvious debt to Stoic and Christian schools of thought, notably in his view of excessive wealth and luxury as enemies of civic virtue, and in his espousal of austerity as a condition of that virtue, Taylor demonstrates that he has nonetheless transformed these developments into a "thoroughly modern position." For, as Taylor writes,

> the distinction of vice and virtue, of good and depraved will, has been aligned with the distinction between dependence on self and dependence on others. *Goodness is identified with freedom, with finding the motives for one's actions within oneself.* (361, my emphasis)

Thus from Rousseau on, selfhood involves a turning inward. The *Sturm und Drang* movement and the German and English Romantics are clearly the inheritors of Rousseau in this sense, with their notion of "an inner voice or impulse," and "that we find the truth within us, and in particular in our feelings." Taylor even characterizes these as "the crucial justifying concepts of the Romantic rebellion" (368-69). Yet with the Romantics the notion of the self also acquires new dimensions. It is here that we see developing those strands underlying our notion of selfhood that have to do with Taylor's second axis of moral thinking: that concerning how to live a full life. With this turn taken by Romanticism, we come to the last crucial aspect of the modern notion of the self, that of self-articulation. Taylor demonstrates that this is a logical development of the idea of nature as source.

> My claim is that the idea of nature as an intrinsic source goes along with an expressive view of human life. Fulfilling my nature means espousing the inner élan, the voice or impulse. And this makes what was hidden manifest for both myself and others. (375)

Taylor stresses that this act is by nature creative: "the direction of this élan wasn't and couldn't be clear prior to this manifestation" (375). It is *through* the act of expressing itself that the self is defined; "it is not just a matter of copying an external model or carrying out an already determinate formulation" (375).

In this way we see emerging one last, and crucial, component to the modern notion of selfhood. Selfhood for us is bound up in self-articulation, which is also self-discovery, and even self-creation. This is of prime importance: this expressive individualism, Taylor writes, "has become one of the cornerstones of modern culture" (376). Moreover, it is "what realizes and completes us as human beings" (377). The active nature of the subject that we saw beginning with the notion of moral autonomy and which is implicit in the idea of an "inner voice" here reaches its completion. In this view, the subject only exists fully through its own act of self-definition or self-creation.

Thus, a study of modern Western thought allows us to identify a complex notion of selfhood which is specific to a particular place and time in the world and in history. To be a person, a self, in this understanding, is to be an agent characterized by moral autonomy, to be motivated by a source that is within, and to be capable of self-articulation, and through this, self-creation. This framework will inform my reading as I trace the accession to selfhood on the part of Colette's narrator in the semiautobiographical works, and the struggle for selfhood on the part of the protagonists of the novels.

Yet having come this far, it is now necessary to stop and return to the original image suggested by Colette's writing, that of paradox. For if modernism has given shape to the notion of the self, postmodernism has given us an understanding of the constraints placed upon it and thus its limitations.

Social constructionism, in particular, has studied the ways in which structures of power, and the language that is inextricably bound up with them, mark and shape the individual. Postmodernism in general cautions against the error in thinking that we are independent of the structures in society that shape us, that we can position ourselves outside it, and decide from such a vantage point whether to be marked by it or not. Thus at first glance the postmodern view seems in conflict with the notion of the self outlined above, characterized by moral autonomy, inwardness, and the potential for self-articulation and self-realization. Yet ultimately I argue that this is not so. While the self is not and cannot exist outside society's structuring, neither is it an entirely passive product of that society. Shaped by and inevitably part of his or her social and linguistic world, the self remains nonetheless an agent, with the capacity of marking, by his or her thought and actions, that same society in which he or she has taken shape. Thus, Taylor's thesis provides a framework through which to understand the nature of the self, and poststructuralist thought allows the tracing of its emergence in society and language.[3]

Specifically, I trace the inscription of self in Colette through the prism of the notions of gender—the cultural institutions of masculinity and femininity[4]—the discourse that creates and regulates it, and the resistance by which it may also be transformed. And these words bring up what seem to be more paradoxes. Discourse, gender, and resistance—in Colette? Perhaps more than any other well-known French woman writer of her day, Colette has persistently been viewed as apolitical, and, specifically, as nonfeminist. To a very large extent, her early reputation as an "instinctive" writer has persisted up to this day. Viewed as a consummate stylist and portrayer of love, nature and sensual experience, but both nonthinking and nonmoral and without ideas on the important social or political questions of her time, Colette has had the curious reputation of being both a great writer, and at the same time, somehow inferior.[5]

The sexism inherent in such a view is clearer to us as we enter the twenty-first century than it was in earlier decades. Another oft-repeated cliché about Colette—the supposedly inevitably biographical nature of her work—aptly illustrates this sexism yet again. Colette did indeed produce a considerable number of works drawing heavily on biographical material and featuring a narrator bearing her own name, and in this she bears an affinity with her contemporary, Marcel Proust. However, as Donna Norell points out, while Proust's "critics and admirers nevertheless succeeded in comprehending that his work was more than a thinly veiled autobiography, in Colette's case . . . there developed in the minds of her readers the habit of identifying the author with her characters and of viewing her books as little more than a series of confessions."[6]

However, from the beginning of Colette's career, a persistent minority has looked beyond these generally held views,[7] and by 1979 Bernard Bray was able to express satisfaction at the appearance of new directions in Colette criticism that increasingly examined not the author's life but her work.[8] This trend has continued. Appreciations of the richness of Colette's language have given way to studies on the complexity and constructed nature of her text. In particular, feminist criticism has begun to recover, from the mystifying characterizations of Colette as the highest embodiment of "feminine literature"[9]—the essence of unanalyzable 'woman,' a skillfully crafted feminine *auctoritas*.[10]

However, while recent work has traced this feminine "I" through the analytical perspectives of both feminist and psychoanalytic thought, little attention has been paid to the inscription of self in Colette in direct confrontation with discourses of power. Yet, as Colette's phoenix image of death and rebirth suggests, the inscription of selfhood in her work was won at the cost of long and at times painful struggle. Indeed an examination of discourse, gender, and resistance is particularly à-propos in Colette, for the life story we read in her semiautobiographical works is a concrete and highly visible metaphor for what remains less discernable, but no less pertinent, elsewhere—the woman writer's entry into language by way of an apprenticeship in masculine discourse.

It is the itinerary of this apprenticeship, and especially the subversion of its goal through the articulation of a feminine presence, which I map in the chapters that follow. While I make reference to a broad range of Colette's works in these essays, the particular objects of this study are Colette's early novels, especially the *Claudine* series (1900-03), her most important mature fictional work, *Chéri* (1920), and her major semiautobiographical works, especially *My Mother's House* (1922), *Break of Day* (1928), *Sido* (1930), *The Pure and the Impure* (1932), and *My Apprenticeships* (1936). I take care to say "*semi*-autobiographical," and we are back at one of the main and long-standing sources of confusion and debate in the reception of Colette's work. Before continuing, I will clarify my understanding of this term, as well as define how this study undertakes an examination of this particular subcorpus of Colette's work.

Philippe Lejeune's study of autobiography provides a starting point for discussion here. Paul John Eakin writes thus of Lejeune's conclusions in the latter's early study, *L'Autobiographie en France* (1971):

> Acknowledging autobiography to be a complex and unstable category, historically speaking, and eschewing any pretense to an essentialist or idealist objective, Lejeune proposed the following working definition of the genre: 'we shall define autobiography as the retrospective prose

narrative that someone writes concerning his own existence, where the focus is his individual life, in particular the story of his personality.'[11]

While aspects of this definition seem relevant to Colette's writings, the incompatibility of her work with Lejeune's framework becomes clear as we continue to explore the latter. In fact, as is well-known among Colette critics, in the same early work quoted by Eakin above, Lejeune specifically excluded Colette from the French autobiographical canon. This because, as he rightly concludes, her work does not enter into the contractual relationship with the reader, which Lejeune calls the autobiographical pact, and which completes his definition of autobiography at this stage of his thought. The autobiographical pact 'concluded' between writer and reader, and which allows autobiography to be read as such, is based on an assumption of authorial sincerity. As Lejeune states, it translates not so much, on the part of the author, as " 'I, the undersigned,' " but as " 'I swear to tell the truth, the whole truth, and nothing but the truth.' "[12] And this is where Colette's work becomes incompatible with Lejeune's definition, for her works combine autobiography and fiction in any number of ways.[13]

Hence the multitude of vantage points from which Colette's work has been studied, for her semiautobiographical writings have been considered everything from traditional autobiography[14] to genuine novels.[15] Moreover, while these works have been characterized alternately as either fiction or autobiography, they have also inspired numerous attempts to unmask them as false examples of one or the other, usually autobiography, and this in spite of the author's own repeated warnings that she is not to be found in her books.[16] A recent example of this tendency is the work of Herbert Lottman, who points to the many ways in which Colette's real, lived childhood is at variance with the one evoked in her books. Yet these unmasking gestures remain as full of contradictions as the works they analyze, as Dana Strand demonstrates in her comments on Lottman's work.

> [C]alling into question the accuracy of Colette's memory, Lottman casts doubt upon the veracity of her autobiographical writings. Nevertheless, throughout his lengthy book, he continually draws upon a vari-

ety of Colette's works, quoting them without hesitation as reliable biographical sources.[17]

The same could be said about Judith Thurman's recent biography, *Secrets of the Flesh*. My point in analyzing these different gestures is not to argue for or against a particular view of what Colette's childhood or life was really like, but rather to clarify the nature of her work. Her semiautobiographical works are difficult to pin down as either autobiography or fiction, for they are rooted in historically accurate names, places, and events, yet they continually invent.[18] In order to gain an understanding of this refusal of generic purity, as well as to appreciate its importance for her writing, let us examine a well-known example, the pink cactus letter from *Break of Day*.

This work opens with a letter to 'Colette's' second husband, Henry de Jouvenel, from the mother character, 'Sido.' In this letter, 'Sido' refuses an invitation to visit her daughter because her pink cactus may flower—a rare event occurring only once every four years—and because 'Sido,' at age seventy-six, may not live to see it flower again. However, as is well-known among critics, the crucial letter that opens the work was in fact rewritten. A similar letter does exist, but in that letter the plant mentioned is not a rare tropical plant that flowers only occasionally, but a "sédum," a wild plant found commonly in the south of France. Moreover, in real life Sido accepts, rather than refuses, the invitation to Paris. What is significant here is the importance of these changes for the passage that follows, and for an overall understanding of Colette's writing. As Lastinger points out in her excellent article on this work, it is not a question of simple embellishments to the letter. Rather, as Lastinger states, these details move the narrator to a statement "which gives the fullest importance to the textual 'Sido,' "[19] a statement in which *the narrator's very identity is shaped:*

> Whenever I feel myself inferior to everything about me [. . .] I can still hold up my head and say to myself: "I am the daughter of the woman who wrote that letter—that letter and so many more that I have kept. This one tells me in ten lines that at the age of seventy-six she was planning journeys and undertaking them, but that waiting for the possible bursting into bloom of a tropical flower held everything up and

silenced even her heart, made for love. [. . .] Let me not forget that I am the daughter of a woman who bent her head, trembling, between the blades of a cactus, her wrinkled face full of ecstasy over the promise of a flower, a woman who herself never ceased to flower, unceasingly, during three quarters of a century." (BD, 5-6)

[Au cours des heures où je me sens inférieure à tout ce qui m'entoure, { . . . } je puis pourtant me redresser et me dire: "Je suis la fille de celle qui m'écrivit cette lettre—cette lettre et tant d'autres, que j'ai gardées. Celle-ci, en dix lignes, m'enseigne qu'à soixante-seize ans elle projetait et entreprenait des voyages, mais que l'éclosion possible, l'attente d'une fleur tropicale suspendait tout et faisait silence même dans son cœur destiné à l'amour. { . . . } Puissé-je n'oublier jamais que je suis la fille d'une telle femme qui penchait, tremblante, toutes ses rides éblouies entre les sabres d'un cactus sur une promesse de fleur, une telle femme qui ne cessa elle-même d'éclore, pendant trois quarts de siècle..." (3: 277-78)]

It is precisely the *fictional* details of the letter that are crucial to the construction of the mother-figure, in relation to whom the daughter then constructs her own identity. The mother and daughter figures are constructions; the story Colette chooses to tell through these characters, whatever they do indeed owe to real memories, is essentially fictional.[20]

In the end, the best description of these texts is Jerry A. Flieger's, who speaks of "fictional autobiography, tales in the first person where 'Colette' herself is identified as the narrator."[21] She goes on to say that in Colette's case this "might be considered a kind of 'autofiction,' the result of a creative act that crafts a textual or narrative persona but that finally reveals few facts about the biographical person" (10). Flieger's definition allows the critic to avoid the pitfalls that have historically claimed many readers of these texts. One has been to exclude them from serious study on the basis of their incompatibility with accepted definitions of autobiography,[22] and another, that of treating them *as* autobiography, but trivialized: as mere confessions rendered all the more enticing for being slightly veiled, rather than a "construction of self."[23]

It is in this latter sense, as "construction of self," that I explore these texts, tracing within them the emergence of a fictional textual 'I.'

My reference to the historical events of Colette's life will be limited to cases where this illuminates the nature of her writing.

In this way my work differs from a number of other recent studies of Colette. In fact, the blurring of genres that we have seen in Colette's work has also been an enduring feature, in a curious mirroring movement, of the body of work written on her. Several different strands can be traced in Colette criticism and commentary with respect to the way in which they blend biography and literary analysis, or privilege one over the other, and reference to these strands will allow me to situate my work among them.

Jean Larnac's *Colette: sa vie, son œuvre*, published by Krâ in 1927, the first "in-depth study" of Colette's work, offers a mixture of biography and literary criticism.[24] This tradition has continued and can be seen in such works as Michèle Sarde's *Colette, libre et entravée* (1978) and Nicole Ward Jouve's *Colette* (1987).[25] Despite her greater emphasis on Colette's novels as opposed to her semiautobiographical works, and her emphasis on a specific aspect of Colette's literary production, Marcelle Biolley-Godino exhibits this approach in *L'homme-objet chez Colette* (1972) as well. An important recent work in this category, which views the study of autobiography and fiction in Colette as inseparable, is Jerry A. Flieger's *Colette and Fantom Subject of Autobiography* (1992). Flieger's interest, however, is less in presenting a balanced, if intertwined, interpretation of both life and work, or in reconstituting Colette's life *through* her work, than in tracing the creative process that in Colette renders autobiography fictional.

Moving along the continuum in one direction towards biography, we find that a very high percentage of the works that have been written on Colette are devoted to telling her life story. These biographies often contain brief analyses of the literary works as they come up, and often with the goal of illuminating, through this analysis, the reader's understanding of Colette as a person. Joanna Richardson's *Colette* (1984) falls into this category; two more recent examples of such biographies are Judith Thurman's *Secrets of the Flesh,* and Claude Pichois and Alain Brunet's highly readable, exhaustively researched *Colette,* both published in 1999.

Finally, moving along the continuum in the other direction, another tradition can be seen, for example, in Elaine Marks's *Colette* (1960), Joan Hinde Stewart's *Colette* (1983, 1996), and Dana Strand's *Colette: A Study of the Short Fiction* (1995), which propose a literary study of Colette's works as distinct from a study of her life. Lynne Huffer's *Another Colette: The Question of Gendered Writing* (1992) is perhaps the most far-reaching representative of this approach. Huffer works in the same terrain as Flieger, the area where autobiography and fiction intersect, exploring "the ways in which Colette's fictional real is constructed through an autobiographical mode"(3). Unlike Flieger, however, her "revisionary rereading" (12) of Colette remains entirely within the realm of language; it is an exploration of Colette *as text.*

My work, like that of Flieger and Huffer, explores Colette's creation of fiction through autobiography. However, my theoretical approach is different from that used in both of these previous studies. In these pages I will concentrate on Colette's texts, rather than on the links between Colette and her creation, as Flieger does. At the same time, I do not, as Huffer does, subsume all of Colette into text, but rather do recognize a subject as referent for the author's name. However, I choose to study Colette's textual production as an entity in itself, rather than the links between it and the woman. This does not involve denial of the existence of the woman, nor of the fact that every author, and certainly Colette, in ways which are particular to her, is inextricably bound up in his or her texts. However, my interest lies elsewhere. While the attempt to read Colette's works in order to reconstruct her life has been perennially popular as an approach to Colette, my work approaches the life-and-work question from the other side of the coin. If Colette's playful literary use of her own presence—and nonpresence—in her texts has given rise to much genuine interest in knowing who the woman responsible for and apparently central to these texts really was, my work explores her *œuvre* from the opposite direction, as it were. Certainly Colette led an exceptionally full, unconventional, and interesting life, and many glimpses of this life are given in her works—although always with an ambiguous stance as to their veracity—and this is indeed part of the reason for the interest in her as a person. At the same time, however, interest, to the extent that we see it, in the real-life woman and author Gabrielle Sidonie Colette, would not exist were it not for the compelling force of the fictional self she created, and which, as has been demonstrated time and time again, shares elements with, but is not to be conflated with, the person of the author herself. What is it in this persona, 'Colette,' that is so powerful, that has struck such powerful chords with so many readers, and has inspired so many to attempt to search for her further? This study will examine the literary aspects of this powerful, mythical 'Colette,' without which an interest in the author's biography and its relation to her works would not exist.

For this reason, since the narrator 'Colette' is not to be confused with Colette the author, I will designate the narrator throughout this study with single quotes, to distinguish her from the historical person. I will do the same with other characters such as 'Sido' and 'Willy,' who also bear the names of real-life individuals.

Thus I will trace within the works selected the emergence of textual selfhood. In particular, I examine "self" in Colette as arising out of language. More specifically yet, I see subjectivity as created by discourse;[26] by which I mean language in its social context, especially in the context of power hierarchies within society. I draw here on Michel Foucault, whose immensely influential work in history and philosophy took the form of "an investigation of the historical constitution of different modes of discourse—particularly medical, psychiatric or literary."[27] We have, in fact, already encountered Foucault's work in this essay through Taylor, who is himself influenced by it. However, at this juncture, and before continuing with my own argument, I will take a moment to summarize *per se* some of the main aspects of Foucault's thought that inform and support my own study.

To begin with, Paul Rabinow notes that Foucault's thought presents a distinct difference from such versions of history as Christianity, Marxism, or the nineteenth-century vision of the continuing march of progress. While all these means of making sense of history posit universal truths, such as human nature, or truth itself, Foucault, as Rabinow states it, is "highly suspicious of claims to universal truths. He doesn't refute them; instead his consistent response is to historicize grand abstractions." Thus, for example, instead of asking the philosophical question, does human nature, or truth, exist? Foucault asks: "How has the concept of human nature [or truth] functioned in our society?"[28]

And in answering this, Foucault refuses to separate knowledge from power. Thus for Foucault, truth is not an ontological notion having to do with what is or is not real, but rather a function of power.[29] In Rabinow's words, Foucault's study of forms of knowledge throughout history attempts to "locate historically and analyze [in domains such as psychiatry or criminal justice, for example] the strands of discourse and practices dealing with the subject, knowledge and *power*" (my emphasis), a practice that he names " 'the genealogy of the modern subject.' " Rabinow continues: "Foucault's most general aim is 'to discover the point at which these practices become coherent reflective techniques with definite goals, the point at which a particular discourse emerged from these techniques and came to be seen as true, the point at which they are linked with the obligation of searching for the truth and telling the truth.' "[30]

Thus discourse, in Foucault, has to do with language as related to power structures, it has to do with the ways in which statements are legitimized, become seen as carriers of truth. In this view, power relations and language are intermingled. Power relations and language work together to create the conceptual framework within which specific questions or issues can be articulated or thought. Arguments and discussions coming out of these conceptual frameworks are what I call discourse. Rather than being purely individual utterances, they participate in, and owe a large part of what they are, to a structuring conceptual framework that is larger than the individual.

Going a step further, I explore not just the self as created by discourse, but also in its *resistance* to discourse, and in the specific context of Colette's work, female resistance to the masculine discourse of a male-dominated society, and thus inherently to the power this discourse wields over women. Here again, reference to Foucault is relevant for my work. Specifically, Foucault's work illuminates not just my understanding of discourse and its relation to power, but the implications this has for social and political questions. Again, Rabinow traces this in Foucault's thinking. Given his understanding of the ways in which power and knowledge are enmeshed, the task for Foucault, he writes, is "to cast aside those utopian schemes, the search for first principles, and to ask instead how power actually operates in society." Rabinow continues, quoting Foucault: " 'It seems to me,' Foucault expounds, 'that the real political task in a society such as ours is to criticize the workings of institutions which appear to be both neutral and independent; to criticize them in such a manner that the political violence which has always exercised itself obscurely through them will be unmasked, so that one can fight them.' " While Colette would certainly have rejected an image of herself as actively, openly engaged in political contestation or struggle, is it not true that part of the enduring fascination of her works is precisely their subtle yet incisive critique, particularly in the realm of gender, of "the workings of institutions which appear to be both neutral and independent," and her criticism of "them in such a manner that the political violence which has always exercised itself obscurely through them [is] unmasked"(6)?

Again this clashes with long-standing popular notions about Colette, for, as mentioned above, she is not generally perceived, nor did she invite perception of herself, as overtly contestatory.[31] Her resistance is characterized by subtlety, and more often takes the form of subversion than overt contestation. For all its subtlety, however, it is unmistakable. It is through discourse and resistance to discourse that a textual selfhood in Colette emerges.

The subjectivity that emerges through this resistant relationship to discourse is further illuminated by reference to the inherently conflictual nature of language itself, and particularly of the language of modern narrative genres as discussed by Mikhail Bakhtin. In his view, the novel as opposed to the epic comes into being in a time when a single world view is no longer universally shared, and the languages of the various positions from which the world is seen, experienced, created, jostle together in the same text, a phenomenon he termed "heteroglossia."[32] This in itself is for him the essential characterizing feature of the novelistic genre.[33]

Equally important for me is the further development Julia Kristeva brings to this idea of language as conflict; that is, the conflictual nature of language not just at the level of discursive passages, but at the very level of the word. Thus even the building blocks, the minimal elements, with which Bakhtin's heteroglossia is constructed, are themselves seen as unstable in their relation to meaning. Kristeva elaborates in the following way as she reads Bakhtin:

> Writer as well as "scholar," Bakhtin was one of the first to replace the static hewing out of texts with a model where literary structure does not simply *exist* but is generated in relation to *another* structure. What allows a dynamic dimension to structuralism is his conception of the "literary word" as an *intersection of textual surfaces* rather than a *point* (a fixed meaning), as a dialog among several writings: that of the author, the addressee (or the character), and the contemporary or earlier cultural context.[34]

Thus added to the notion of heteroglossia, we see here, articulated in Kristeva's reading, the notion of this same meeting of diverse languages, but which here make up, not just the novel, but the word itself. Further, in the passage quoted above, this word exists as meaningful *as* an active result of this process. We also see that these converging meanings, which create the word, include that of the reader, as well as of the writer and of the cultural context. It is this that Kristeva terms intertextuality. Language—through which the subject voices its being and imposes its direction on the ebb and flow of discourse—is dynamic; it is the locus of a conflictual negotiation of meaning. While language acquires meaning through this process, the subject, as well, emerges only in so far as he or she assumes his or her role in it. This active participation and resistance to the discourses of others is what characterizes Colette's textual selfhood.[35]

A series of five chapters will discuss this process through the exploration of different areas of confrontation of the self with language. Selfhood will first be analyzed as resistance to and consequent autonomy within discourse in the context of reading, in a study of passages from *My Mother's House*. The presence in these texts of two young female subjects who read allows for the positing of two opposing models of reading in Colette. It is the character 'Colette' who resists discourse and achieves a measure of autonomy as a result. While she remains in an active relation to the texts she reads, the older sister 'Juliette' approaches books with no sense of self; she seeks instead to be defined by the texts she reads.

Learning to read reveals itself as an apprenticeship in negotiating with discourse and in selfhood itself. Gender complicates the process; in the case of both 'Colette' and 'Juliette' the texts read are not neutral, but vehicles of the discourse of a patriarchal society. Resistance involves contesting these discourses, but most importantly, it necessitates an autonomy vis-à-vis discourse in general. While 'Juliette' is unable to achieve this, 'Colette' negotiates more successfully with the dangers inherent in reading. Interventions by both father and mother mediate her relationship to texts. While the censorship of the father proves disempowering, the mother's modeling of the fictionality of fiction and the power inherent in the role of narratee[36] allows 'Colette' to accede to maturity as a reader.

Chapter 2 studies the apprenticeship of 'Colette' not as reader but as writer. Different relationships of the adult writing self to language are foreshadowed in two vignettes from *My Mother's House* describing childhood experiences. In one, language is used not as a carrier of meaning, but instead as an expression of drives. The child 'Colette' who uses language in this way is in a powerful mode in relation to language. However, when discourse enters the picture, that is, when language is manipulated not just for the pleasure of creating sounds and venting aggression, but in a way that takes into account what it says, the child loses her powerful role. The meaning of the ready-made language into which she steps and with which she plays overcomes her. She is left feeling empty and "debased," lost in a language-inspired, potentially alienating desire. It is the force of the maternal that will pull her back into the familiar and ground her.

Chapter 2 goes on to examine the apprenticeship of 'Colette' as an adult, not in speech now, but in writing. We might expect asserting herself within language as discourse or carrier of meaning to be the goal and outcome of this apprenticeship. However, as announced by the childhood experience, this first apprenticeship as writer will prove alienating, for it consists again of stepping into ready-made language. The *Claudine* series, and specifically the discourses of femininity and sexuality that inform them, are examined in the light of the coercive presence of 'Willy' under whom 'Colette' wrote these first works as a hack. I analyze this coercive overseeing presence as it is described in *My Apprenticeships*. My conclusion is that these first novels do not trace the achievement of selfhood. Rather, they constitute a flight from selfhood, as a result of the various forces besieging 'Colette' at this time. The discourses of femininity and sexuality within which the *Claudine* series remains confined prove to be a dead end for the female writing subject.

Chapter 3 examines the works in what Huffer refers to as the "maternal cycle," *My Mother's House, Break of Day,* and *Sido,* in light of the feminist psychoanalytic notions articulated by Jessica Benjamin.[37] *Break of Day,* for example, both explores and elaborates a model of female selfhood, desire, and voice. Attaining the dawn functions in this novel as a metaphor for the attainment of death and consequent rebirth, into what is not necessarily a different desire, but as Benjamin argues, a different "*relationship* of the self to desire" (95). The mother provides the daughter with a model for the solitude and renunciation necessary to experiencing desire as being one's own. Desire and renunciation of desire are thus part of a cyclical movement. Neither one is posited as a fixed and unchanging aim in and of itself. The dichotomy set up between mother and daughter is also found to be fluid and changing. The daughter seeks to imitate the mother's purity in order to achieve the renunciation of love. However, the mother is in turn contaminated by the daughter's impurity. Thus while the mother models renunciation for the daughter, the daughter in her turn proves the means of bringing the mother back to the object of the renunciation she (the mother) has attained—the experience of desire. This chapter concludes that the mother/daughter relationship in *Break of Day* functions as a complex figure participating in more than one story, and through which the text explores and elucidates models of femininity, sexuality and selfhood constructed within a female-centered context.

Chapter 4 examines love and self in Colette's 1920 novel *Chéri*. This work is analyzed within the context of Colette's mature fiction viewed as an ensemble, in which the love story does not end in romantic bliss, but rather proves the battleground on which the mettle of the self is tried. *Chéri* presents an unusually problematic example of gender subversion in Colette's work, for it offers characters whose unconventional relation to gender reverses the traditional roles, but does not alter the reality of hierarchy. Symbols such as the pearl necklace and mirrors offer the means of tracing the itinerary of both major characters as regards selfhood and love. The socioeconomic order in which they exist as "parasites" precludes the existence of both; it is in spite of the world in which they exist and evolve, rather than because of it, that their love achieves a momentary expression, and through this acquires the quality of nobility.

Chapter 5 examines the question of the female subject's relation to the conventional discourses of gender and sexuality as this question is posited in *The Pure and the Impure*. 'Colette' in this collection of vignettes investigates both "real and phony mysteries,"[38] the real one being the nature of sexuality, which she calls "the Inexorable." Ostentatious veils purporting to cover a scandalous sexuality and an unorthodox means of living one's gender are lifted and found to hide familiar scripts instead. However, different seers lead 'Colette' along the road of the real mystery—the way travelled by those who neither deny the world of difference (the here and now world in which there exists gender), nor submit to the discourses that construct the "masculine" and the "feminine" in their conventional form. The key to the mystery of a sexuality that does not constitute a "vain flight" lies in the notion of power. It is in confrontation with a rival female power that the protagonist and her "rival" achieve mutual and self-recognition and experience desire.

Thus I trace the construction of a textual selfhood arising through resistance to discourse, through the themes of reading, writing, and sexuality. This analysis reveals that identity in Colette emerges through an assertion of self *in relation* to discourse and to the power it represents and creates and that this in turn has an effect on that discourse and that balance of power. However, identity in Colette is ultimately fluid; it exists through the process of its becoming and is never posited as fixed and immutable.

In the final analysis, paradox in Colette makes itself felt once again as we review the direction taken by recent Colette scholarship. Those very qualities that lent themselves to her dismissal from the canon of the truly great reveal an unexpected contemporaneity seen through a fresh perspective. The play that her texts offer makes us share the same experience these works relate. With them, we also embark on an apprenticeship in discourse, in reading and in dialog, in sensitivity, openness, resistance, and self-reliance—in short, the practice of an ever-continuing construction of self.

Although this study is not biographical in nature, a brief summary of Colette's life will help the reader to situate her and her work in history. Colette's mother, Adèle-Eugénie-Sidonie Landoy, was born in Paris in 1835. Her childhood and youth was spent in part in the Yonne region of Burgundy, where Colette herself grew up, and in part in Brussels, in the home of two older brothers who were involved in journalism, literature, and liberal politics. There Sidonie, or 'Sido,' as she was known, was exposed to a lively and free-thinking intellectual and cultural atmosphere. At age twenty-one, as a result of a contract between the two families, she married Claude Jules Joseph Robineau-Duclos, a landowner and a violent, unsociable alcoholic twenty years her senior. They settled in the Yonne, in the village of Saint-Sauveur-en-Puisaye. In a letter to Colette written many years later, Sido recounts that early in their marriage Robineau-Duclos attempted to beat his new wife, but that she responded by seizing all objects within reach and hurling them at his head, effectively putting an end to his attempts at domestic violence.[39]

A child was born of this marriage in 1860, a girl, named Juliette. In the same year, a Captain Jules Joseph Colette moved to the village of Saint-Sauveur. Captain Colette had been born in Mourillon, near Toulon, in 1829. He had pursued a military career, which had taken him on campaigns to the Crimea, North Africa, and finally Italy, where at the Battle of Melegnano (Marignan in French) he lost his left leg. A position as tax-collector in Saint-Sauveur was accorded him in compensation for his services. By all accounts, he and Sidonie Robineau-Duclos became intimate soon after his arrival in the village.

In 1863 Sidonie gave birth to a boy, Achille, who bore the name Robineau-Duclos, but was rumored to be the son of Captain Colette. Jules Robineau-Duclos died in January of 1865, and in December of that year Sidonie married Captain Colette. In 1866 a son, Léopold, or Léo, was born. On January 28, 1873, Sido gave birth to her fourth and last child, Sidonie-Gabrielle Colette.

Gabrielle, or Gabri, as she was known in the family, grew up in Saint-Sauveur-en-Puisaye where she attended the village school. At age sixteen she was among the eight out of twenty-six students to pass the exams necessary for graduation. She thus earned the "brevet élémentaire" and the "certificat d'études primaires supérieures," the highest level of formal education she would attain.

When Gabrielle was seven her father retired from his civil service position. He attempted—unsuccesfully—to enter local politics, and to write. The family finances also suffered during this time, and when Gabrielle was seventeen, the family had to sell the home in Saint-Sauveur and move to Châtillon-sur-Loing, now Châtillon-Coligny, where Achille was practicing medicine.

On May 15, 1893, Gabrielle married Henry Gauthier-Villars, 'Willy,' a well-known Parisian music critic and a prolific publisher of light, salacious fiction through his stable of hacks. He was thirteen years her senior. The marriage did not prove a happy one, and after a lengthy separation, the two were divorced some seventeen years later. However, through this marriage, Colette—as she was soon to be known—made the acquaintance of the literary and cultural world of the capital and also got her beginnings as a writer. Possibly as a result of her husband's suggestion, she produced a work of fiction based on her school days, *Claudine at School,* which was published in 1900. The book enjoyed immense popularity, inspiring whole lines of "Claudine" products including perfume and clothing, as well as more than one stage adaptation. *Claudine at School* was followed by three other books featuring the same heroine. The exact nature of the relationship between Colette and Willy, which led to the publication of the *Claudines,* has been the subject of much debate and may never be known with certainty. It seems clear that there was collaboration between the two; this aspect of the relationship is moreover treated by the narrator of *My Apprenticeships.* It is also clear that Colette was exploited. The books were first published bearing Willy's name alone, and at their divorce he sold the rights to all four novels to other publishing houses, thus effectively preventing Colette from reaping any financial benefit from them.

As the marriage dissolved, Colette began a career on the music-hall stage. She took lessons in mime and appeared in revues at the Théâtre Marigny, the Théâtre des Arts, and the Moulin-Rouge in Paris, among others. A certain amount of scandal is attached to these years; in some acts she danced seminude, and after the first performance of *Rêve d'Egypte* in January of 1907, which ended with a kiss between Colette and the woman who was then her lover, the ex-Marquise de Belbeuf, known as Missy, the act as it had been performed was prohibited by the Paris Prefect of Police.

Colette continued to write during this period, producing some of the first significant works written independently of Willy, including *Tendrils of the Vine* (1908) and *The Vagabond* (1911). She also began contributing fiction as well as journalistic pieces and theater criticism to the newspaper *Le Matin* owned by Henry de Jouvenel. In 1912 she and de Jouvenel were married. This year also saw the death of Colette's mother. The following year, on July 3, 1913, Colette gave birth to her only child, a girl, Colette-Renée de Jouvenel, known in the family as Bel-Gazou.

The following decade saw the publication of some of Colette's most important works, including *Chéri* (1920), and the series of works— *My Mother's House* (1922), *Break of Day* (1928), and *Sido* (1930)—that are undoubtedly Colette's masterpieces. These last works center on one of Colette's most powerful and evocative literary creations, the character 'Sido,' which draws much from, but is not to be conflated with, Colette's own mother. In 1932 she published what was in her own estimation her finest work, *The Pure and the Impure. My Apprenticeships*, in which she treats her formative years as a writer and her life with Willy, appeared in 1936.

The marriage between Colette and Henry de Jouvenel ended in divorce in 1925; in that same year Colette made the acquaintance of Maurice Goudeket, a gem seller sixteen years her junior. They married on April 3, 1935. This marriage lasted until Colette's death some twenty years later.

During the exodus from northern France before the advancing German army in June of 1940, Colette and Goudeket, who was Jewish, fled to the Corrèze district in the south, where Bel-Gazou was living. They returned to Paris in September. In December of 1941 Goudeket was arrested by the Germans and interned at Compiègne, northeast of Paris. He was released in February of 1942. Apart from the three months she spent in the south in 1940, Colette spent the war years in occupied Paris, in her apartment in the Palais-Royal.

During her lifetime Colette produced some seventy works, including semiautobiographical works, novels, theater and journalism, and the outstanding quality of her writing is attested to by the honors she received throughout her lifetime. In 1920 she was made a chevalier of the French Légion d'honneur; in 1928 the rank was elevated to officer and in 1936 to commander. She was received in the Royal Belgian Academy of French Language and Literature in 1936, and in 1945 became the first woman to be elected to France's most prestigious literary academy, the Goncourt Academy. In 1949 the Goncourt Academy elected her president, and in 1953 she was made a grand officer of the Légion d'honneur. Colette died in Paris on August 3, 1954. She did not ask for the last rites according to Catholic tradition and did not receive a religious burial, but she became the first woman in French history to be given a state funeral. She is buried in the Père Lachaise cemetery.[40]

1

Reading: Domination, Resistance, Autonomy

In the last twenty-five or thirty years reading has been increasingly the object of examination and discussion in literary theory, and at the same time increasingly problematized. From Barthes's introduction of the notion of the erotic into reading theory to the claims by de Certeau of the need to politicize the act of reading, we find ourselves continually more distant from the Enlightenment's view of the text as the container of a specific and identifiable meaning and as the educative tool of an elite, a tool which, if disseminated widely enough, will imprint on its receivers—the readers—the desired message, and achieve the transformation of society.[1]

This movement in the study of reading is not only a fascinating object of study on its own, but is also of prime importance for understanding Colette. Reading constitutes a theme in certain of Colette's works, such as *The Innocent Libertine* and *My Mother's House*. This theme in turn presents the Colette reader with an entry to the problematic her semi-autobiographical works develop: the movement toward a gendered discursive autonomy on the part of the protagonist. A review of some of the important ideas from Roland Barthes, Ross Chambers, and Michel de Certeau provides a springboard to an analysis of reading in Colette. Barthes's *The Pleasure of the Text* presents a starting point to a survey of this work.

Not only does Barthes break away from established theories of the reading of texts in a decisive and refreshing way, but his work is the origin of many of the ideas later taken up and elaborated on by other thinkers.

The Pleasure of the Text immediately introduces a change in the traditionally accepted criterion of the reader faced with the text, theorizing a shift away from moral judgment (does the work conform to standards that make it worthy?) and towards that of pleasure (do I keep reading it or do I turn away?). According to Barthes, the locus of this pleasure is not so much in the text itself as object, as in the relationship between writer and reader. The writer seeks the reader, and a "site of bliss" is created.[2] Here, where things are not fixed, there is the possibility of play.

Thus for Barthes, the text is infinitely plural, the reader creates it through play, and the motivation is pleasure. Peter Brooks, in *Reading for the Plot,* carries on some of these ideas, with a slightly different agenda. Going back to the distinction between "fabula" and "szujet" of the Russian Formalists, he notes that the "fabula," what "really happened," as opposed to the "szujet" or plot that the author makes of it, is actually in itself a mental construct and nothing more, since it is only through the "szujet" that we ever know anything of its "fabula." However, Brooks argues that the "differing status of the two terms by no means invalidates the distinction itself." Rather this distinction is important for the analysis of narrative because it allows us to see two modes of ordering (ordering by the narrator of 'events,' and ordering by us readers of the 'real events' we construct as lying behind that 'artificial' plot), and hence to understand how "ordering takes place."[3] So for Brooks, plot is not the more simplistic idea of something the writer has created out of reality, but rather the *work* of the reader, who reads the narrator's ordering, and who constructs, in his own turn, a 'reality' behind that ordering. For Brooks "plot is the interpretive activity elicited by the distinction between 'szujet' and 'fabula,' the way we *use* the one against the other" (13). Thus he joins Barthes in saying that plot is an *interpretive activity,* not a static, constructed thing; it is something the reader participates in creating.

Ross Chambers in *Story and Situation* in his turn picks up a number of Barthes's threads but carries them in some slightly different directions. He stresses the importance of situational phenomena, that "the narrative act is always available as a vehicle whereby people may 'do things'—that is . . . *relate.*[4] His work with texts takes the particular form of examining the narrative techniques texts deploy to seduce the reader and to produce their point, particularly strategies of mirroring and *mise-en-abyme.* Again, we note how much Chambers owes to Barthes. In particular, we continue to see the notion of the text as mediator in relationships of desire and in part as a creation of the reader.

With Michel de Certeau's "Reading as Poaching" in *The Practice of Everyday Life,* we come to an approach to reading concerned more overtly with the idea of resistance. This notion is implicit in the thinking of Barthes, Brooks, and Chambers, since all three stress the active nature of reading and the partial creation by the reader of a text's meaning. Yet all talk about this being done most especially with "writerly" texts, and by readers who have the literary baggage to perform this act of "reading for the plot." De Certeau is the first to stress reading as an activity practiced by ordinary people in resistance to a commercially produced mass culture.

De Certeau is the first in this context to mention an elite involved in the production of culture. While he does not refute the fact that it is only this elite with access to power who decides or creates what appears on the television or in the newspapers, he *does* refute the idea of a passive consumer of this culture. Rather, de Certeau speaks of "consumers" as "unrecognized producers"; he compares their "signifying practices" to the "wandering lines" drawn by autistic children. He writes that:

> In the technocratically constructed, written and functionalized space in which the consumers move about, their trajectories form unforeseeable sentences, partly unreadable paths across a space. Although they are composed with the vocabularies of established languages (those of television, newspapers, supermarkets, or museum sequences) and although they remain subordinated to the prescribed syntactical forms (temporal modes of schedules, paradigmatic orders of spaces, etc.), the trajectories trace out the ruses of other interests and desires that are neither determined nor captured by the system in which they develop.[5]

This activity, rather than passivity, on the part of the consumer, who is often a reader, is then the point of entry for de Certeau into a critique of the separation of reading and writing in our society and the privileging of writing within this hierarchized separation. Writing seen as creation, or self-creation—as opposed to reading, the passive reception of messages from another, allowing oneself to be created by the other—is even seen by François Furet (qtd. in de Certeau 168) as the figure itself of modernity. De Certeau summarizes the actual impact of writing thus: "The generalization of writing has in fact brought about the replacement of custom by abstract law, the substitution of the State for traditional authorities, and the disintegration of the group to the advantage of the individual." In addition, de Certeau notes that this "transformation took place under the sign of a 'cross-breeding' between two distinct elements, the written and the oral." Very interesting for the study of reading in Colette are the connections he makes not only between oral tradition, reading, and writing, but also, tellingly, between all of this and gender. The female is encoded as passive within this hierarchized duality privileging writing and characterizing the modern age. De Certeau writes: "Furet and Ozouf's recent study has indeed demonstrated the existence, in the less educated parts of France, of a 'vast semi-literacy, centered on reading, instigated by the Church and by families, and aimed chiefly at girls' " (168).

Important for our dismantling of this hierarchy, and the encoded female passivity within it, is the evidence de Certeau points to that undermines the cleanness and separateness of the distinction between oral tradition on the one hand, and literacy—reading and writing, on the other. We will find later that the oral tradition in Colette is strongly associated with the mother and will be crucial to the character 'Colette' in her apprenticeship of autonomy, both as a reader and writer. De Certeau writes that research in cognitive psycholinguistics distinguishes two acts in reading: lexical and scriptural. This research

> [S]hows that the schoolchild learns to read by a process that *parallels* his learning to decipher; learning to read is not a *result* of learning to decipher: *reading* meaning and *deciphering* letters correspond to two different activities, even if they intersect. In other words, cultural memory (acquired through listening, through oral tradition) alone makes possible and gradually enriches the strategies of semantic questioning whose expectations the deciphering of a written text refines, clarifies, or corrects. From the child to the scientist, reading is preceded and made possible by oral communication, which constitutes the multifarious "authority" that texts almost never cite. (168)

Thus reading depends on prior acculturation and experience with language through listening; we could say that it depends on a kind of intertextuality.

Armed with this tool for understanding, reading can take place, a reading that is itself a kind of writing in that it is creation. While the written text modifies it, reading is creation, is writing in itself.

So, de Certeau as well fits into the evolution of reading theory since Barthes. Furthermore, he becomes the most explicit of the theorists discussed so far in relating the general notion of resistant reading to actual social structures of power such as class and gender.[6] He thus takes us the farthest toward an analysis of *gendered* reading in Colette. Reading has traditionally been defined as negative—passive and therefore feminine; de Certeau points to concrete historical evidence for this. As we take up the theme of reading in Colette, we will see that the character of the older sister will actually *read* this meaning of reading in the culture around her. She will assume in reading her gendered position defined by culture and its discourses on reading. This assumption of her preinscribed role will prove deadly. 'Colette' on the other hand becomes a resistant reader, as does the character of the mother, 'Sido.' 'Colette' reads as the theorists describe, announcing their discoveries. This gives her the strength to resist the depersonalizing effects of subservience to discourse, called forth, as we shall see, by the father's interdiction, symbolized not only through his actions in "My Mother and the Books," but also in the content of the texts his interdiction forbids.

> With my hair plaited Alsatian fashion, two little bows swinging at the ends of my two plaits and a parting down the middle of my head, disfigured by my uncovered temples and by ears too distant from my nose, I would sometimes climb the stairs to visit my sister with the long hair. At noon she would already be reading, as luncheon finished at eleven o'clock. In bed, in the morning, she would still be reading. The sound of the opening door would hardly win a glance from her absent, slanting black eyes,[7] blurred with some tender romance or blood-thirsty adventure. A candle stump bore witness to her night-long vigil. The wallpaper, pearl-grey with a design of cornflowers, showed traces, near the bed, of the many matches that my long-haired sister, with a rough and heedless hand, had struck on its surface. (*MMH* 70)

[Nattée à l'alsacienne, deux petits rubans voletant au bout de mes deux tresses, la raie au milieu de la tête, bien enlaidie avec mes tempes découvertes et mes oreilles trop loin du nez, je montais parfois chez ma sœur aux longs cheveux. A midi, elle lisait déjà, le grand déjeuner finissant à onze heures. Le matin, couchée, elle lisait encore. Elle détournait à peine, au bruit de la porte, ses yeux noirs mongols, distraits, voilés de roman tendre ou de sanglante aventure. Une bougie consumée témoignait de sa longue veille. Le papier de la chambre, gris de perle à bleuets, portait les traces, près du lit, des allumettes qu'y frottait la nuit, avec une brutalité insouciante, ma sœur aux longs cheveux. (2: 1014)]

The most immediately visible figure of a reader in Colette's semi-autobiographical works, particularly in *My Mother's House,* is that of the older half-sister 'Juliette,' "[m]y sister with the long hair." The relationship between the older sister and books forms a subplot to the main plot we are investigating here, namely, the coming of age of 'Colette' in respect to reading. Her coming of age is recounted in the chapter from *My Mother's House* called "My Mother and the Books." This is set off by the story involving 'Juliette' and her relationship to texts, told in the chapter of the same work entitled "My Sister with the Long Hair." The subplot involving 'Juliette' stands as a "means of warding off the danger of short-circuit ['the wrong solution to the problems'], assuring that the main plot will continue through to the right end."[8] While 'Colette' *resists* the texts she reads, remains *in relation* to them, the older sister approaches books with no sense of self. She seeks instead to be *defined* by the texts she reads.

'Juliette,' as we have seen in the passage above, is identified continually and almost ritualistically by her long hair. In fact, this metonymic feature comes almost to stand in for the person herself. We shall return to the question of the choice of hair as metonymic feature. However, for now let us consider how this nonperson who has first been effaced by her long hair subsequently searches for her self through reading.

As continual and as ritualistic as the references to her long hair are the references to the older sister's complete absorption in reading. "My sister with the too long hair might read for ever with never a pause; the two boys would brush past her as though they did not see the young girl sitting abstracted and entranced, and never bother her" (*MMH* 8). "On

Thursday mornings, then, towards ten o'clock, I would often find my long-haired sister still abed and reading. . . . She took no more heed of my arrival than of the cries of, 'Get up, Juliette!' coming from below stairs. She would read on . . ." (*MMH* 72). "Novels were stuffed among the cushions, wedged into the work-basket, or languished forgotten in the garden, soaked by the rain. My long-haired sister no longer spoke, ate scarcely anything, seemed surprised to meet us about the house, and woke with a start if a bell rang" (*MMH* 73). The sinister, unhealthy nature of this complete evacuation of the sister into reading erupts into outright disaster when she falls physically ill. It is, moreover, her insatiable desire to read that brings illness on.

> My mother lost her temper, sat up of nights to put out the lamp and confiscate candles; my long-haired sister caught a cold, demanded a night-light in order to prepare hot infusions and read by the night-light's glimmer. After the night-light, there were boxes of matches and the moonlight. After the moonlight, my long-haired sister, exhausted by romantic insomnia, became feverish, and her fever refused to yield either to compresses or purgative draughts. (*MMH* 73)
>
> [Ma mère se fâcha, veilla la nuit pour éteindre la lampe et confisquer les bougies : ma sœur aux longs cheveux, enrhumée, réclama dans sa chambre une veilleuse pour la tisane chaude, et lut à la flamme de la veilleuse. Après la veilleuse, il y eut les boîtes d'allumettes et le clair de lune. Après le clair de lune, ma sœur aux longs cheveux, épuisée de romanesque insomnie, eut la fièvre, et la fièvre ne céda ni aux compresses, ni à l'eau purgative. (2: 1016)]

The doctor is called in and diagnoses typhoid, leaving the mother "vaguely shocked and astonished." Yet this surprise at the gravity of the illness is only a foreshadowing of the shock the mother feels when the full extent of her daughter's self-effacement and alienation is revealed. The mother and 'Colette' return to the sister's room after the doctor leaves, and the mother busies herself about the sickroom, talking cheerfully to her daughter, offering to bring her a glass of cool lemonade or to plump up her pillows. 'Juliette,' however, makes no direct response. When she does speak, she leaves the mother and the younger sister stunned by her incoherent ramblings, for it becomes clear that rather than addressing them she is conversing with the authors of the books she has read.

She addresses Catulle Mendès, mentions to him a visit she has received from Octave Feuillet, and in general carries on an incoherent conversation full of coquetry, references to other men and simultaneous protestations that he, Catulle, is the only one. The mother is filled with horror as she watches "this stranger, who in her delirium called only for unknown persons" (*MMH* 75). Catching sight of the younger daughter, 'Colette,' whose presence she had forgotten, she brusquely orders her downstairs, and "as though overcome with shame . . . buried her face in her hands" (*MMH* 75).

The relationship of the older sister to books allows us to return to the notion of narrative as understood by Chambers, that is, narrative as mediating relationships of desire. In a postmodern cultural landscape, the alienated or autonomous text does not exert authority over the reader as does Barthes's readerly text. Rather it is dependent on the other, the narratee, who will engage with the narrator through the mediation of the text, and thus allow the text to acquire meaning and to come into being. However, since the reader will not be moved by the text's authority, s/he must be "seduced" into entering the role of narratee. And as Chambers puts it, "[w]hen we are seduced, are we not always seduced into conforming ourselves with an image: the simulacrum of one whom we believe can be loved?"[9]

The fictionalized level that a reader and writer must attain before the interchange takes place that will actualize the text—and incidentally the reader and writer as well—is worth clarifying here. To begin with, a writer and reader—both concrete, physical beings—are necessarily involved. The writer must assume a narrative voice in order to produce a text of fiction. The reader must equally play the role of narratee if the pact between narrator and narratee, on which the reading of the text as fiction depends, is to remain good. Thus the reader of fiction is not only dealing with the fictionality of the characters or plot. S/he is also dealing with the fictionality of the narratee or "seducee" produced within . . . [the] literary text as the object of its seduction" with whom the reader makes a provisional identification in order to engage the narrative and construct meaning (15). In the case of the sister, illness and delirium bring to light, and stand as a figure of, an involvement with the text that does not recognize fictionality. In fact, the sister skips two levels that normally distance the reader from the story read. Not only does she fail to recognize the fictionality of the "seducee" with whom the reader normally identifies in a provisional way, she fails even to recognize the fictionality of the characters and events. She bypasses both fictional constructions, and enters into a direct, unmediated relationship with a fantasized figure of the author. She assumes the identity of the loved one within the discourse of romantic love that his text transmits. She does not take the role of the *other* necessary to reading as Chambers sees it. She seeks instead to become the *same* as the text, to be defined by it.

Thus we see that once the sister submits to playing a gendered role as reader, she is confronted in the texts with a gendered identity. She does not approach this identity as an active, questioning other, but as a nonperson seeking definition. We thus see her assuming the feminine role in what Rachel DuPlessis calls "romantic thralldom." DuPlessis defines this term in the following manner:

> Romantic thralldom is an all-encompassing, totally defining love between apparent unequals. The lover has the power of conferring self-worth and purpose upon the loved one. Such love is possessive, and while those enthralled feel it completes and even transforms them, dependency rules. The eroticism of romantic love, born of this unequal relationship, may depend for its satisfaction upon domination and submission. Thralldom insists upon the differences between the sexes or partners, encouraging a sense of mystery surrounding the motives and powers of the lover. Because it begins and ends in polarization, the sustenance of different spheres is both a cause and effect of romantic love. Viewed from a critical, feminist perspective, the sense of completion or transformation that often accompanies such thralldom has the high price of obliteration and paralysis. This kind of love is socially learned, and it is central and recurrent in our culture.[10]

We will return later on in this chapter to the implications of the sister's approach to reading, but let us for now discuss the notion of hair, the other of the sister's two metonymic extensions that come to engulf and replace her as a person. For not only is her long hair associated with her continually, not only does the mention of her long hair come almost to replace her name as the means by which she is identified, the hair itself almost effaces her. And, in fact, this is not surprising. Hair, and particularly long hair, is of course a symbol of femininity within the context of nineteenth-century France. If the sister takes the same submissive, docile position vis-à-vis her hair, which she allows to dominate and define her, as she does to the text, which she also allows to dominate and define her, there is a logical connection. In fact, in both cases she is submitting to a discourse of femininity, or the symbol of one, generated by patriarchal culture.

'Colette' relates in describing the sister that "her low forehead, her ears and the nape of her neck, all of her that was faintly anaemic white flesh, seemed foredoomed to be overrun by her hair" (*MMH* 70). This idea of the excessive, invasive nature of hair is repeated in the image created when 'Juliette' is having her hair brushed. At these moments, the loosened hair forms a "tent," covering her from head to toe. The reaction of the neighbors is one of pity. "Poor little wretch!" exclaims one. Another asks her if she can't put her hat straight, and concludes: "Of course I know that with your hair. . . . Life can hardly be worth living, I should say, with hair like yours" (*MMH* 71).

The chapter entitled "My Sister with the Long Hair" actually contains towards the beginning a series of general comments on this traditional symbol, hair. These comments are at first, and overwhelmingly, critical. Long hair is time-consuming to maintain; it is a burden:

> At seven o'clock on dark winter mornings I would fall asleep again, sitting before the wood fire, while my mother brushed and combed my nodding head. From those mornings I date my invincible hatred of long hair. (*MMH* 69)
>
> [Les noirs matins d'hiver, à sept heures, je me rendormais assise, devant le feu de bois, sous la lumière de la lampe, pendant que ma mère brossait et peignait ma tête ballante. C'est par ces matins-là que m'est venue, tenace, l'aversion des longs cheveux... (2: 1013)]

The narrator continues, in images in which hair begins to have a destructive life of its own:

> Long hairs would be discovered tangled in the lower branches of the trees in the garden, long hairs attached to the cross-beam from which hung the trapeze and the swing. A pullet in the barnyard was supposed to be lame from birth, until we ascertained that a long hair, covered with pimply skin was bound tightly around one of its feet and atrophying it. (*MMH* 69)
>
> [On trouvait de longs cheveux pris aux basses branches des arbres dans le jardin, de longs cheveux accrochés au portique où pendaient le trapèze et la balançoire. Un poussin de la basse-cour passa pour estropié de naissance, jusqu'à ce que nous eussions découvert qu'un long cheveu, recouvert de chair bourgeonnante, ligotait étroitement l'une de ses pattes et l'atrophiait...[11] (2: 2013)]

What is the purpose of maintaining this burdensome, destructive hair?[12] It is a symbol of sexuality, which women represent in patriarchal discourse, even though at the same time they must not express or even feel any manifestation of it in themselves. Hair works as a figure of this relationship of women to sexuality in patriarchal society—they maintain this (actually burdensome) symbol signifying them as sensual, sexual beings, beings in whom the metonymic (partial) aspect of sexuality comes to stand for the whole. This sends the message to the other that here is where sexuality, sexual pleasure is found, for the other. But it is not meant to signify that here is a being who is sexual herself. As Susan Cohen has said about a similar symbol in *Gigi,* the long skirt, it "is the sign of the taboo on female genitals, a taboo that applies not to men but to women themselves, and it is the sign of entry into the social system."[13] Thus hair signifies woman as object of pleasure for another. Since hair stands as a figure of the entire relationship of women to sexuality, it is this relationship that is being criticized as we continue to read about the destructive, deadening effects of long hair, even in the realm for which it is supposedly maintained, that of sensuality and sexuality:

> Long hair, barbaric adornment, fleece to which clings an animal smell, hair that one cherishes in secret for secret purposes, that one displays when twisted or plaited and conceals when it is dishevelled; who bathes in your torrent rippling to the waist? A woman surprised when she is

doing her hair, flies as though she were naked. Amorous dalliance sees no more of you than the passerby. Unbound, you fill the bed with a mesh that irritates a sensitive epidermis, trailing weeds that confuse a wandering hand. (*MMH* 69-70)

[Cheveux longs, barbare parure, toison où se réfugie l'odeur de la bête, vous qu'on choie en secret et pour le secret, vous qu'on montre tordus et roulés, mais que l'on cache épars, qui se baigne à votre flot, déployé jusqu'aux reins? Une femme surprise à sa coiffure fuit comme si elle était nue. L'amour et l'alcôve ne vous voient guère plus que le passant. Libres, vous peuplez le lit de rets dont s'accommode mal l'épiderme irritable, d'herbes où se débat la main errante. (2: 1013)]

Even in bed, long hair, or what it represents, this particular relationship of women to sexuality, where she must represent to the other what she is not allowed to feel herself, is a "mesh" ["rets"], a net or trap, which catches one in it and either domesticates or kills.[14]

We have the impression that it is the man's hand that is caught in this "mesh" or these "weeds," and we thus feel the suggestion of the destructive effects for men of this discourse of female sexuality. However, above and beyond that, this "mesh" catches women. They must bear the burden of being the sign of this sexuality for the other, although it stifles them. No point could be made more strongly than that 'Juliette' is effaced by her hair. The images of her invisible beneath her hair are reinforced by her eventual obliteration. This is the case for both the Juliette of real life and the literary character. She marries a man her mother dislikes, a man who requires her to cut herself off from her family completely, and her life ends in suicide.

Let us now return once again to 'Juliette' and texts. Her submersion under hair only renders clear and imaginable for us the real problem, her submersion under discourse. And as I have already demonstrated, we see this primary submersion in her relationship to the texts that transmit discourse in a verbal way (the romance novels she never stops reading). It is the same gesture in both cases, with the same issues at stake. In both cases, she is dominated by a male-centered discourse that eventually obliterates her. However, the problem with the sister and texts, with this subplot standing as a "means of warding off the danger of short-circuit ['the wrong solution to the problem']," as Brooks expresses it, is not so much submission to the content of a particular discourse, but one of subservience to discourse. It is true that the discourse by which she seeks to be defined is one in which she will identify with an image of herself that will objectify and subjugate her as woman. However, her subjugation exists and perhaps with the most important and serious consequences on another level, that of her subjugation, her nonautonomy, to discourse in general. This is contrasted in both cases by the behavior of 'Colette.'[15] However, before turning to our main plot, 'Colette' and books, let us first briefly contrast her relationship to hair to that of 'Juliette'; as in the case of books, this also provides the other side of a coin.

In fact, the chapter entitled "My Sister with the Long Hair" actually begins with a description of 'Colette' and her hair; she is standing within this particular chapter as the subplot to the main plot involving 'Juliette.'

> I was twelve years old, with the manners and vocabulary of an intelligent, rather uncouth boy, but my gait was not boyish because my figure already showed signs of development, and above all because I wore my hair in two long plaits that swished through the air around me like whips. These I used indiscriminately as ropes from which to hang the picnic basket, as brushes to be dipped in ink or in paint, as whips for a recalcitrant dog or as ribbons to make the cat play. (*MMH* 69)
>
> [J'avais douze ans, le langage et les manières d'un garçon intelligent, un peu bourru, mais la dégaine n'était point garçonnière, à cause d'un corps façonné déjà fémininement, et surtout de deux longues tresses, sifflantes comme des fouets autour de moi. Elles me servaient de cordes à passer dans l'anse du panier à goûter, de pinceaux à tremper dans l'encre ou la couleur, de lanières à corriger le chien, de ruban à faire jouer le chat. (2: 1013)]

What strikes the reader first in this paragraph is a confusion of gender. At age twelve, the end of childhood, her manners and language are those of a boy. Thus she is a girl who looks like a boy. However, she is eventually marked as feminine by "two long plaits"—long hair, the privileged symbol of conventional femininity itself. Yet these two braids are characterized as "swish[ing] . . . like whips," certainly a very masculine, warlike symbol. They are not a burden, as long hair is to 'Juliette,' nor are they a sign by which 'Colette' is passively marked. Rather they are tools, weapons even, as we have just seen, by which she marks the world: alternately ropes serving as basket-carriers, paintbrushes, and again, the lashes of whips.

But what are we to make of this masculine imagery, which verges at times on the warlike, as we have noted? The question becomes more interesting when we note that it is her mother who is particularly in favor of 'Colette' wearing these braids. "My mother wailed to see me maltreat these two golden brown stirrups . . ." (*MMH* 69, translation modified). Even the word "stirrups" fits into the pattern of imagery we have been remarking. They are a conventionally more masculine than feminine image, associated as they are with horseback-riding, movement, and action. 'Colette' continues to identify them with such images, and to make use of them accordingly, but her mother bemoans this masculine, active use of them. Therefore, it seems to be against her mother that 'Colette' rebels with her hair.

If 'Colette' is rebelling against her mother in the business of long hair, the tension becomes stronger when her hair is finally cut, an event she recounts in *My Apprenticeships*.

> From the day when, following Mr. Willy's instructions, I cut off my too long hair, a number of clever people discovered that I bore a strong likeness to Polaire. . . .
>
> To be strictly honest, I must admit I was not sorry to lose the great inconvenient rope of hair that was weighing me down, feeding on my strength. Once rid of it, the only thing that spoilt my pleasure was a letter from 'Sido.' She rebuked me in strangely grave terms: "Your hair was not your own. It was mine, the work of twenty years of care and attention. You have disposed of a precious trust that I had confided to you." (*MA* 97)
>
> [A partir du jour où, obéissant aux suggestions de M. Willy, je coupai mes trop longs cheveux, maint observateur avisé me découvrit une ressemblance avec Polaire. . . .

> Pour ne pas mentir, je ne demandais qu'à voir tomber ma grande corde incommode de cheveux, qui se nourrissait de moi. Le coup de ciseaux donné, je goûtais un plaisir que seul gâta une lettre de Sido. Elle flétrit mon geste en termes étrangement graves : "Tes cheveux ne t'appartenaient pas, ils étaient mon œuvre, l'œuvre de vingt ans de soins. Tu as disposé d'un dépôt précieux, que je t'avais confié..." (3: 1049-50)]

In fact, hair seems to be a troublesome symbol, and if we keep in mind that it is a figure of women's relationship to sexuality, it is not surprising. The burdens 'Colette' sheds with her long hair are several. It is not just a physical burden, but a mark of oppression, defining her as feminine in the conventional way, as a being who is sexual for the other although not in herself, and as an object of exchange. It is also what subjugates her to her mother, for this mark of femininity that the mother treasures is a means by which she (the mother) identifies with her daughter to an excessive and perhaps even stifling degree. Yet when 'Colette' cuts her hair and rejoices in its shortness, she is helping 'Willy' exploit her; he shows her off with her 'twin' Polaire (the actress who played Claudine on stage) as a publicity stunt. While short hair is associated with this merging of 'Colette' and Claudine and with the discourse of female sexuality imposed by 'Willy' in the writing of the *Claudine* series, it does not seem to have anything more to do with autonomy than does long hair. 'Colette' struggles to free herself from the various subjugating interferences represented by hair but does not find an easy solution. However, there does come a moment in which Colette muses on long hair in a way that allows it to represent whatever one might want, free of the domination or manipulation of the other.

> There is just one moment, in the evening, when the pins are withdrawn and the shy face shines out for an instant from between the tangled waves; and there is a similar moment in the early morning. And because of these two moments everything I have just written against long hair counts for nothing at all. (*MMH* 70)
>
> [Il y a bien un instant, le soir, quand les épingles tombent et que le visage brille, sauvage, entre des ondes mêlées,—il y a un autre instant

> pareil, le matin... Et à cause de ces deux instants-là, ce que je viens d'écrire contre vous, longs cheveux, ne signifie plus rien. (2: 1013-14)]

Here, hair is a symbol of a different relationship of women to sexuality—one in which sensuality plays a part, one that is desirable and gives pleasure, and this forms a provisional conclusion to all the battles Colette has waged with this sign. We have seen that Colette engages with the sign that is hair. She has an active relationship to the discourse that assigns it meaning, first through the character of the young 'Colette,' who makes use of hair for things for which it is not intended by the culture she grows up in. We see in her de Certeau's "silent, transgressive, ironic or poetic activity of readers (or television viewers) who maintain their reserve in private and without the knowledge of the 'masters,' "[16] "trac[ing] out the ruses of other interests and desires that are neither determined nor captured by the systems in which they develop (xviii)." Colette then continues this transgression with the figure of an adult woman. Susan Cohen has already mentioned hair as a symbol of a positive, spontaneous, infantile sexuality in *Gigi*, but which will be domesticated by Lachaille in the final scene of that work.[17] But here, in this last quote from *My Mother's House*, hair is associated positively with female sexuality in *women*—and thus we see a new discourse created out of the symbol. This very act bears witness implicitly to the fictionality of discourses, which Colette recognizes she has the ability to create like anyone else. Thus she subverts the traditional meaning of hair as she also assigns it a new one.

If 'Colette' seems to have no difficulty maintaining her independence in relation to hair, the question of books is different. While hair as a symbol of patriarchy is more easily managed and controlled by the young female subject, books, with their complex discourses and their power to cast a spell, prove a more formidable adversary.

As we turn to the topic of 'Colette' as apprentice reader, we are struck first of all by the title of the chapter in *My Mother's House* devoted to it. Like so many others in the same work, the title contains the words "my mother"; here, we read "My Mother and the Books." 'Colette' will pass through several stages in the process of coming of age in relationship to texts. The last ones will involve mediations by both father and mother. Significantly, however, it is the mediation by the mother that is privileged in the title of the chapter itself.

The mother's relationship to texts is introduced thus: "The twenty-odd volumes of Saint-Simon replaced each other nightly at my mother's bedside; their pages provided her with *endlessly renewed pleasure,* and she thought it strange that at eight years old I should sometimes fail to share in her enjoyment" (*MMH* 35, emphasis added). The mother reads for *pleasure,* and she reads and rereads the same texts. The pleasures she finds in engaging the texts are *familiar* pleasures—the texts are in fact like family. 'Colette' relates to texts as does her mother. Books for her as well are associated with home and family; they are, for example, the "warm covering of the walls of the home in which I was born" (*MMH* 35, translation modified). "Books, books, books. It was not that I read so many. *I read and reread the same ones,*" she recalls in another moment (*MMH* 34, my emphasis). "Lost, stolen or strayed, I could catalog them today. Almost every one of them *had seen my birth,*" she continues (*MMH* 33, translation modified, my emphasis). Thus for 'Colette' also, the books are integrated into the world of interpersonal relationships. They are like parents; she has similar relationships to them. And if I have switched from talking about texts to talking about books, it is with reason, for as a young reader, 'Colette' relates simply to the books themselves as physical objects.

> There was a time, before I learned to read, when I would curl up into a ball, like a dog in its kennel, between two volumes of Larousse. (*MMH* 33-4)
>
> [Il y eut un temps où, avant de savoir lire, je me logeais en boule entre deux tomes du Larousse comme un chien dans sa niche. (2: 988)]

The image of the books covering the walls of the home is intensified here; the books no longer decorate the walls of the "home in which [the child] was born," they themselves become the walls of a "kennel" or home even closer and tighter than those of the real house, to the point where 'Colette' and the 'house' seem to merge into one. We name this stage in her relationship to books (not yet to texts) the preimaginary—that stage at which the child as yet perceives no difference between itself and the outside world.

Gradually, this relationship is replaced by another, the imaginary, the stage at which the child perceives itself as separate, whole unto itself;

falsely confident in fact of this separateness and self-sufficiency, and locked into a dualistic relationship with the other.[18]

> No love lost between me and Dumas, save that the *Collier de la Reine* glittered for a few nights in my dreams upon the doomed neck of Jeanne de la Motte. Neither the enthusiasm of my brothers nor the disapproving surprise of my parents could persuade me to take an interest in the Musketeers.
>
> ... I read the story of the Hind and that of Beauty only in Walter Crane's pure, fresh illustrations. The large characters of his text linked up picture with picture like the plain pieces of net connecting the patterns in lace. But not a single word ever passed the barrier that I erected against them. What becomes in later life of that tremendous determination not to know, that quiet strength expended on avoidance and rejection? (*MMH* 34)
>
> [Point d'amour entre Dumas et moi, sauf que *Le Collier de la Reine* étincela, quelques nuits, dans mes songes, au col condamné de Jeanne de la Motte. Ni l'enthousiasme fraternel, ni l'étonnement désapprobateur de mes parents n'obtinrent que je prisse de l'intérêt aux Mousquetaires...
>
> ... Je n'ai lu l'aventure de la Biche, de la Belle, que dans les fraîches images de Walter Crane. Les gros caractères du texte couraient de l'un à l'autre tableau comme le réseau de tulle uni qui porte les médaillons espacés d'une dentelle. Pas un mot n'a franchi le seuil que je lui barrais. Où s'en vont, plus tard, cette volonté énorme d'ignorer, cette force tranquille employée à bannir et à s'écarter?... (2: 988)]

In this imaginary stage, it is the *images* she reads, not the words. It is the image of Jeanne de la Motte's necklace that she retains, rather than the story surrounding it—images that are likened to the *holes* in a length of lace. These 'holes' or images are the important part, which the words, or cloth (both are 'texts' or *tissus*), serve only to support, as a means of providing a place in which to mark them. These 'holes' render the fascination, and, at the same time, the fictionality of the images—beginning with her own—that the child has progressed to the point of perceiving in this imaginary stage. This stage is also characterized by a false, yet at this stage salutary, notion of the subject's separateness and inviolability, as well as that of the other in the relationship (30). This as well we see reflected here. 'Colette' speaks of "that tremendous determination not to know, that quiet strength expended on avoidance and rejection." She reports that "not a single word ever passed the barrier that I erected against them." Nothing persuades her to permit the Musketeers to her intimacy. And, interestingly, if she is serenely virginal, with unquestioned defenses against intrusion and invasion, so also at this stage are the books.

> Perhaps those most hermetically sealed were the dearest. I have long forgotten the name of the author of a scarlet-clad Encyclopedia, but the alphabetical references marked upon each volume have remained for me an indelible and magic word: *Aphbicécladiggalhymaroidphorebstevanzy*. And how I loved the Guizot whose ornate green and gold was never opened! And the inviolate *Voyage d'Anacharsis!* If the *Histoire du Consulat et de l'Empire* ever found its way to the Quais, I wager that a label would proudly proclaim its condition as "mint." (*MMH* 34-5)

> [Les plus hermétiques ne m'étaient-ils pas les plus chers? Voilà longtemps que j'ai oublié l'auteur d'une Encyclopédie habillée de rouge, mais les références alphabétiques indiquées sur chaque tome composent indélébilement un mot magique: *Aphbicladiggalhymaroidphorebstevanzy*. Que j'aimai ce Guizot, de vert et d'or paré, jamais déclos! Et ce *Voyage d'Anarchsis*, inviolé! Si l'*Histoire du Consulat et de l'Empire* échoua un jour sur les quais, je gage qu'une pancarte mentionne fièrement son 'état de neuf' ... (2: 989)]

Thus books as well are virginal. They resist or at any rate have not known invasion, violation. Moreover, their very closed and secretive nature is the key to their fascination for 'Colette.'

At a certain point this changes.

> Labiche and Daudet wormed their way early into my happy childhood, condescending teachers who played with a familiar pupil. Mérimée came along with them, seductive and severe, dazzling my eight years with an incomprehensible light" (*MMH* 34).

["Labiche et Daudet se sont insinués, tôt, dans mon enfance heureuse, maîtres condescendants qui jouent avec un élève familier. Mérimée vint en même temps, séduisant et dur, et qui éblouit parfois mes huit ans d'une lumière inintelligible" (2: 988).]

We see that 'Colette' begins to be aware of books as containing discourse, rather than simply the mysterious, alluring promise of discourse. She becomes aware of *texts,* rather than just books. With this comes the beginning of conflict—gone is the relationship between two distinct entities who have the power to remain mutually impenetrable if they so desire. Labiche and Daudet "worm their way" into her happy childhood. There is the beginning of a violation of her perceived complete self-sufficiency and self-containment. We are on the verge, with 'Colette,' of a stage where discourse begins to be perceived, on some level, as holding power, as incarnating a law. This is a law described in terms suggestive of masculine dominance—"condescending teachers," "seductive and severe," "incomprehensible light."

At this point we begin to note the intervention of both parents in their daughter's apprenticeship. The mother's is the more important in terms of the space devoted to it in Colette's text, as well as in terms of the privileged place her intervention has in the title of the chapter. The mother is giving 'Colette' an apprenticeship. The example she sets is one of pleasure in the text and of dialogue with it, for the mother proves to be a very Barthesian reader.

If the mother takes pleasure in reading, they are pleasures she would like to share with her daughter—"she [thinks] it strange that at eight years old [her daughter] should sometimes fail to share in her enjoyment" (*MMH* 35). This is illustrated again in the scene in which the mother asks the narrator if she's read a certain ghost story. 'Sido' wonders if there could be anything prettier than the page where the ghost is "wandering by moonlight in the churchyard." She continues: "A ghost must be a wonderful thing to see. I only wish I could see one; I should call you at once if I did" (*MMH* 34). The text is a source of pleasure, and the pleasure is one to be shared.

As for dialogue, in discussing the texts with 'Colette' the mother takes the discourses within them to task.

> Beautiful books that I used to read, beautiful books that I left unread . . . I learned, long before the age for love, that love is complicated, tyrannical and even burdensome, since my mother grudged the prominence they gave it.
> "It's a great bore—all the love in these books," she used to say. "In life, my poor Minet-Chéri, folk have other fish to fry. Did none of these lovesick people you read of have children to rear or a garden to care for? Judge for yourself, Minet-Chéri, have you or your brothers ever heard me harp on love as they do in books? And yet I think I ought to know something about it, having had two husbands and four children!" (*MMH* 35)
>
> [Beaux livres que je lisais, beaux livres que je ne lisais pas. . . . J'y connus, bien avant l'âge de l'amour, que l'amour est compliqué et tyrannique et même encombrant, puisque ma mère lui chicanait sa place.
> "C'est beaucoup d'embarras, tant d'amour dans ces livres, disait-elle. Mon pauvre Minet-Chéri, les gens ont d'autres chats à fouetter, dans la vie. Tous ces amoureux que tu vois dans les livres, ils n'ont donc jamais ni enfants à élever, ni jardin à soigner? Minet-Chèri, je te fais juge : est-ce que vous m'avez jamais, toi et tres frères, entendue rabâcher autour de l'amour comme ces gens font dans les livres? Et pourtant je pourrais réclamer voix au chapitre, je pense; j'ai eu deux maris et quatre enfants!" (2: 989)]

Close exploration of the narrator's words is particularly revelatory here. "I learned, long before the age for love, that love is complicated, tyrannical and even burdensome . . ." We have the impression that the books mediate between 'Colette' and experience: it is in them that she learns about love, even before the age of experiencing it. But reading on we see that is not the full picture. "I learned, long before the age for love, that love is complicated, tyrannical and even burdensome, since my mother grudged the prominence [books] gave it." It is not directly from the texts that 'Colette' learns something about this love, it is through her mother's reaction to the way it is presented in texts, in discourse. It is her mother's mediation of the daughter's relationship to texts that is crucial in her apprenticeship as resistant reader. Unlike 'Juliette,' the mother *does* assume the role of narratee, as her daughter watches and listens. She must in order to read the texts as fiction. However, she does it grudgingly, in critiquing it, as she critiques the text that her role as narratee would produce. Thus 'Colette' as apprentice learns the fictionality of this role and the text it produces—its noninfallibility, its contingency, its nonnecessity.

It is this contestation of discourse that she witnesses that gives her an entry into the idea of the *pushiness* of discourse. This is also what initiates her into the act of reading as dialogue with it and as resistance.[19]

This is the first step in the apprenticeship 'Colette' undergoes under her mother's guidance—a recognition of the fictionality of fiction, and of the necessary combativeness of reading. The mother's implicit empowerment of her daughter as reader becomes, however, even more explicit and direct:

> I hardly know what literary coldness, healthy on the whole, protected me from romantic delirium, and caused me—a little later, when I sampled certain books of time-honoured and supposedly infallible seductiveness—to be critical when I should by rights have fallen an intoxicated victim. There again I was perhaps influenced by my mother, whose innate innocence made her inclined to deny evil, even when her curiosity led her to seek it out, and to consider it, jumbled up with good, with wondering eyes.
>
> "This one? Oh, this isn't a harmful book, Minet-Chéri," she would say. "Yes, I know there's one scene, one chapter . . . But it's only a novel. Nowadays writers sometimes run short of ideas, you know. You might have waited a year or two before reading it, perhaps. But after all, Minet-Chéri, *you must learn to use your judgment.* You've got enough sense to keep it to yourself if you understand too much, and perhaps there are no such things as harmful books." (*MMH* 36-37, emphasis added)
>
> [Je ne sais quelle froideur littéraire, saine à tout prendre, me garda du délire romanesque, et me porta un peu plus tard, quand j'affrontais tels livres dont le pouvoir éprouvé semblait infaillible, à raisonner quand je n'aurais dû être qu'une victime enivrée. Imitais-je encore en cela ma mère, qu'une candeur particulière inclinait à nier le mal, ce-

pendant que sa curiosité le cherchait et le contemplait pêle-mêle avec le bien, d'un oeil émerveillé?

"Celui-ci? Celui-ci n'est pas un mauvais livre, Minet-Chéri, me disait-elle. Oui, je sais bien, il y a cette scène, ce chapitre... Mais c'est du roman. Ils sont à court d'inventions, tu comprends, les écrivains, depuis le temps. Tu aurais pu attendre un an ou deux, avant de le lire... Que veux-tu! *débrouille-toi là-dedans*, Minet-Chéri. Tu es assez intelligente pour garder pour toi ce que tu comprendras que trop . . . Et peut-être n'y a-t-il pas de mauvais livres..." (2: 990, emphasis added)]

Crucial here is the direct empowerment of the daughter by the mother: "you must learn to use your judgment. You've got enough sense to keep it to yourself if you understand too much, and perhaps there are no such things as harmful books." The daughter is empowered to enter the fray and do battle with discourse, on the assumption that she is capable of it. Her intelligence mentioned is not cited as an asset because it will allow her to understand. This is already taken for granted. Rather it will allow her to preserve social conventions, which are the only real obstacles to her reading certain books; for her ability to understand is not an obstacle, nor her ability to hold her own with the discourses they contain. The mother actually strips discourse of much of its power: "But it's only a novel . . . perhaps there are no such things as harmful books." She questions even the discrete categories of good and evil that might be used to describe them— she sees "evil . . . jumbled up with good, with wondering eyes." It is curiosity (again, a form of pleasure) that motivates her to contemplate them, not a desire to judge or to order reality.

If the mother is a revisionist Pandora, curious about and investigating all, yet not unleashing evil, but rather questioning the very categories of good and evil, then 'Colette' is a revisionist Eve. Curiosity in the face of interdiction is her reaction to the mediation of the father in her relationship to texts, yet the result of her actions is not perpetual pain and misery, but the toughening necessary to survive.

"And perhaps there are no such things as harmful books."
Nevertheless, there were those that my father locked away in his thuya-wood desk. *But chiefly it was the author's name that he locked away.*

"I fail to see the use of children reading Zola!"

Zola caused him a problem, and rather than seek in his pages for reasons that would explain why he allowed or forbade us to read him, he placed upon the index a vast, complete Zola, periodically increased by further yellow deposits.

"Mother, why aren't I allowed to read Zola?"

Her grey eyes, so unskilled at dissimulation, revealed their perplexity.

"It's quite true there are certain Zola's that I would rather you didn't read." (*MMH* 37, translation modified, my emphasis)

["Et peut-être n'y a-t-il pas de mauvais livres..."

Il y avait pourant ceux que mon père enfermait dans son secrétaire en bois de thuya. *Mais il enfermait surtout le nom de l'auteur.*

"Je ne vois pas d'intérêt à ce que les enfants lisent Zola!"

Zola l'ennuyait, et plutôt que d'y chercher une raison de nous le permettre ou de nous le défendre, il mettait à l'index un Zola intégral, massif, accru périodiquement d'alluvions jaunes.

"Maman, pourquoi est-ce que je ne peux pas lire Zola?"

Les yeux gris, si malhabiles à mentir, me montraient leur perplexité:

"J'aime mieux, évidemment, que tu ne lises pas certains Zola..." (2: 990-91, emphasis added).]

The first thing we note in the act of censorship that constitutes the father's intervention in the daughter's coming of age as reader is that "chiefly it was *the author's name* that he locked away" (emphasis added), and this is significant. For Foucault, "[t]he author's name manifests the appearance of a certain discursive set and indicates the status of this discourse within a society and a culture."[20] It seems to be a particular discourse that the father forbids, rather than simply a text or a book, and, if we were to carry further the application of Foucault's idea, the "status of this discourse within a society and a culture." Since the discourse in question is, as we shall see, disempowering of women, and since it enjoys strong social credence, we conclude that the father in forbidding it seeks to protect his daughter. In any case, for Foucault, in forbidding a discourse, he would be seeking to protect 'Colette' not only from the discourse itself, but from the power that discourse wields in society and will thus, in the father's view, wield over her as well. Since the father appears here as having an excessive respect for discourse that leaves no place for the free and easy dialog with—and resistance to—it, he seems closer here to 'Juliette' than to the mother.

Paradoxically, it is his desire to protect her from discourse that invests the discourse with the power to cause fear. Interdiction drives young 'Colette' to purloin and to read in secret one of the forbidden Zola novels, and we read:

> I went out into the garden with my first pilfered book.[21] Like several others by Zola it contained a rather insipid story of heredity, in which an amiable and healthy woman gives up her beloved cousin to a sickly friend, and all of it might well have been written by Ohnet, God knows, had the puny wife not known the joy of bringing a child into the world. She produced it suddenly, with a blunt, crude wealth of detail, an anatomical analysis, a dwelling on the colour, odour, contortions and cries, wherein I recognized nothing of my quiet country-bred experience. (*MMH* 37-38)
>
> [Je m'en allai au jardin, avec mon premier livre dérobé. Une assez douceâtre histoire d'hérédité l'emplissait, mon Dieu, comme plusieurs Zola. La cousine robuste et bonne cédait son cousin aimé à une malingre amie, et tout se fût passé comme sous Ohnet, ma foi, si la chétive épouse n'avait connu la joie de mettre un enfant au monde. Elle donnait le jour soudain, avec un luxe brusque et cru de détails, une minutie anatomique, une complaisance dans la couleur, l'odeur, l'attitude, le cri, où je ne reconnus rien de ma tranquille compétence de jeune fille des champs. (2: 991)]

Crucial here is not only the censorship of the father but also the feeling of powerlessness before the text that this engenders in 'Colette,' and especially the fact that this powerlessness is related in particular to gender. For as we have just seen, it is in the act of reading in violation of her father's interdiction that 'Colette' first feels herself not only powerless, but in a gendered position vis-à-vis the text. The father's interdiction combines with an essentially male discourse of pregnancy and childbirth as disease[22] found in the forbidden Zola novel in question and 'Colette' continues: "I felt credulous, terrified, threatened in my dawning *femininity*" (*MMH* 38, emphasis added). Particularly suggestive for my argument are not only the fact that she feels menaced as a gendered being, but also the word "credulous"; 'Colette' no longer feels able to dialog with discourse, she finds herself believing it, subject to it, no longer in a position of being able to chose whether or not to take its message, but succumbing to believing it in spite of herself.

Colette's story does not give much detail surrounding the reasons for the father's interdiction of the text. We know only that he puts it off limits. Whatever his objection to Zola is, his solution to the question, unlike the mother's ("perhaps there are no such things as harmful books") is to judge, to condemn and to forbid. This very gesture implies a belief in the power of discourse; otherwise there would be no reason to forbid.

Thus the lesson of the intervention of the father in his daughter's apprenticeship as a reader is one that reinforces the notion of the power of discourse, and of that power as coming from the male, or the father. As we saw earlier in the case of 'Juliette,' this type of gendered passive and submissive involvement with the text is coupled with the reading of an actual text, the content of which reproduces this passivity, helplessness, and victimization in a gendered way. The gendered nature of the interdiction, coming from the father, sends not only the message of the power of discourse over the reader, in this case the female child, but also of that power as being something to which he as father is presumably privy, for he has the right to allow or forbid access to it. This is echoed by the gendered nature of the distribution of power and helplessness presented in the text—where, as we have noted, the female character becomes an object in an essentially male discourse of pregnancy and childbirth as disease. Sido remonstrates with the discourse, after 'Colette' faints:

> "There, there now. There's nothing so terrible as all that in the birth of a child, nothing terrible at all. It's much more beautiful in real life. The suffering is so quickly forgotten, you'll see! The proof that all women forget it is that it is only men—and what business was it of Zola's, anyway?—who write stories about it." (*MMH* 39)
>
> ["Laisse donc, laisse donc... Ce n'est pas si terrible, va, c'est loin d'être si terrible, l'arrivée d'un enfant. La peine qu'on y prend s'oublie

si vite, tu verras!... La preuve que toutes les femmes l'oublient, c'est qu'il n'y a jamais que les hommes—est-ce que ça le regardait, voyons, ce Zola?—qui en font des histoires..." (2: 992)]

For Sido, pain in childbirth has a different significance. Rather than signifying woman's near-fatal enslavement to her biology, it foretells the bond between the mother and child:

"When you came into the world, my last born, Minet-Chéri, I suffered for three days and two nights. When I was carrying you I was as big as a house. . . . But I've never regretted my suffering. They do say that children like you, who have been carried so high in the womb and have taken so long to come down into the daylight, are always the children that are most loved, because they have lain so near their mother's heart and have been so unwilling to leave her." (*MMH* 38)

["Quand je t'ai mise au monde, toi la dernière, Minet-Chéri, j'ai souffert trois jours et deux nuits. . . . Mais je n'ai jamais regretté ma peine: on dit que les enfants, portés comme toi si haut, et lents à descendre vers la lumière, sont toujours des enfants très chéris, parce qu'ils ont voulu se loger tout près du cœur de leur mère, et ne la quitter qu'à regret..." (2: 991)]

Thus, we come full circle, back to the role of the mother in the process of 'Colette' coming of age as reader. Once again she models the recognition of the fictionality of fiction, and of dialog with it and resistance; she assumes the power inherent in the role of narratee. Reading for the mother is primarily aesthetic (having to do with pleasure and the senses—the "lovely ghost"); the father's reading seems more tied to ideology—meaning and judgment. The father recognizes a power in discourse and feels overawed by it; the mother does not—she even goes so far as to read Corneille in church, substituting a text of her choice for the sermon of the priest, as well as debating points with him on which she is not in agreement (*MMH* 112). Thus, under the influence of her father's intervention, 'Colette' experiences reading as disempowering and threatening, even to the point of making it impossible at the time of reading under his intervention to call up "the exorcising voice"—that of Sido, with her alternate version of the tale of childbirth. But after the bout with physical collapse (as with 'Juliette,' this method of reading seems to make the reader physically ill), it is Sido's voice that welcomes her back to the world, dispelling not just the content of the frightening text read, but the power of discourse in general that this episode of interdiction had served to set up. In conclusion, while the father's intervention in her apprenticeship disempowers 'Colette' as a reader and as a female being, the mother's empowers her, as both.

Thus I have argued that a positively connoted reading in Colette, that learned by the character of the same name, involves an engagement of the self with the other, while a negatively connoted reading, exemplified by Juliette, involves a loss of self. From a feminist perspective, the point goes beyond aesthetics alone and engages the question of ethics. Reading involves survival of the self within structures of domination that can be seen in ways of reading as well as in the content of texts read. As the case of Juliette and her "wrong solution" to the problem illustrates, reading in Colette carries a polemical message, challenging readers of any gender to read for the "right solution," that is, the construction of an intact self.

2

Writing as Other

Colette, Gabrielle, Colette de Jouvenel, the Little One, Minet-Chéri, Colette Willy, Claudine, Bel-Gazou . . . 'Colette' has passed through and given herself many names. The multiplicity of identities suggested by the proliferation of names challenges us to the question—where is the origin of the discourse that is Colette's work? The humanist convention of stable identity is unsettled, just as the legal convention of naming undergoes subversion, by the work of this particular "author."

Indeed Colette's texts construct, rather than an identity, an exploration of the problematic of identity. We as readers, and particularly feminist readers, might, however, be tempted to place a definitive identity upon her in our attempt to recover her as a woman writer. Her story as a writer, as she recounts it in *My Apprenticeships,* has in fact all the elements of the story of a hero. Her beginnings as a hack writer under her husband, and especially the participation that this experience entailed in a certain discourse of women and of feminine sexuality, lead, through struggle and hard work, to her eventual legal independence[1] as well as freedom from coercion as a writer, not to mention great success. The very clarity of the tale on a certain level tempts us to assign to it a simple meaning—of triumphant victory over alienation from self and writing as other. As a matter of fact, I do argue a move in Colette's work away from the production of a conventional patriarchal discourse of women and sexuality and towards greater experience, questioning, self-awareness, strength, and independence, and thus, for me, hers is indeed a success story. At the same time, the self that is constructed in her works is not in the end a single and stable identity. It is the experience of having created herself through a discourse that the protagonist does not choose or create that later gives rise to a need for self-definitions *in resistance* to this initial alienating experience of writing. That the subjectivity presented in Colette is always to be rethought, always created anew, is the logical result of that first experience of writing within another's definition of the self.

This chapter will discuss in particular the initiatory experiences in speech of the child 'Colette,' as they are narrated in two chapters of *My Mother's House*—"The Priest on the Wall" and "The Little One." It will then move to a discussion of her apprenticeship as a writer, through an examination of the *Claudine* series, read through the filter of the narrator's discussion of them and the conditions of their creation in *My Apprenticeships*.

Nicole Ward Jouve's interpretation of "The Priest on the Wall" in *My Mother's House* provides us with a starting point from which to trace the development of the speaking and writing self. Both "The Priest on the Wall" and "The Little One" lead to the same state of questioning, in terms of the status of the subject, as does proliferation of names for 'Colette.' Not only is subjectivity in language put into doubt, but these chapters also open up the question of desire in language. Jouve writes:

> Early on in *My Mother's House,* little Colette is described as relishing the sound of unknown words. She delights in 'presbytery,' hurling it at people as an insult from the top of the garden wall. It's the 'semiotic' all right: the child revels in the sound, she vents aggression through it, not knowing what it 'means.' The signifier functions independently from the signified, carrying 'archaic' drives.[2]

In this chapter, as Jouve analyzes it, language is not the servant of a subject who consciously manipulates and controls it to say what she 'means.' Yet if it is true that a traditional subjectivity within language is in this way undermined here, what I find most interesting in this passage is that the protagonist 'Colette' is in a powerful mode within this language.

This scene is reminiscent of her earliest, prereading contact with those purveyors of discourse already discussed—the books in the family library. There, her first contact was not with books as containing discourse, but with them as physical objects, which she used to create a safe and enclosed space for herself. Here again, the spoken language is not a container of discourse but a physical, sensual pleasure. And again, 'Colette' uses this language which does not 'mean' to make a space for herself, since it is used aggressively towards imaginary others—"invisible outlaws" (*MMH* 31), and thus to create in play a safe space for herself. This premeaning language as translator of drives is a means of imposing her will, and gratifying her desire. Precisely because the words have no meaning for her, she is freer to do with them what she will. She is the powerful one in this situation, not the words.[3]

"The Little One" presents us with a similar situation. Here language is also play and is also used in the service of drives. Yet whereas in "The Priest on the Wall" she is in control of the words, in "The Little One" the words, which she is now able to understand, overcome her, filling her with an identity that she takes on, that evacuates her, and then leaves her "debased." The words also inspire her with desire—an alienating, frightening desire.

This particular chapter opens with the end of a day of play among six little girls, a day that is not coincidentally a Thursday, for what the little girls have been indulging in is the "full license of Thursday" (*MMH* 22). In the France of this time this was a day off from school, and this is therefore a day of freedom, but without the restraining influence of the special clothes that make Sundays "empty days of idle dreaming" (*MMH* 21). Thursday's ordinary clothes permit a "degrading pursuit of pleasure," which is the particular pleasure of playing at being someone else.

This game involves what Kristeva calls intertextuality, the notion that language is always made up of other language. The little girls become the mouthpiece for the language of the adults around them. "Not a single event of village life that they have not declaimed and mimicked with passionate intensity!" (*MMH* 22), writes the narrator. It is in fact through language that the little girls are able to effect their disguise and to adopt the personae of different individuals in the village.

> One of them has played at being the invalid, another has sold coffee to a third, a horse-dealer, who in return has sold her a cow. "Thirty louis and a gift at that! Swine to you if you say it isn't!" Jeanne has got inside the skin of Grandpa Gruel, the dealer in tripe and rabbit-skins, while Yvonne has impersonated his lean daughter, a wretched and dissolute hag. Scire and his wife, Gruel's neighbors, have looked out through the eyes of Gabrielle and Sandrine, and all the filth of a village street has poured forth from six childish mouths. (*MMH* 22)
>
> [L'une fit la malade, l'autre vendit du café à une troisième, maquignonne qui lui céda ensuite une vache : 'Trente pistoles, bonté! Cochon qui s'en dédit!' Jeanne emprunta au père Gruel son âme de tripier et de préparateur de peaux de lapin. Yvonne incarna la fille de Gruel, une maigre créature torturée et dissolue. Scire et sa femme, les voisins de Gruel, parurent sous les traits de Gabrielle et de Sandrine, et par six bouches enfantines s'épancha la boue d'une ruelle pauvre. (2: 979)]

Much in this child's use of language is reminiscent of what Colette describes in "The Priest on the Wall." The meaning of the words is less the function of language here than its use as a vehicle for the expression of aggression or drives. Yet, at the same time, meaning begins to intervene here in a way that it did not in the other story. For, although the little girls are stepping into ready-made language, as it were, for the fun of mimicking adults, without thinking too much about what it means, they are not at this point *unaware* of its meaning. This differentiates this play from that in "The Priest on the Wall," for this language with its meaning does, as the afternoon wears on, penetrate them and effect a change in them so that it becomes the motor force in their play rather than the girls themselves. Moreover, this change is a distinctly negative one that leaves them "sick" and "debased." This negative change or deterioration is the direct result of assuming the roles or personae that go with this ready-made language, as we see in the following passage:

> Today [the Little One] is ugly, and feels upon her face the passing ugliness of . . . above all, the successive mimicries that have linked her with Jeanne, with Sandrine, with Aline, the daily dressmaker, with the chemist's wife and the postmaster's daughter. For the children had

crowned the afternoon's sport with a long game of "What shall we be when we're grown up?" (*MMH* 23)

[Aujourd'hui, [la Petite] est laide, et sent sur son visage la laideur provisoire que lui composent . . . surtout des ressemblances successives, mimétiques, qui l'apparentent à Jeanne, à Sandrine, à Aline la couturière, à la dame du pharmacien et la demoiselle de la poste. Car elles ont joué longuement, pour finir, les petites, au jeu de 'qu'est-ce qu'on sera.' (2: 980)]

Not only does language become the motor force in their play rather than the girls themselves, but, especially as it leads to the adoption of others' roles or identities, it makes them ugly.

Intertextuality is, therefore, construed as negative in this particular case, for here the 'other language' of which language is inevitably made up is so strongly and exclusively that of another. While according to the Kristevan notion of intertextuality the language we use is inevitably in part other language, is always dialog, the participation of the girls here is not enough.

Thus while this passage undermines the idea of subjectivity in language, it does more than that. The particular type of nonsubjectivity in language that this passage illustrates is not presented as an aesthetic solution to this writer's quest for textual selfhood, but a false path. This chapter sketches the potential dangers of loss of self in language, a danger that the subject must confront.

This becomes more apparent as the potential danger of loss of self in ready-made language is linked to the question of desire. "The Little One" suggests that desire can become another possible conduit for loss of self when the desire expressed has as its object, once again, a role, a place that is ready-made, already formed, and that will therefore constrain, alienate, and even efface the subject who enters into it.

During the course of this game of "What shall we be when we're grown up," the Little One announces that in the future she will be a sailor. The reason for this choice lies in the fascination of certain images that incarnate the sailor for her. In fact, she recounts in the following manner the reason for her choice:

> [S]he sometimes dreamed of being a boy, and wearing trousers and a blue béret. The sea, of which Minet-Chéri knows nothing, the ship breasting a wave, the golden island and the gleaming fruit, all that surged up much later, to serve as a background to the blue blouse and the cap with a pompom. (*MMH* 23-24)
>
> [{E}lle rêve parfois d'être garçon et de porter culotte et béret bleus. La mer qu'ignore Minet-Chéri, le vaisseau debout sur une crête de vagues, l'île d'or et les fruits lumineux, tout cela n'a surgi après, que pour servir de fond au blouson bleu, au béret à pompon. (2: 980)]

Just as images—clothes in particular, make the difference between the behavior of the girls on Thursdays and on Sundays, clothes, an outfit, the image it constitutes for the Little One, and the further images it calls up, are at the base of this desire to be a sailor.

This desire comes out of a ready-made image, and it leads to further images. It is a process of simulation that is going on, in Jean Baudrillard's meaning of the word: "the generation by models of a real without origin or reality: a hyperreal."[4] For him this is a process that feeds upon itself, and he asserts that "the age of simulation . . . begins with a liquidation of all referentials—worse: by their artificial resurrection in systems of signs" (167).

In like manner, the initial seduction of the Little One by appearances, by simulacra, pulls her into the further generation of simulacra. Her thoughts take the form of further referent-less images generated within the system of signs that is language. After announcing her future profession, the Little One repeats to herself: " 'I shall be a sailor, and on my voyages...' " (*MMH* 24). The lack of referent to this is explicitly commented upon. Her playmates gone, she sits down, still under the sway of seduction.

> She sits down on the grass to rest and reflect. Travel? Adventure? For a child who, twice a year at the periods of the great spring and winter provisioning, leaves the confines of her district, and drives in a victoria to her country town, such words have neither force nor value. They evoke only the printed page, the coloured picture. The Little One, now very tired, repeats the words "When I go round the world..."

automatically, just as she would say, "When I go gathering chestnuts..." (*MMH* 24)

[Assise dans l'herbe, elle se repose et pense peu. Le voyage? L'aventure?... Pour une enfant qui franchit deux fois l'an les limites de son canton, au moment des grandes provisions d'hiver et de printemps, et gagne le chef-lieu en victoria, ces mots-là sont sans force et sans vertu. Ils n'évoquent que des pages imprimées, des images en couleur. La Petite, fatiguée, se répète machinalement : "Quand je ferai le tour du monde..." comme elle dirait : "Quand j'irai gauler des châtaignes..." (2: 980)]

She is at this point tired and unaware of what she is saying. Language has overcome her, her very desires inspired from it. She has become an empty vessel, like the one she dreams of sailing in. She has become the vessel, and language the sailor who is sailing her, through the desires it calls up in her.

Here the focus of the story shifts, symbolized by the shift in light in the garden caused by a lamp being lit inside the house. The result of this lamplight is described thus: "All that had looked green up to the moment before, now turns blue around this motionless red flame" (*MMH* 24). This new light cast creates a new garden, one that is suddenly unrecognizable, hostile, and frightening: "The garden, grown suddenly hostile, menaces a now sobered little girl with the cold leaves of its laurels, the raised sabres of its yuccas, and the barbed caterpillars of its monkey-puzzle tree" (*MMH* 24). What the Little One focuses on, now that the garden has become dark, is the light inside the house, and a hand "wearing a shining thimble," which passes again and again before the light (*MMH* 24). It is the maternal hand, sewing, that she sees. In the now darkened garden, watching this figure in the lighted window, bent over the lamp light and stitching, 'Colette' becomes aware that outside the circle of maternal light "all is danger, all is loneliness" (*MMH* 25). It is the force of the maternal that pulls her back into the familiar and grounds her.

Again, we are reminded that in her early encounters with reading, 'Colette' drew the strength to resist the alienating and depersonalizing effects of discourse from her mother. We see a similar situation here, where with her sewing gestures Sido symbolically pulls towards her and attaches to herself her child, binds her to warmth, familiarity, maternal love, and security, banishing the hostile garden, and dispelling the emptying desires that the children's play in a rootless, referent-less language had called up.

The mother thus functions here as guarantor, until such time as the child finds her own language. This foreshadows the role the mother figure will play in Colette's later construction of herself as writing subject, undertaken after she has gone beyond the voice used in the creation of the *Claudines*. In that later construction, the mother's language, inextricably intertwined with the daughter's, is what allows her to base her self-definition in a feminine voice. In chapter 3, we will return to this question of the figure of the mother who grounds the narrator within the darkened, frightening garden of alienating discourse, when we tackle the question of the narrator's move from loss of self in the discourse of another towards autonomy within discourse. However, for the moment, I will continue to examine the narrator's initial ventures into discourse, as a writing rather than speaking subject now, and especially within the framework of the loss of self mentioned above.

If the mother brings the daughter back to familiarity from a potentially alienating and frightening venture into discourse, the father, on the other hand, provides an encouragement for these ventures. In fact, preliminary ventures into critical mastery of language are offered both by the father, and later 'Willy.' 'Colette' recounts in *Sido* that:

> I was still quite small when he began to appeal to my critical sense. Later on, thank goodness, I proved less precocious, but I well remember how severe a judge I was at ten years old.
>
> "Listen to this," my father would say, and I would listen, very sternly. Perhaps it would be a purple passage of oratorical prose, or an ode in flowing verse, with a great parade of rhythm and rhyme, resounding as a mountain storm.
>
> "Well?" my father would ask. "I really believe that this time. . . . Go on, say!"
>
> I would toss my head with its fair plaits, a forehead too high to look amiable, and a little marble of a chin, and let fall my censure: "Too many adjectives, as usual!"
>
> At that my father exploded, thundering abuse on me: I was dust, vermin, a conceited louse. But the vermin, unperturbed, went on: "I

told you the same thing last week, about the *Ode à Paul Bert*. Too many adjectives!"

No doubt he laughed at me behind my back, and I daresay he felt proud of me too. But at the moment we glared at each other as equals, already on a fraternal footing. (*Sido* 176)

[J'étais encore petite quand mon père commença d'en appeler à mon sens critique. Plus tard, je me montrai, Dieu merci, moins précoce. Mais quelle intransigeance, je m'en souviens, chez ce juge de dix ans...

"Ecoute ça," me disait mon père.

J'écoutais, sévère. Il s'agissait d'un beau morceau de prose oratoire, ou d'une ode, vers faciles, fastueux par le rythme, par la rime, sonores comme un orage de montagne...

"Hein? interrogeait mon père. Je crois que cette fois-ci!... Eh bien, parle!"

Je hochais ma tête et mes nattes blondes, mon front trop grand pour être aimable et mon petit menton en bille, et je laissais tomber mon blâme : "Toujours trop d'adjectifs!"

Alors mon père éclatait, écrasait d'invectives la poussière, la vermine, le pou vaniteux que j'étais. Mais la vermine, imperturbable, ajoutait :

"Je te l'avais déjà dit la semaine dernière, pour *l'Ode à Paul Bert*. Trop d'adjectifs!"

Il devait derrière moi, rire, et peut-être s'enorgueillir... Mais au premier moment nous nous toisions en égaux, et déjà confraternels. (3 : 517)]

Although 'Colette' recounts herself as being spontaneous in her desire to judge, it is nevertheless a behavior *called forth* by the father's invitation to her to exercise her "critical sense." The child seems to have understood on some instinctive level what is expected here, and is not perhaps entirely unaware that this behavior causes her father to "feel proud." This role of judge that the father invites her to fill is one that will later be taken over by 'Willy,' a second, textual father, "the 'Father of Claudine,' as he liked to be called" (*MA* 64). If this role of judge or censor is one that 'Colette' learns to play from the father, and that 'Willy' will later play in relation to her own writing, these two men have another characteristic in common, for both are themselves incapable of writing.

Already much discussed in Colette scholarship are the passages in *Sido* that recount the discovery by the narrator, in a séance, that she had become what her father had most wanted to be, a writer. Equally commented on is the scene of the discovery, after his death, of the truth of her father's 'works'—that the already bound volumes on the family library shelf—an entire row—are completely empty, except for the dedication page, which is found to read:

> TO MY DEAR SOUL,
> HER FAITHFUL HUSBAND:
> **JULES-JOSEPH COLETTE**
> (*Sido* 197)

In a strikingly similar situation 'Colette' recounts that 'Willy' had more talent than those whose works he signed (*MA* 72), but that he as well feared the blank page.

> Between the wish, the need to produce saleable printed matter, and the act of writing, this strange author encountered an obstacle that I have never been able to picture—some barrier of a peculiar shape and quality, unknown, possibly terrifying. His letters express only the *refusal* to write. (*MA* 72)
>
> [Entre le désir, le besoin de produire une denrée imprimée et la possibilité d'écrire, s'élève chez cet auteur étrange, un obstacle dont je n'ai jamais distingué la forme, la nature, peut-être terrifiantes. Sa correspondance ne révèle que le *refus* d'écrire. (3: 1032)]

The narrator elaborates on this:

> I have often thought that M. Willy suffered from a sort of agoraphobia, that he had a nervous horror of the blank page. His correspondence shows a preference for postcards, letter-cards, half- or quarter-sheets of notepaper, the flaps of envelopes, triangles cut off and used just as they are, even newspaper wrappers. And again, on these scraps,

the writing is huddled in the far corners. Sometimes he scribbles the answers in the margins of the letters he has received and so posts them back. (*MA* 76-77)

[J'ai souvent songé que M. Willy souffrait d'une sorte d'agoraphobie, qu'il eut l'horreur nerveuse du papier vierge. Sa correspondence hante de préférence les pneumatiques, les cartes, les demis et les quarts de feuillets, les abattants d'enveloppes, détachés en forme de triangles, même les bandes de journaux. Encore, sur ces bribes, son écriture se réfugie-t-elle dans les angles. Il écrit souvent dans les marges des lettres qu'il a reçues, et le tout retourne à la poste. (3: 1035-36)]

In light of the fact that in both cases these "fathers" exercised, or caused to be exercised, a judge or censor role toward writing or literary creation, and that they both proved incapable of producing their own discourse, it is logical to conclude that they exercised the same judge or censor role towards themselves as towards others. It remains for the daughter, through her initiation by the mother, to accomplish what they could not. However, before returning to this initiation through the mother, I will first discuss the initial phase as a writer 'Colette' experiences under her first husband.

In *My Apprenticeships,* 'Colette' recounts her beginnings as a hack writer under her husband, 'Willy,' or Henry Gauthier-Villars. I will examine this reflection on her early writing, made within this later work. However, before doing so, an examination of the voice used to make these reflections will prove revelatory. Early on in *My Apprenticeships,* 'Colette' writes:

I can only be thankful today, that I absorbed nothing from my shadowy friends, learned no effective lessons either in dazzling virtue or resplendent vice, remained immune to influences insidiously diffused and even to direct infection. Occasionally, in my extreme youth, I found myself sighing to "be somebody." If I had had the courage to express my wish fully, I should have said "somebody else." But I soon gave it up. I have never succeeded in becoming somebody else. Dear patterns of a passionate excellence! Dear evil counsellors! Was it all I could do, to love you with a love and a horror that was equally disinterested? Forceful personalities have passed before me, paraded and given of their light. Not in vain, since they remain luminous and pleasing. But I discouraged them. Not to copy is always to discourage. An attention that goes only to feed curiosity looks like impertinence. And I have copied neither the good nor the others. I have listened to them, watched them.... (*MA* 7-8)

[Qu'il n'y ait pas eu, de mes ténébreux amis à moi, enseignement efficace d'une vertu ou d'un vice éclatants, osmose ni même simple contagion, je ne puis maintenant que m'en réjouir. Dans le temps de ma grande jeunesse, il m'est arrivé d'espérer que je deviendrais "quelqu'un." Si j'avais eu le courage de formuler mon espoir tout entier, j'aurais dit "quelqu'un d'autre". Mais j'y ai vite renoncé. Je n'ai jamais pu devenir quelqu'un d'autre. Chers exemples effrénés, chers conseillers néfastes, je n'aurai donc pu que vous aimer, d'un amour ou d'une horreur également désintéressés? Des personnages péremptoires ont devant moi passé, paradé et émis leur lumière, non point en vain puisqu'ils me demeurent agréables et lumineux. Mais je les ai découragés. On décourage toujours ceux qu'on n'imite point. L'attention qui n'alimente que la curiosité passe pour impertinence. Or je n'ai imité ni les bons, ni les autres. Je les ai écoutés, regardés. (3: 986-87)]

This passage clarifies a number of the aspects of the voice used here. First of all, this narrating voice declares itself autonomous, independent, free from vulnerability to "infection" by others. Moreover, this voice, a present voice, declares that even in the past, this was always so, although she did not always wish it to be so.

Thus 'Colette' here assumes the persona of an observer, an analyst, a decipherer of others. Moreover, she declares that this is not only true for the present of this narration, but also for the past. At the same time, the 'Colette' of the present plays in this narrative the role of the analyst, the observer, of this earlier self.

In the reflections on her earlier self, that self that produced her first writings, she compares her present ability as analyst reading signs and symbols to an earlier lack of the same skill. We read:

> The memories of my first and second years of marriage are clear and fantastic, like the impressions that dwell in the mind after some confused dream in which every detail, beneath its apparent incoherence, is plainly and fatally symbolic. But I was twenty-one and kept forgetting the symbols. (*MA* 34)
>
> [De la première, de la seconde année de mon mariage, je conserve un souvenir net et fantastique, comme l'image que l'on rapporte du fond d'un rêve désordonné dont tous les détails, sous une incohérence apparente, contiennent des symboles clairs et funestes. Mais j'avais vingt et un ans et j'oubliais à chaque moment les symboles. (3: 1005)]

If this earlier self was already unable to succeed in becoming someone else ("The Little One" also recounts the failure of that attempt), she had not, however, yet completed her apprenticeship in learning how to read. It is this she must learn to do anew, now in the adult world, if she is to attain again, at this level, a measure of autonomy. But first in the two-fold process of reading, in order to dialog with, to resist, the signs, she will have to learn to interpret them. It is the later self who has learned to read the signs. It is 'Colette' who takes upon herself the task of going back to read and interpret for us readers the meaning of the initiating experiences of that earlier self. It is this voice that narrates her initiation into writing.

The protagonist of this tale, the earlier self, since she has declared herself impermeable to the influence of others, must then necessarily have been coerced to write a discourse that she later disavows. This process is in fact recounted in *My Apprenticeships*. We will examine for this process the importance of two elements: the domination by another, which the later self specifically alludes to, and an immature selfhood, which seeks itself in paths that will later be rejected, something that the later self only hints at. These two are linked.

'Colette' describes in *My Apprenticeships* her beginnings as a writer—her start as a hack under her first husband.

> Figures, figures.... Where did you take me—I who paid so little heed to you? We had been married a year or a year and a half when M. Willy said to me: "You ought to put down what you remember of your

> board-school days. Don't be shy of the spicy bits. I might make something of it. Money's short. (*MA* 19)

> [Questions de chiffres, questions de chiffres... Où m'ont-ils menée, moi qui ne m'occupais pas d'eux? Un an, dix-huit mois après notre mariage, M. Willy me dit: "Vous devriez jeter sur le papier des souvenirs de l'école primaire. N'ayez pas peur des détails piquants, je pourrais peut-être en tirer quelque chose... Les fonds sont bas." (3: 994-95)]

This passage makes clear that the reason for writing the *Claudine* series is money, that the money that will come of it will go to someone else—to 'Willy,' and that the "détails piquants," the discourse of women and sexuality that he encourages her to include, is one that is to be falsified in order to exploit.[5]

'Colette' produces a manuscript, but 'Willy' does not at first consider it worth publishing. It is stuffed into the back of a drawer, and it is months or even years later before it is discovered again. 'Colette' recounts that it is after returning from a vacation that 'Willy' decides to straighten out the contents of his desk. It is interesting to note that the artificiality and ugliness of the desk repeat the falseness of the discourses that the manuscripts contain:

> The odious piece of furniture, hideous in its red baize cover and sham ebony paint, was turned out, the whitewood drawers appeared, disgorging a compressed mass of papers, and there came to light the forgotten set of copy-books I had so industriously blackened: *Claudine à l'Ecole*. (*MA* 58)

> [L'affreux comptoir peint en faux ébène, nappé de drap grenat, montra ses tiroirs de bois blanc, vomit des paperasses comprimées, et l'on revit, oubliés, les cahiers que j'avais noircis : *Claudine à l'école...*]

'Willy' leafs through them again, rereads snatches, and finally curses himself for an idiot. The scene ends thus:

> He swept up the scattered copy-books just as they were, grabbed his flat-brimmed top hat and bolted to his publisher's. And that is how I became a writer. (*MA* 58)
>
> [Il rafla en désordre les cahiers, sauta sur son chapeau à bords plats, courut chez un éditeur... Et voilà comment je suis devenue écrivain. (3: 1022)]

As 'Colette' thus begins her career as hack in earnest, 'Willy' becomes more "pressing and precise" in his coercive suggestions. 'Colette' describes them thus:

> "Couldn't you add a little to these—er—childish affairs?" M. Willy said to me. "A tender and overintimate affection, for instance, between Claudine and one of her friends?" (his actual words were brief and clear). "And dialect, lots of dialect. And rather more playfulness.... D'you see what I mean?" (*MA* 59)
>
> ["Vous ne pourriez pas, me dit M.Willy, échauffer un peu ce... ces enfantillages? Par exemple, entre Claudine et l'une de ses camarades, une amitié trop tendre..." (il employa une autre manière, brève, de se faire comprendre). Et puis du patois, beaucoup de mots patois... De la gaminerie... Vous voyez ce que je veux dire?" (3: 1023)]

Here, the discourses that are to be falsified, distorted, in order to sell, are more clearly described. In fact, the "spice" that 'Willy' requests, the addition of a more explicit sexual content, is to be linked to childishness on the part of the female protagonist and narrator. This position of inferiority in a situation of domination that the protagonist is to occupy is underscored by the insistence on dialect, for in the mentality of the capital, the provinces are another kind of child or inferior.

About her complicity in this project, this later self writes:

> Young women who write seldom have much sense of moderation (neither have old women, for that matter). And there is nothing that gives more assurance than a mask. The origin and anonymity of 'Claudine' seemed a rather indelicate joke that amused me and that I *obediently* made broader and broader. (*MA* 59, emphasis added)

> [Il n'est pas coutumier que les jeunes femmes (les vieilles non plus) aient, en écrivant, le souci de la mesure. Rien d'ailleurs ne rassure autant qu'un masque. La naissance et l'anonymat de "Claudine" me divertissaient comme une farce un peu indélicate, que je poussais *docilement* au ton libre. (3: 1023, emphasis added)]

Again, we note the extent to which the production of these discourses is in obedience to the directives of another. The protagonist of the *Claudine* series, and the discourses that inform her story, are consciously felt to be a mask.

The amusement that this work behind a mask affords her is elaborated on in the following passage. We see that her production of another's discourse, in particular the rendering of the character Maugis, reaches such a level of mastery that the reader is defied to distinguish between it and the original:

> "If you want my help for Maugis," said M. Willy, "leave gaps."
> I left no gaps. A challenge has provided entertainment for many an anonymous toiler, many a captive. My 'in the manner of —' held together perfectly, my Maugis talked pure, original Maugis.
> "Bravo!" said M. Willy, coldly. (*MA* 68)[6]
>
> ["Si vous avez besoin de moi pour Maugis, me dit M. Willy, laissez des blancs."
> Je n'en laissai pas. Car la gageure est un divertissement commun à bon nombre de captifs et d'anonymes. Mon "à la manière de..." se tenait fort bien, mon Maugis parlait le pur Maugis d'origine...
> "Bravo, dit froidement M. Willy." (3: 1029)]

However, if 'Colette' becomes expert at and diverts herself in producing "pure, original Maugis," she continues to maintain distance from her literary production, as the following passage reveals:

> To form a habit does not mean to become blinded; I did not think very highly of my first book, or of its three sequels. Time has not changed my opinion, and my judgment on all the *Claudines* is still severe. They frisk and frolic and play the giddy young girl altogether too

freely. The work reveals, indeed, an irrepressible youthfulness, if only in its lack of technique. But I do not like to rediscover, glancing through these very old books, the suppleness of mood that understood only too well what was required of it, the submission to every hint and the already deft manner of avoiding difficulties. . . . And I blame myself when I see how certain things in the *Claudines*—allusions, features that are caricatured yet recognizable, tales that come too near the truth—betray an utter disregard of doing harm. (*MA* 60)

> [Habitude ne veut pas dire aveuglement : je ne trouvai pas mon premier livre très bon—ni les trois suivants. Avec le temps, je n'ai guère changé d'avis, et je juge assez sévèrement de toutes les *Claudine*. Elles font l'enfant et la follette sans discrétion. La jeunesse, certes, y éclate, quand elle ne ferait que se marquer par le manque de métier. Mais il ne me plaît guère de retrouver, si je me penche sur quelqu'un de ces très anciens livres, une souplesse à réaliser ce qu'on réclamait de moi, une obéissance aux suggestions et une manière déjà adroite d'éviter l'effort. . . . Et je m'en veux que par allusions, traits caricaturés mais ressemblants, fables plausibles, ces *Claudine* révèlent l'insouciance de nuire. (3: 1024)

Thus the narrative voice of *My Apprenticeships* comes to the point of disavowing its earlier participation in this discourse, of clearly stating that it no longer identifies with it. The reason for this participation, namely coercion, has already been clearly stated.

Yet this later self also hints at other reasons for this participation. We read a direct allusion to this other motivation for participation in the following:

> Is it hard to understand how to have gone from a village home to the life I led after 1894 was an adventure so serious that it could bring a child of twenty to despair? Despair or a wild intoxication. It is true that, at first, ridden by youth and ignorance, I had known intoxication—a guilty rapture, an atrocious, impure, adolescent impulse. *There are many scarcely nubile girls who dream of becoming the show, the plaything, the licentious masterpiece of some middle-aged man.* It is an ugly dream that is punished by its fulfilment, a morbid thing, akin to

the neuroses of puberty, the habit of eating chalk and coal, of drinking mouthwash, of reading dirty books and sticking pins into the palm of the hand. (*MA* 23, my emphasis)

> [Comprendra-t-on que le fait d'échanger mon sort de villageoise contre la vie que je menais à dater de 1894 est une aventure telle, qu'elle suffit à désespérer une enfant de vingt ans, si elle ne l'enivre pas? La jeunesse et l'ignorance aidant, j'avais bien commencé par la griserie—une coupable griserie, un affreux et impur élan d'adolescente. *Elles sont nombreuses, les filles à peine nubiles qui rêvent d'être le spectacle, le jouet, le chef d'œuvre libertin d'un homme mur.* C'est une laide envie, qu'elles expient en la contentant, une envie qui va de pair avec les névroses de la puberté, l'habitude de grignoter la craie et le charbon, de boire l'eau dentifrice, de lire des livres sales et de s'enfoncer des épingles dans la paume des mains. (3: 997-98, my emphasis)]

The young girl's dream that this passage talks about, of being "the show, the plaything, the licentious masterpiece of some middle-aged man," sums up very well a large part of the contents of the *Claudine* series.[7] Curiously enough, the habits that accompany girls at this stage according to 'Colette,' particularly that of eating chalk, reappear, not this time in the later commentary on these early texts, but in one of the texts themselves, namely *Claudine at School*. However, chalk-eating is mentioned in connection not with Claudine, but with her schoolmate Anaïs (*C at S* 28, see also 98). Thus this young girl's dream, a masochistic one, is linked initially with Anaïs rather than Claudine, at least through its accompanying habits. Moreover, while Anaïs, through this chalk-eating habit, is linked to masochism, Claudine on the other hand, is most often sadistic in her behavior towards her schoolmates, including Anaïs. This sadism goes along with a pseudo-maleness. The name of the protagonist is the diminutive of her father's name, for he is called Claude. The protagonist is also motherless. She is oriented in her identity not toward the female but toward the male, but with a difference. Her move from female to male in identification is motivated by her desire for power in a hierarchical world where the male is the powerful one. Yet she remains inferior, since she remains all the same irrevocably female. She joins the club, but not as a full-fledged member—she can be at best a diminutive male. This status as male, but with all its ambiguity, is reflected in the precariousness of Claudine's initially dominant position within the framework of the sadomasochistic relationships we see in these early works.

Sadism and masochism are of course two sides of the same coin. Freud, in *Instincts and their Vicissitudes,* speaks of how instincts turn around upon themselves. Scoptophilia-exhibitionism as well as sadomasochism are two examples of pairs of such opposites, and both are much present in the *Claudine* series. Sadism can be seen as an "exercise of violence or power upon some other person as its object." Later, "this object is abandoned and replaced by the subject's self. Together with the turning round upon the self the change from an active to a passive aim is also brought about." And finally, "another person is sought as object; this person, in consequence of the alteration which has taken place in the aim of the instinct has to take over the original role of the subject." This latter case "is the condition commonly termed masochism."[8]

We see Claudine in both the position of the sadist and later of the masochist. In fact, in the *Claudine* series, an aspiration to an immature selfhood through masochism struggles with a simultaneous desire to disavow the dominated position. What happens is that Claudine desires to dominate—among those that in patriarchy are her inferiors by virtue anyway of not being her superiors—other women, or female-like characters such as Marcel. The masochistic desire—the immature aspiration to selfhood through masochism—comes into play with a suitable figure to bestow transcendence: a father-figure, Renaud. Thus while Claudine exposes, abuses, humiliates, and abandons her female companions, this dominance, based on behavior complicit with patriarchy, in the end serves only to make her, alone among women, worthy to become the "plaything" of Renaud.

It is here that the *Claudine* series seem to enter its real plot—the charting of this desire for transcendence through masochism. In her essay "Master and Slave: The Fantasy of Erotic Domination," Benjamin explicitly ties this fantasy, and both the sadism and the masochism involved, to subjectivity. "However disturbing or perverse their form," she writes, "the impulse to erotic violence and submission express deep yearnings for selfhood and transcendence."[9]

The key notion for Benjamin in selfhood is recognition. This is what the infant needs to receive from its first caretakers, for example, in order to "become [a] human being." The process of acquiring a self or a sense of identity, she continues, "occurs against the background of such [a recognizing] presence. This acquisition of selfhood she terms differentiation, which she describes in the following terms:

> Differentiation means developing the ability to see ourselves and others as independent and distinct beings; it means that we have learned that our acts and intentions can have an impact on others, and theirs on us. Perhaps the most difficult part of this process is, as Simone de Beauvoir put it, coming to terms with the existence of the other—recognizing her without effacing ourselves, asserting ourselves without effacing her. (281-82)

Psychological domination, she argues,

> is ultimately a failure to recognize the other person as like, although separate from oneself. The self that is strong enough to define itself not only through separateness but also through commonality with other subjects is able to recognize other subjects. This self is able to differentiate and need not objectify the other in order to separate. It is able to feel that it exists when it is with the other and when it is alone. (283)

If sadism and domination come out of a failure to achieve a mature selfhood, so does masochism. Benjamin paraphrases de Beauvoir as saying that

> masochism is essentially a desire for subordination to another person, rather than for the experience of pain as such. Masochism is a search for recognition of the self by an other who alone is powerful enough to bestow this recognition. . . . The masochist is unable to give herself freely and must or wishes to be forced to do so. But the desire for transcendence, the hope of being recognized, is discernable behind the masochist's submission. (286-87)

If it becomes clear that this plot—the tracing of this masochistic desire on the part of Claudine in relation to Renaud—is the logical conclusion of the discourses contained in the *Claudine* series, we also note at the same time that the narrative voice seems ill at ease with this story. Claudine here seems confused. On the one hand, the only culminating plot available for the series seems to be a heterosexual love of this sort, for aspiration to recognition by the dominant male in the gender hierarchy is what animates Claudine and the other female characters. The sexual relations portrayed between two women—Claudine and Luce, for example, and later Claudine and Rézi—do not really go outside the bounds of the discourses that we have described. However, since it takes shape within the discourses already set up by the *Claudine* series, this plot of heterosexual love can hardly be one in which the woman is anything but an object. In *Claudine Married*, we see an unresolved tension between the need to carry this plot through to its logical end, and a resistance to this, an inability to write this plot.

Thus Claudine enunciates sentiments like the following:

> My liberty oppressed me. . . . what I had been searching for months . . . with absolute clarity, was a master. Free women are not women at all. (*CM* 189)
>
> [Ma liberté me pèse. . . . ce que je cherche depuis des mois . . . c'était sans m'en douter, un maître. Les femmes libres ne sont pas des femmes. (1: 364)]

Yet without any direct contestation of this sort of discourse, Claudine also begins to voice sentiments such as the one quoted below:

> [G]o home! Have I no real dwelling then? No! I live here with a man, admittedly a man I love, but I am living with a man! (*CM* 57)
>
> [{R}entrer! Je n'ai donc pas de demeure? Non! J'habite ici chez un monsieur, un monsieur que j'aime, soit, mais j'habite chez un monsieur! (1: 420)]

This tension in *Claudine Married* is finally dissipated after Claudine, inevitably we feel, becomes a victim. Claudine's own affair with Rézi had in fact taken place under the controlling eye of Renaud. At the knowledge that she desires Rézi, he exclaims that

"No, it isn't the same thing at all [as adultery with a man]! You women can do anything. It's charming and it's of no consequence whatever...."

"I mean what I say and I'm right! Between you pretty little animals it's a ... how can I put it? ... a consolation for *us,* a restful change.... If I dared ... I would say that certain women need women in order to preserve their taste for men." (*CM* 99)

[—Non, ce n'est pas la même chose! Vous pouvez tout faire, vous autres. C'est charmant, et c'est sans importance....

—Si, je dis bien! C'est entre vous, petites bêtes jolies, une... comment dire?... une consolation de nous, une diversion qui vous repose.... Si j'osais ... je dirais qu'à certaines femmes il faut la femme pour conserver le goût de l'homme. (1: 453-54).]

Having established that this is not adultery, as no real sexual satisfaction can be had between women, he then sets about orchestrating the affair—renting the apartment in which they meet, retaining the key to it, escorting them to it, and playing host to them in it, and in general acting according to a manner that Claudine qualifies as having a "touch of the *voyeur*" (*CM* 99). This affair on the part of Claudine, taken over by Renaud and invested with the meaning he gives it, orchestrated by him finally for his own pleasure, can thus in no way signify a rebellion on the part of Claudine or a questioning of his power and authority over her. Rather, it is co-opted, and becomes no more than one more means of subordinating her to his desire. Infidelity on the part of Renaud, however, is of a different sort. The affair between Renaud and Rézi, which Claudine eventually discovers, is not one that she had known of, sanctioned, or controlled, in the way he had hers. Claudine thus feels betrayed and experiences pain upon the discovery of this act on the part of Renaud.

At this point, a half gesture of independence is used to resolve the situation. Claudine, after discovering Renaud's infidelity, goes back to Montigny, her childhood home. This foreshadows Colette's own behavior later—she will return to childhood through the writing of *My Mother's House, Sido,* and other works to a lesser extent. After Claudine's departure, Renaud is penitent and wants her back. She remains in Montigny however, where he joins her when he can. Thus she establishes her space in which she is the powerful one—*he* comes to see *her,* and only in this space.

Yet this solution does not quite ring true. First, we are not given a convincing reason for this change in the power relations between them, as Renaud has up until that point called all the shots. In addition, this change in the power relations between Renaud and Claudine, which is presented as a resolution, falls short of satisfying, for it fails in fact to give Claudine authentic power. She is in retreat, and remains in state of retreat, with no purpose to her existence in Montigny except remembering and reliving her childhood. She is no longer in a relationship of trust with Renaud, but she remains tied to him; she is unable to move on to anything else. This solution, which we feel is the best that could be devised within the confines of the discourses within which this series was written, has a semblance of making Claudine independent, and of providing a solution to the dialectic of domination and rebellion of the books. But as we have seen, it is in the end unconvincing, and in this way the contradictions of the *Claudine* series are revealed. When they emerge, there is no convincing way to write their resolution without coming out of the framework of the *Claudines*. A false solution is set up, which reveals the inevitable dead-end for the female writing subject of the discourses within which these books remain confined.

The way out of this dead end will be the subject of the following chapter. If Claudine's return to Montigny does not ring true in terms of being a satisfying solution to her tale of domination and humiliation, the return to and recreation of childhood through writing on the part of Colette (particularly in *Sido* and *My Mother's House*) *will* in fact trace—or create—the story of the female writing subject; of how a feminist and independence-achieving voice is first attained, and where it can always be found again. It is with this voice that Colette's work will tackle anew, having broken the constraints of the discourses of the *Claudines*, the questions of gender, sexuality and "romantic love."

3

Writing through the Mother

If 'Colette' makes her first attempts at writing under domination, and through coercion, gendered in both cases, it is to the same-gendered mother/daughter relationship that she turns afterwards, both as a source of material about which to write and a means to construct a feminine selfhood, desire, and voice.

Feminist psychoanalysis provides a helpful theoretical model to understand this step. While the apprenticeship of 'Colette' as a writer can be seen as having taken place within what Benjamin describes in "A Desire of One's Own" as symbolic structures, the search for a different and feminine voice is illuminated by reference to what she calls the intersubjective mode. As these ideas are complex, some background information is required.

The type of "ideal love" of a woman for a man in an unequal situation that Benjamin discusses in "Master and Slave: the Fantasy of Erotic Domination" provides a starting point to this new argument in "Desire." She begins again with an examination of "women's contradictory position," that is the fact that, because of the responsibility of care for children they are "more skeptical about detachment [than men], less committed to idealizing absolute separation, . . . yet ready to idealize the man who represent[s] and g[ives] them vicarious access to transcendence."[1] The result of this is the crux of the problem for Benjamin: women lack a desire of their own. They enter instead into a subordinate relationship with an idealized other who is desiring, who is an agent, and thus for them desire appears only as envy. However, for Benjamin and indeed for feminists in general, the "partial truth" (84) of this Freudian notion exists not inevitably, but as a result of social and cultural arrangements that create the psychic organization of biological selves, arrangements she intends to counteract.

In Benjamin's view, individuality, rather than taking the form of an autonomy that denies all dependency, is "properly, ideally, a balance of separation and connectedness, of the capacities for agency and relatedness," and she suggests that "the self does not proceed from oneness to separateness [as orthodox psychoanalytic theory would have it] but evolves by simultaneously differentiating and recognizing the other, by alternating between 'being with' and 'being distinct'" (82).

Again, "in the here and now of patriarchal culture," this is not the selfhood that society constructs. Specifically, Benjamin attributes the lopsided development in society of, on the one hand, the idealization of an autonomy that denies dependency, and on the other, dependency and envy, to the influence of these same already existing structures on the developing child, in what is thus a circular movement.[2] Within the context of a holding, nurturing, and at the same time profoundly desexualized mother, and a desiring, willing father representing freedom and the excitement of the outside world, the toddler at a certain stage is led to split, to "assign contradictory strivings to different objects" (88). Thus the mother becomes the object of desire, and the father the subject of desire, in whom the child recognizes itself. In fact, the toddler of either sex, Benjamin argues, once it has discovered its separateness from its mother, and at the same time its dependency, desires to deny this dependency, to be recognized as independent. Toddlers of both sexes also experience this desire within a holding and nurturing presence and a desire to retain this presence. Hence the paradoxical desire "to be recognized as independent by the very person you once depended upon" (86-87). This is achieved by identifying with the father. However, this split in the psyche only "makes sense" completely for the boy child, for the identification with the father is fully approved by both father and mother only in his case. The idealizing love of the child for the father remains untainted by submission only for the boy because only he can receive the message from the "wonderful, exciting father" that " 'yes, you are like me' " (88).

Among the different conclusions that Benjamin draws from this model, is the following, that under the present gender system, the girl's wish to identify with the father, even if it is satisfied, leads to myriad problems. As long as the mother is not articulated as a sexual agent, identification with the father's agency and desire must appear illegitimate and stolen; furthermore, it conflicts with the cultural image of woman-as-sexual-object and with the girl's maternal identification. It will not correspond with what she knows about her mother's position in her father's eyes. (89)

Benjamin draws several conclusions from these observations. She asserts that the "solution to this dilemma of woman's desire [. . .] has to do with the need for a mother who *is* articulated as a sexual subject, who is an agent, who does express desire." She challenges both the idea that "the mother cannot be a figure of separation and a subject of desire for her children," and also the idea that "the father cannot offer himself as a figure of identification for his daughter." Ultimately, this challenge extends to the very "structure of heterosexuality as it is formed through the differential meanings of mother and father, rooted in the early acquisition of gender, and shaped by the earliest splitting of the psyche" (89-90).

This challenge leads to her real interest—the question of whether women have a desire of their own. Here she returns to the importance of the phallus, not as sole "organiz[er] of gender and sexuality,"(91) an inevitable and immutable role attributed to it that she contests, but as that which "still has the power to represent desire, to represent the idealized force of paternal liberation" (91). She counters the position of Juliet Mitchell, whom she paraphrases as saying that "until that [gender] division is overcome, there is no other way to represent desire or difference or separation [than the phallus]" (91). She does this, however, not by identifying another way of representing desire, for she finds that "[t]he representation of women's sexuality does not seem to have its own symbolic structures but rather seems to be incorporated into the system organized by phallic structures" (92). She seeks instead to find "an alternative to the phallic structures," indeed to the "symbolic [representational] mode," and that means *an alternative mode of structuring the psyche, not just a symbol to replace the phallus*" (92). She therefore proposes another mode, which she calls intersubjectivity.[3]

In exploring the emergence of woman's desire within intersubjectivity, Benjamin makes reference to "aspects of the self that each individual brings with her from infancy—agency and receptivity toward the world" (93). This self exists before the other, but its development requires the other, and recognition of the separateness of the other. Benjamin quotes D. W. Winnicott here who asserts that the "moment . . . of really recognizing the other as existing outside the self . . . is the decisive aspect of differentiation" (93). She contends that this same experience, that is, "the reciprocal recognition that intensifies the self's freedom of expression, is actually the goal of erotic union" (93).

Benjamin then turns to spatial metaphors in her argument for an emergence of woman's desire within intersubjectivity (93). It is through spatial metaphors that she demonstrates the emergence of a desire that is linked with women, "with femininity as now constituted and known" (94). She begins by underscoring the importance of female inner space, and the "idea of *self-discovery* that is associated with having an inside" (95). This idea of self-discovery "points to the side of the self preoccupied not with gender but with whether the drives I feel are really my own, whether they come from within me," (95) she continues. Self-discovery within intersubjectivity leads her to further analysis of the importance of space, and here she turns again to Winnicott. His spatial metaphors for developmental experiences provide another step in her argument. Winnicott identifies a space between mother and baby he calls the "holding environment," and later the "transitional area," which is "the child's area of play, creativity and fantasy." "The transitional space," Benjamin paraphrases him as saying,

> is suffused with the mother's protection and one's own freedom to create. . . . Given safety without intrusion, the infant can be in a state of relaxation—that well-known inward gaze—where its own impulses or drives are experienced as coming from within and feeling real. It is in this way . . . that drives become one's own desire. (94)[4]

Benjamin then returns to "the contrasting figures of infancy, the holding mother and the exciting father," to argue "the equal importance of each: recognition in and by the exciting other, and the holding that allows the self to experience this desire as truly inner" (96). She goes on to say that an "important component of women's fantasy life centers around the wish for a holding other whose presence does not violate one's space but permits the experience of one's own desire, who recognizes it when it emerges of itself" (96). She adds that this source of security, and possibility of self-discovery, can also take the shape of spatial containment, within rooms, for example (96-97). Lastly, she refers to the work of Carol Gilligan who notes, in Apulius's version of the Psyche myth, a "description of woman's sexual awakening occurring in a state of benign aloneness," a safe space in which she is paradoxically alone and yet under the protective influence of an invisible presence (97). Thus, for Benjamin, "spatial metaphors may articulate the search for a desire of one's own. In them, a union or balance of holding and excitement is finally achieved. Within this space one's own desire can emerge"(97).[5] As she concludes, it is not a different desire that is at stake, but rather "a different relationship of the self to the other" (97). It is this that permits the emergence of desire.

With these elements of feminist psychoanalysis in mind, I will now turn again to Colette. Having examined her initial ventures as a writer within symbolic structures, I will now illuminate her structuring of a textual "I" that is the voice of a feminine subject with reference to Benjamin's notion of intersubjectivity and to her discussion of female selfhood in general.

The questions raised by feminist psychoanalysis as outlined by Benjamin constitute the central issues within what Lynne Huffer calls Colette's "maternal cycle"—*My Mother's House, Break of Day,* and *Sido*. These texts are important for their examination of the mother/daughter relationship (and of the father/daughter relationship), as well as their comments on the act of writing—the self-articulatory component of selfhood as outlined by Charles Taylor. These two subjects of discussion are of course linked, and the link between them has been the object of much comment.[6]

What I propose here is to study these aspects, but through the lens of feminist psychoanalysis. This theoretical tool illuminates the creation in these texts of a feminine subjectivity and a feminine desire, which I link to the issue of writing. Each of these texts in fact brings a different dimension to the multifaceted and ever-changing questioning and answering of precisely the issues outlined by Benjamin. The development of the female self, within both symbolic structures and intersubjectivity, the role played in this development by mother and father, the alternation in female selfhood between "being with" and "being distinct," all figure in these works, and will figure in our analysis of them as the search by the narrator for a voice with which to express a feminine subjectivity and a feminine desire.

The works in Colette's "maternal cycle"—*My Mother's House* (1922), *Break of Day* (1928), and *Sido* (1930)—are not in fact the first in which a new construction of female selfhood is attempted, as an overview of Colette's early work reveals. A plot revolving around the conflict between heterosexual love and autonomy is experimented with and refined in a number of early novels. Through this chronological overview, we see Colette moving, stage by stage, towards the project of constructing a female "I" within structures other than those inherited in writing the *Claudines*.

The end of *Claudine Married* (1902) already presents us with a female subject who has chosen 'autonomy' over love, but with the contradictions and limitations already mentioned in the previous chapter. *Retreat from Love* (1907), the first work written by Colette independently of Willy, is surprisingly close, at least at first glance, to the later *Break of Day* in its problematic and the solutions it proposes. It again makes an attempt at the creation of an autonomous textual "I," but is also hampered by the use of the same characters inherited from the *Claudine* series.

The plot of *Retreat from Love,* like that of *Break of Day,* centers around an aging female protagonist (an older Claudine) who renounces love with a man who desires it with her (an older Renaud), to turn herself towards "life":

> "People don't die of anything," declared Marthe in a penetrating voice, "and certainly not of grief! Nobody dies of grief! Look at Claudine, now—when Renaud died, everyone said to one another: 'It'll kill her, you can be sure!' And thank goodness, it didn't! She's got too much common sense, really, she enjoys life too much." (RL 197)
>
> ["On ne meurt de rien, déclara la voix coupante de Marthe, et surtout pas de chagrin! Ainsi, tenez, Claudine... Tout le monde s'est dit, au moment de la mort de Renaud : 'Elle va en claquer, pour sûr!' Et,

Dieu merci, elle n'en a rien fait! Elle a trop de bon sens au fond, trop de goût à vivre..." (1: 939-40)]

Love, construed as the opposite of living fully, is already present here as it will be in *Break of Day,* as is its renunciation by a heroine who will turn to the other more satisfying pleasures of nature and solitude.[7] Yet this story of the tension between "being with" the other and "being distinct" again fails to satisfy. Although it is the first work acknowledged as having been written independently of Willy, it nevertheless remains within the limitations of the *Claudine* series, as it is written with the same characters. As this novel stays within this framework, it again fails to break free of the discourses that inform the *Claudine* series, into which these characters and this story must somehow be made to fit. Claudine is still capable of saying, in referring to Renaud, "[d]on't I owe him all my thoughts? But they belong to him, since they come from me, and I depend on him" (*RL* 56). Thus, even though Claudine here is on her own with Annie in the country, while Renaud, ill, languishes in a sanatorium, pines for her, and writes her letters, she still situates herself as dependent within this relationship between the two of them. While the plot eventually liberates Claudine through Renaud's illness and eventual death, Claudine herself never confronts him or challenges the patriarchal discourses within which their relationship is inscribed.

The Vagabond (1911) construes another textual feminine self who grapples with the issues of autonomy versus love. Here at last we have a story that is lifted completely out of the framework of the *Claudine* series. Its heroine, suggestively named Renée Néré, has left her unfaithful husband. This is convincingly portrayed as a gesture of strength, in a way that Claudine's flight from Renaud was not. Renée successfully earns her living as a music hall artist, is independent of the constraining ties of love, and writes. These are all well thought-out, freely undertaken choices, rather than reactive decisions to events beyond her control, that victimize her. *The Vagabond* is thus already much more convincing in its depiction of autonomy than the earlier *mises en scène* of the protagonist's choice of autonomy over love.

If we see the successive rewritings of this plot—culminating in the fully mature 1928 work *Break of Day*—as a series, another element of *The*

Vagabond becomes significant. In line with the idea of selfhood as outlined by Taylor, the purpose of autonomy for the protagonist here becomes the task of becoming a writer, of finding her own voice.[8] Doing this is associated with returning to childhood, to an earlier—and nobler, purer—self. While traveling with her show, Renée writes to her lover, with whom she has not yet broken off, and makes the following confession:

> "My darling, I've just passed through, without stopping, a region which belongs to me because I spent my childhood there. . . .
>
> "Nothing has changed here. A few new roofs, bright red, that's all. Nothing has changed in my part of the world—except me. Ah, my darling love, how old I am! Can you really love such an old young woman? I blush for myself here. Why did you not know the tall child who used to trail her regal braids here, silent by nature as a wood nymph?" (*Vagabond* 175-76)
>
> [Mon chéri, je viens de traverser, sans m'y arrêter, un pays qui est le mien, celui de mon enfance. . . .
>
> Rien n'y a changé. Quelques toits neufs, d'un rouge frais, c'est tout. Rien n'a changé dans mon pays—que moi. Ah! mon ami chéri, que je suis vieille! Pouvez-vous bien aimer une aussi vieille jeune femme? Je rougis de moi, ici. Que n'avez-vous connu la longue enfant qui traînait ici ses royales tresses, et sa silencieuse humeur de nymphe de bois? (1: 1198)]

It is this same return to childhood, in the construction of a feminine self and voice, that Colette herself carries out in her writing, with *My Mother's House,* and later *Sido*. And it is here that the missing element in these constructions finally appears—the mother.

The importance of the mother figure in these works and in Colette's work in general has been the subject of much discussion, and is in any case self-evident.[9] What interests me here, in *My Mother's House* and *Sido,* is the importance of the mother/daughter relationship in the development of female selfhood. With these works, I will study the role the mother figure plays in textual construction of selfhood, specifically in light of what feminist psychoanalysis brings to our understanding of it.[10]

For it is, as we have already noted, precisely the mother who is conspicuously absent from the *Claudine* series. If we return to Benjamin's identification of the twin needs of children in the achievement of selfhood and in arriving at the "conviction of owning [their] own desire"—the holding other, and the exciting other, then we see the importance of reinstating the mother figure. The move toward the exciting other by Claudine—that is, identification with the father—does indeed ultimately reveal itself as "illegitimate and stolen" since it is achieved through abuse of other female characters. Moreover it does not provide her with a selfhood capable in the end of allowing her to be an independent female-gendered person. Similarly, the lack of the holding other is also suggestive for the failure and eventual renunciation of love. It sheds another light on why love—inevitably within the *Claudine* series, we feel—must prove unsatisfying. Without the achievement of a selfhood in which this holding presence has played a part, desire is never experienced by the protagonist as her own.[11]

The textual importance of the mother changes, beginning with *My Mother's House* and with *Sido*. The mother here is not only present but by far the dominant figure in these works, having as a common theme the protagonist's childhood. The mother is also strongly linked with nurturance. In *My Mother's House* and *Sido,* she is in fact almost deified as a protector of life in all its forms.[12]

'Sido' is also, however, linked to space in very interesting ways. She is the center of a circle of light towards which she draws 'Colette' by means of her sewing needle ("The Little One," *My Mother's House*); in *Sido* she is the center of the cosmos for the child 'Colette.' A closer look at pertinent passages of this latter work reveals in addition that she is not merely passively the center of these already existing circular spaces. Rather this world as a self-contained world, a cosmos, is called into being by 'Sido.'

> My childish pride and imagination saw our house as the central point of a Mariner's Chart of gardens, winds and rays of light, no section of which lay quite beyond my mother's influence. (*Sido* 157-58)
>
> [Mon imagination, mon orgueil enfantins situaient notre maison au centre d'une rose de jardins, de vents, de rayons, dont aucun secteur n'échappait tout à fait à l'influence de ma mère. (3: 503)]

This is the transitional area, suffused with maternal protection. Rather than an actual physical area in space, or only that, it is a space capable of providing its inhabitants with an illusion, with faith, with security—it is a space that provides a particular state of well-being for the child. Moreover, it exists by the power of the mother. It is "merely because she held sway there and watched over it all" that "the walls grew higher" and "the enclosures which I had so easily traversed by jumping from wall to wall and branch to branch, became unknown lands," she writes (*Sido* 158). Through the mother and her influence, quite ordinary, everyday space is divided into the safe, the secure, and the suddenly unknown and potentially hostile. We are reminded here of "The Little One"—it is when the light encircling the mother is turned on in the house, in a moment when the child is already feeling tired and emptied, that the garden, which is suddenly thrown into shadow, becomes threatening and overwhelming. In another scene from *Sido* 'Colette' recounts that it is in going out to experience the dawn *under her mother's benediction* that she feels herself in a state of grace.

> For even then I so loved the dawn that my mother granted it to me as a reward. She used to agree to wake me up at half past three and off I would go....
>
> At half past three everything slumbered still in a primal blue, blurred and dewy, and as I went down the sandy road the mist, grounded by its own weight, bathed first my legs, then my well-built little body, reaching at last to my mouth and ears, and finally to that most sensitive part of all, my nostrils. I went alone, for there were no dangers in that free-thinking countryside. *It was on that road and at that hour that I first became aware of my own self, experienced an inexpressible state of grace*, and felt one with the first breath of air that stirred, the first bird, and the sun so newborn that it still looked not quite round.
>
> "Beauty," my mother would call me, and "Jewel-of-pure-gold"; then she would let me go, watching her creation—her masterpiece, as she said—grow smaller as I ran down the slope." (*Sido* 156, my emphasis)

[Car j'aimais tant l'aube, déjà, que ma mère me l'accordait en récompense. J'obtenais qu'elle m'éveillât à 3 heures et demie, et je m'en allais. . . . .

A 3 heures et demie, tout dormait dans un bleu originel, humide et confus, et quand je descendais le chemin de sable, le brouillard retenu par son poids baignait d'abord mes jambes, puis mon petit torse bien fait, atteignait mes lèvres, mes oreilles et mes narines plus sensibles que tout le reste de mon corps... J'allais seule, ce pays mal pensant était sans dangers. *C'est sur ce chemin, c'est à cette heure que je prenais conscience de mon prix, d'un état de grâce indicible* et de ma connivence avec le premier souffle accouru, le premier oiseau, le soleil encore ovale, déformé par l'éclosion...

Ma mère me laissait partir, après m'avoir nommée 'Beauté, Joyau-tout-en-or'; elle regardait courir et décroître sur la pente son œuvre—'chef-d'œuvre,' disait-elle. (3: 501-02, my emphasis).]

I will return later in this chapter to the dawn as the moment at which this state of grace is attained; for now it is the space within which this occurs that interests me. For here even as the daughter is leaving she remains in her mother's world, within the mother-centered space; as she is sped on her way, we see her from the mother's point of view, getting smaller as she runs away. I am arguing for an interpretation of the mother figure here as occupying the role of holding other as Benjamin defines it, with the power to create space with what is retrospectively recognized as an "illusory" magical, paradisical quality—of safety, peace and well-being—the world within which 'Colette' as a child lived as "queen of the earth" (1: 1033, my translation).

This literary recreation of the safe space of Winnicott's and Benjamin's transitional area is more than an autobiographical attempt to portray a particular lived experience. It is a necessary component to Colette's textual construction of a feminine selfhood no longer confined within the patriarchal discourses that limited the scope of the *Claudine* series. That indispensable component of childhood for the construction of selfhood, the holding other—here, as most typically in real life, personified by the mother—is reinstated. Significant is the idealization both of this mother, and of the childhood state of grace that 'Colette' lived in while within her sphere of influence.

While one centrally important aspect of the mother in these texts is thus her link to a safe, protecting space, another important aspect is her presence in the texts themselves, *as text,* through her discourse. In fact, if the mother's role as holding other is fundamental to developing the protagonist's sense of selfhood and authentic desire, the mother's linguistic and literary activity is crucial as well. For as we saw in the chronological overview of Colette's successive reworking of the same plot, the goal of selfhood is ultimately writing—the creation of that voice through which the self expresses itself. It is the model of the mother that allows her to construct the voice used for self-expression *as feminine,* and that allows her to speak from that place, rather than through the voice created for her by the other.

Thus, the mother is present not only as holding and nurturing other, she is also present as initiator into literary activity, and will be constructed as the very model, for the female subject, of the creative use of language for self-definition and self-expression. I will examine the mother in this role as well as her counterpoint, the father. First, however, it is interesting to note that prior to her own initiation into literary creation, and into the contesting of discourses that this inevitably entails, the daughter first witnesses the performance of discourse through a sort of 'literary creation' on the part of another. It is the presence of the holding other in this experience that plays the crucial role in her reception of this creation, and the discourses that it performs.

This can be seen in the vignette from *My Mother's House* called "Father and Madame Bruneau." In this story, 'Colette' listens to a romantic interaction between a man and woman, her father and a neighbor, in what seems almost a theatrical performance. The discourse that informs this type of romantic interaction is the basis of the novels 'Juliette' reads, for instance, and is what 'Colette' in her own later creation of selfhood will challenge and subvert. In this vignette, however, what we note is not contestation of this discourse, but rather its irrelevance and unreal quality as 'Colette' witnesses the scene from within her mother's sheltering presence.

In this vignette, 'Colette' sits in the garden against her mother's knee on a summer evening, sleepy but unwilling to go to bed. It is from this perspective that she witnesses her father's ribald teasing of the neighbor Madame Bruneau. The vignette describes at length the feeling of protection 'Colette' feels here. She closes her "useless eyes" (*MMH* 44), and leaning against her mother, sheltered within her space, apprehends the presence and activities of those around her through sound and scent, and in the case of her mother, who smooths her hair and playfully pinches her ear, through touch.

The father on the other hand, when he appears, is seen. Moreover, in contrast to the realism and the detail in the descriptions of what 'Colette' senses with her eyes closed, the father is lit by a moon's ray as if by a theatrical spotlight. The staginess of this scene is accentuated by the nature of the light, which seems artificial and makes him look green: "The rays of the rising moon fall at last on the angular silhouette of a man standing on the terrace. One hand, so white that it appears green in the moonlight, grips a bar of railing" (*MMH* 45). The father appears fake rather than human, a stage prop, nothing more than a stiff silhouette.

He sings a slightly off-color love song, and Madame Bruneau sighs in admiration to 'Sido,' saying that "[t]he Captain's voice would really grace any theater" (*MMH* 45). She continues, confiding to 'Sido' the following: "To grow old beside a husband like my poor husband. To tell myself that I will die without ever having known love" (*MMH* 46). The father then intervenes in the conversation between 'Sido' and Madame Bruneau, to remind her that he maintains his proposition: "Sixpence and a packet of tobacco as payment for teaching you the meaning of love" (*MMH* 46).

While the tone of the vignette is light, and the scene is comic, the relationship of Mme Bruneau to "The Captain" is nonetheless reminiscent of that of 'Juliette' to the authors of the romance novels she reads. The father "launches one more romantic couplet at the moon" (*MMH* 46), even after Madame Bruneau has already fled these "risky pleasantries that she comes here to seek on fine summer nights" (*MMH* 46). She continues after her flight this particular evening to avoid him, but cannot escape the cynical glance and attention that she seeks and that causes her pain:

> [N]ext day, . . . all the days that follow, our neighbour, Madame Bruneau, no matter how careful a watch she keeps, peering out before dashing across the road as though under a shower, will not escape her enemy, her idol. (*MMH* 46)

> [[L]e lendemain, . . . tous les jours qui suivent, notre voisine, Mme Bruneau, a beau guetter, tendre la tête et s'élancer, pour traverser la rue, comme sous une averse, elle n'échappe pas à son ennemi, à son idole. (2: 997)]

The story ends with her eventual departure from the village; taking with her "her ludicrous husband, she departed to live far away from us, up in the hills, at Bel-Air" (*MMH* 47).

Certainly Mme Bruneau remains a largely comic character, for the reason given for her flight is that "[t]here are souls with an almost endless capacity for hiding their suffering and their trembling responsiveness to the lure of sin" (*MMH* 47). Mme Bruneau, in bourgeois fashion, is afraid of being revealed as willing to listen to this improper behavior, rather than being properly shocked by it. Yet there is a hint of the pathetic in the word "suffering"—stagy and comic though this scene is, the romantic interaction played out and which Mme Bruneau comes to seek on fine evenings is nonetheless one that ridicules her. She is the butt of the joke.

Yet the most interesting aspect of this *mise en scène* of male seduction and female ideal love ("her idol") is its irrelevance and unreal quality for 'Colette' as she witnesses it from within the maternal space: "gradually I cease to hear him, forgetting, as I sleep against the knees so careful of my repose" (*MMH* 46). The danger of loss of self in Benjamin's "symbolic structures"—tragic in the case of 'Juliette,' comic in that of Mme Bruneau—cannot touch her in her safe world. It has no power over her, indeed no reality at all, while she is within the mother's space.

Thus the dominant discourse of patriarchy is present, but irrelevant, while 'Colette' lives within the sphere of her mother. However, quite obviously, this state cannot last. As I have argued, in her first experiences as a writer, this discourse is not only present, but the extent of its power is such that it defines her production. It is other childhood experiences that provide her with a weapon to counteract this—the modeling by the mother of a gendered relationship to language and literary creation.

Perhaps the most striking feature of the mother's literary activity is its interactive aspect. 'Sido' is in fact the possessor of oral literature and the teller of tales. *Sido* and *My Mother's House* are filled with the mother's verbal presence, in the form of conversations with the daughter, remarks, admonitions, and tales. *Break of Day* does not contain the same vignettes, featuring the protagonist 'Colette' as a child living in her mother's world, of the other two works. Its story unfolds in another place and time. However the mother still retains her verbal presence, through remembered conversations reported by the daughter, and through the presence of her letters in the text. All of these genres: the tale, the letter, the adage, the proverb, are interactive in nature. The letter is clearly so, and this is no less the case for the tale and the proverb, as they come out of the implicitly interactive tradition of oral genres.

The mother's literary creation is not only interactive, it is also, in terms of its presentation within the daughter's text, unmediated. The relation of the daughter to the parents in "Father and Madame Bruneau" is once again suggestive here. In that vignette, the mother's presence is felt by the narrator, rather than seen, as she and the mother are physically contiguous. The father, on the other hand, is seen at a distance. He is moreover doubly removed from the narrator by the mediation of a certain theatricality, which puts him on stage. In a similar way, the manner in which the mother's literary creation, or participation in literary forms and genres, is present in the daughter's text, contrasts with the way in which we see the father's. There is also a difference in what the two parents produce.

The reader learns that the father tells tales, but we do not see them in the text. The family learns stories of his life before he knew them, but through the intermediary of outsiders, his military friends. The father sings, and the words of the songs he sings do appear in the text. However, these songs are not his creation; here he interprets common cultural property. Moreover, the words of these songs appear separated, apart from the text itself.

The mother's literary creation most often does not. Tales she tells form part of the flow of the narrative. As we saw with reading and writing, the father initiates the daughter into the ability to judge according to certain aesthetic standards of a bookish, literary nature. There is a hint that the daughter seeks his approval through this, and an initiation into a literary fraternity. In reading, the mother seeks to share pleasure with her daughter, and rather than teaching her a certain aesthetic standard, she initiates her daughter into remaining in relation to, and contesting, what she reads. With literary creation, again, 'Sido' is not teaching the daughter mastery. Rather her interactive activity teaches another purpose to literary creation. For her it is a means of communicating, of forming and retaining relationships, and this is based on subjectivity.

Thus, in literary creativity, as in reading, two approaches are exemplified through the mother and father figures, and once again we find a strong and explicit valorization of the mother's with its orientation toward selfhood and independence vis-à-vis discourse. The mother, for example, creates her own proverbs and tales, and while the father's more 'literary' creation (slated for book form, to be executed according to received literary standards) remains forever unstarted, the mother's creation literally pours from her. While the discovery of 'the Captain' as unfulfilled writer closes the section developed to him to *Sido,* the first section, devoted to the mother, is opened by the mother's speech, which flows almost uninterrupted through the opening three paragraphs of the work. Through her speech she is the central presence here, displacing the narrator, who exists at this point only in the second person, as "you," and who appears finally in the third paragraph only to identify the opening speech as that of "my mother."

The inclusive, interactive creation of the mother pours forth—the exclusive, literary creation of the father is never realized. The same connectedness, sharing, and pleasure—discernable in the mother's approach to reading with her daughter—is present in her approach to literary creation. This maternal approach is moreover highly valorized. The narrator of *Break of Day,* in speaking of her mother, explicitly asks: "Between us two, which is the better writer, she or I? Does it not resound to high heaven that it is she?" (*BD* 141).

Thus, Colette proposes a path toward feminine voice and creativity diametrically opposed to the "matrophobic" one of many women writers discussed by Jean Wyatt.[13] The mother in Colette is in fact explicitly posited as the daughter's literary source, and even idealized in this role. Once again, we read this not as simple autobiographical mirroring of reality. Rather the valorization of the mother, the necessary and different role (to that of the father) that she plays, both in the child's development in general, and more specifically in the child's relationship to discourse, is part of the telling—and the creating—of the female self.

However, at this point, the story becomes more complicated, the "plot thickens." If the mother's creativity is idealized, and if she is explicitly named as the source of the daughter's vocation, the story is not as simple as it might be, for 'Colette' does not, in unproblematic fashion, follow her example. Instead, the narrator of *Break of Day* confesses a different ambition.

> Love and respect for living creatures could be read in my mother's letters and in her heart. So I know where the spring of my vocation lay, a spring which I muddied as soon as I was born through my passion for touching and stirring up the depths lying beneath the pure stream. I accuse myself of having from an early age, not content with loving them, wanted to shine in the eyes of these, my kin and my accomplices. It is an ambition I still have. (*BD* 46)
>
> [Dans le cœur, dans les lettres de ma mère, étaient lisibles l'amour, le respect des créatures vivantes. Je sais donc où situer la source de ma vocation, une source que je trouble, aussitôt née, dans la passion de toucher, de remuer le fond que couvre son flot pur. Je m'accuse d'avoir voulu, dès le jeune âge, briller—non contente de les chérir—aux yeux de mes frères et complices. C'est une ambition qui ne me quitte pas... (3: 304)]

This desire to shine, this desire for glory, is in fact more characteristic of the father and his approach to writing, than of the mother. Moreover, the daughter identifies herself here with masculine figures—"mes frères et complices" ["my kin and accomplices"]. Thus, even as she idealizes the mother's example, the daughter sets herself up in the father's place, in opposition to her mother.

In this way *Break of Day* sets up a tension rather than a conflation between mother and daughter. As we have seen, the reinstating of the mother figure in *My Mother's House* and *Sido* serves as a means of constructing a gendered, specifically feminine, selfhood and voice, and the figure of the mother continues to play that role in *Break of Day*. At the same time, here, now that the narrative voice has established itself as feminine, the mother figure is used to another purpose, as well. The mother/daughter relationship in this novel serves as the means by which the narrator works through the issues she sets out to articulate, in particular that of the tension between separation and connection.

This novel, the last in the series that had begun with *Claudine Married* in 1902, brings us back to the plot surrounding the conflict between autonomy and love. Here at last Colette's work proposes a resolution to, or perhaps it would be more accurate to say, a more thorough exploration of, the questions that she had grappled with in all the previous rewritings of this plot. *Break of Day* posits a cyclical movement between autonomy and connection, a back and forth movement between the two, for the achievement of which the mother serves as the daughter's model, and vice versa. The autonomy attained by the mother, to which the daughter aspires, will prove in fact the prerequisite for the experience of desire, which the mother will attain in her turn through contamination by the daughter. Each end of the back and forth movement, in order to be realized, ultimately proves to need its opposite. I will begin my discussion of these issues by turning to one of the novel's main stated concerns—heterosexual love.

This is one of the most complex issues discussed in this work, not least because of the many textual messages on how to interpret it. *Break of Day* is rich in indications of how the novel, and Colette's or anyone's work in general, should be read. We will begin with an examination of passages that explore the question of reading women's writing, and within it, writing on the theme of love.

This has of course already been discussed in chapter 2 as regards the *Claudines*. We have seen that in *My Apprenticeships* the narrative voice furnishes an account of the conditions of their creation. The narrator of *Break of Day* makes a brief allusion to these same conditions, in the following passage:

> Not long before his death Catulle Mendès said to me: "You won't be able to gauge until much later the power of the literary type you've created." Why did I not *ignore all masculine suggestions* and create a type which by its simplicity and even by its resemblance would have been much more worthy to endure? (*BD* 64, my emphasis)
>
> ["Vous ne mesurerez que plus tard", me disait Mendès peu avant sa mort, "la force du type littéraire (Claudine) que vous avez créé". Que n'en ai-je, hors de *toute suggestion masculine*, créé un qui fut, par sa

simplicité, et même par sa ressemblance, plus digne de durer! (3: 316, emphasis added)]

We thus see here a reiteration of the comments made by the 'Colette' of *My Apprenticeships* on her first work, expressing the need to read these works with caution—bearing in mind the conditions under which they were written, and the falsification of the 'feminine' self that they depict. In the following passage, we see similar remarks made on the subject of women's writing in general.

> Why should I stop my hand from gliding over this paper to which for so many years I've confided what I know about myself, what I've tried to hide, what I've invented and what I've guessed? At no time has the catastrophe of love, in all its phases and consequences, formed a part of the true intimate life of a woman. Why do men—writers or so-called writers—still show surprise that a woman should so easily reveal to the public love-secrets and amorous lies and half-truths? By divulging these, she manages to hide other important and obscure secrets which she herself does not understand very well. The spotlight, the shameless eye which she obligingly operates, always explores the same sector of a woman's life, that sector tortured by bliss and discord round which the shades are thickest. But it is not in the illuminated zone that the darkest plots are woven.[14] Man, my friend, you willingly make fun of women's writings because they can't help being autobiographical. On whom then were you relying to paint women for you, din them into your ears, debase them in your eyes, in short make you tired of them? On yourself? You have become my friend too recently for me to give you my opinion on that. (BD 62-63)

> [Pourquoi suspendre la course de ma main sur ce papier qui recueille, depuis tant d'années, ce que je sais de moi, ce que j'essaie d'en cacher, ce que j'en invente et ce que j'en devine? La catastrophe amoureuse, ses suites, ses phases, n'ont jamais, en aucun temps, fait partie de la réelle intimité d'une femme. Comment les hommes—les hommes écrivains, ou soi-disant tels—s'étonnent-ils encore qu'une femme livre si aisément au public des confidences d'amour, des mensonges, des demi-mensonges amoureux? En les divulguant, elle sauve de la publicité des

> secrets confus et considérables, qu'elle-même ne connaît pas très bien. Le gros projecteur, l'œil sans vergogne qu'elle manœuvre avec complaisance, fouille toujours le même secteur féminin, ravagé de félicité et de discorde, autour duquel l'ombre s'épaissit. Ce n'est pas dans la zone illuminée que se trame le pire... Homme, mon ami, tu plaisantes volontiers les œuvres, fatalement autobiographiques, de la femme. Sur qui comptais-tu donc pour te la peindre, te rabattre d'elle les oreilles, la desservir auprès de toi, te lasser d'elle à la fin? Sur toi-même? Tu es mon ami de trop fraîche date pour que je te donne grossièrement mon opinion là-dessus. (3: 315-16)]

This passage suggests that the masculine shaping of woman's discourse continues to exist even in situations where it is less obvious than in the writing of the *Claudines*. This is not only a general observation on women's writing, but one that is applicable to 'Colette' in her own work as well. She admits openly that her 'self-portrayal' is a mixture of many things—invention, guessing, and falsification through hiding. However, most interesting is the reason given to explain why: the remark addressed to "Man," reproaching him for his ridicule of women's writings, which "can't help being autobiographical." The narrator's reproach continues, as she asks him, essentially, why not? Who, after all, she reasons, will speak for women, if it isn't women themselves? Is it not to be expected, rather than ridiculed? This patronizing criticism, called into being once it is a question of women's writing, is thus given as the reason why this writing functions as a mask. Women hide behind a mask, the passage relates, in order to save from publicity—and criticism or ridicule—the most important part of themselves. This is then said, however, to be something that women themselves do not know—this secret part is secret even from themselves.

At this point, Benjamin's reference to the Psyche myth as discussed by Carol Gilligan is once again illuminating. Psyche's sexual awakening occurs in a state of benign aloneness. She tells her father not to weep for the events that have caused this to happen to her. Instead he should have wept for her when she was an object on display, an object of adulation, for it was then that she was truly dead.[15] A very similar observation is made here in Colette's text. Women's writing about love, which she likens to exhibitionism, to putting oneself on display, is what women do in order *not* to expose their real selves. Thus 'Colette' suggests that women's writing about love is not "autobiographical" but rather the opposite, it is, in fact, another *Claudine* discourse, generated by a masculine power implicit in patriarchy, of which the interference made by 'Willy' was only a more concrete symbol. Even the ironic reproach to man by 'Colette,' where she asks him who if not woman he expected to write about women, contains nuances leading us to this conclusion. For 'Colette' suggests that writing about love, although it is a discourse 'by and about' women, is nonetheless one that will do women a disservice in men's eyes ("debase them in your eyes"). Women's writing, 'Colette' suggests here, tends, within a hostile atmosphere, to hide women, or to serve them badly, using the means of a false exposure of a falsely important aspect of themselves—love—to do so.

But let us return to the most suggestive aspect of this whole passage—the notion that all this hiding or camouflaging that women undertake effectively ends up hiding them from themselves. The end result is that they do not know themselves, or even have a 'self' to know. We are back to the problem produced by the desire to break out of the confines of the discourses that generated the *Claudines*. The mother figure is reinstated in Colette's work, allowing the narrative voice to construct itself as feminine. Yet this is not, so to speak, the whole battle. On the one hand, the reinstatement of the mother, while indispensable, does not alone constitute the construction of selfhood. Mothering is indispensable, in Colette's construction, but the subject must go on from there, and create herself in relation and interaction with the world, that "here and now of patriarchal culture," as Benjamin expresses it. Thus *Break of Day* reasserts the problem of woman's voice, the expression of woman's desire, and cautions us against thinking it has been too easily achieved. Most particularly, we are cautioned against thinking it is too easily found in the most stereotypically feminine of discourses, that of love.

This is illustrated again in the following passage:

> I've been told often enough that to live first as love dictates, then as the absence of love dictates, shows the most overweening conceit. (*BD* 52)
>
> [On m'a assez affirmé que vivre selon l'amour, puis selon l'absence de l'amour, était la pire outrecuidance. (3: 308)]

If external pressures mean that women's writing hides more than it reveals, then this remark brings a particular confirmation of that for the most typically feminine of subject matters—love. Love as subject matter constitutes a double-bind for the woman writer—she is damned if she does talk about it—it is a trivial and feminine matter, and damned if she doesn't— she is then unnatural and unfeminine. If the external pressures surrounding this subject matter are especially strong, then this discourse is the one to arouse the most suspicion in reading women's writing. How then— in light of indications in the text that we are not to take writing on love at face value—to interpret this novel, which 'Colette' suggests to us might at last be the "code for life as a couple" that her second husband always urged her to write (*BD* 22)?

This statement is at first glance enigmatic, for superficially *Break of Day* does not resemble a "code for life as a couple" at all; it is rather the story of a renunciation of love, and preparation for death. However, more careful scrutiny reveals this puzzling statement to be key to a reading of the novel as a theoretical exploration of the questions of woman's selfhood, desire, and voice. In its exploration of the balance between separation and connection, this novel posits two kinds of love. The movement from one to the other is assimilated to the movement between death and rebirth, and both passages will take place at dawn.

Colette herself said about *Break of Day*, in answer to André Billy, "one cannot hide anything from your clear-sightedness: you have sensed that in this novel the novel does not exist."[16] It is composed partly of narrative, partly of philosophical musings, partly of comments addressed directly to two different interlocutors, 'Sido,' and 'Man,' and partly of letters from 'Sido' to 'Colette,' which structure the novel, and give the model of the behavior and approach to life to which 'Colette' strives to conform.

Love figures importantly in all of these elements. The narrative recounts in part the story of the love between 'Colette' and a younger man, Vial, a love that 'Colette' renounces. The philosophical musings also often concern love, its real nature, its role in life, and its importance. And the mother's attitude and behavior as regards love are posited as the model, and appear both in the daughter's remembrances, and in the letters.

In fact love is neither entirely valorized, nor entirely denigrated. But rather two types of loving are posited, the one positively connoted, the other negatively. Most visibly and noticeably, love is valorized when it does not try to achieve a permanent transcendence—when one does not try to make permanent what is not, or possess in a concrete way what cannot be so possessed. Thus the idealized 'Sido' points the way to 'real' love:

> There is no doubt that my mother, who only learned, as she said, "by getting burnt," knew that one possesses through abstaining, and only through abstaining. (*BD* 24)
>
> [A n'en pas douter, ma mère savait, elle qui n'apprit rien, comme elle disait, "qu'en se brûlant", elle savait qu'on possède dans l'abstentation, et seulement dans l'abstentation. (3: 290)]

And as an abstaining lover, she is a "great lover" (*BD* 24). This "great love" is characterized by three things: the ability to resist the desire to know, to avoid becoming fixated by a single object of desire, and the ability to be for oneself as well as with the other. The relationship of the widowed 'Sido' to her neighbor, friend, and partner at chess the "wool-seller," recounted in *Break of Day*, is contrasted with the behavior of 'Colette' towards objects she should not touch. The pleasure that 'Sido' takes in the company of her neighbor during their games of chess is based on *not* knowing what is "imprisoned in that fat little man." She continues: "It makes me curious. But I have to resign myself to never knowing, though I'm very glad to feel sure there's something, and to be the only one to know it" (*BD* 131).

'Colette' eulogizes this attitude on the part of her mother. "Flair, instinct for hidden treasure. Like a diviner she went straight to what shines only in secret," she writes (*BD* 131). 'Sido' is able to recognize what is of value, what is precious. Yet she is also able to resist unearthing it and looking at it in the light of day. In contrast, in *Sido,* 'Colette' recounts her mother's rebuke when she, sensing buried treasure, cannot resist the desire to bring it to light, and in so doing, to destroy it. The form that treasure takes in the case of this incident is a spring bulb. Since her mother has forgotten what she planted, 'Colette,' curious, digs into the ground to unearth it and find out. What she really seeks is knowledge, and the thrill of unearthing the bulb is that of "lay[ing] bare and bring[ing] to light something that no human eye before mine had gazed upon" (*Sido* 163). She continues:

> She knew then that I was going to scratch on the sly in her trial-ground until I came upon the upward-climbing claw of the cotyledon, the sturdy sprout urged out of its sheath by the spring. I thwarted the blind purpose of the bilious-looking, black-brown chrysalis, and hurled it from its temporary death into a final nothingness.
>
> [J'allais donc, grattant à la dérobée le jardin d'essai, surprendre la griffe ascendante du cotylédon, le viril surgeon que le printemps chassait de sa gaine... Je contrariais l'aveugle dessein que poursuit la chrysalide d'un noir brun bilieux et la précipitais d'une mort passagère au néant définitif.]

Her mother responds in the following fashion, a verbal punishment that for 'Colette' is harsh enough:

> "You don't understand... you can't understand. You're nothing but a little eight-year-old murderess. . . . You just can't understand something that wants to live." (*Sido* 163)
>
> ["Tu ne comprends pas... Tu ne peux pas comprendre... Tu n'es qu'une petite meurtrière de huit ans. . . . Tu ne comprends rien encore à ce qui veut vivre..." (3: 507)]

In a similar fashion, in *Break of Day* 'Colette' remembers a dialog she had with herself as a child, in which she tried to teach herself to resist a similar temptation, yet once again failed:

> "Never touch a butterfly's wing with your finger."
>
> "I certainly won't... or only just lightly... just at the tawny-black place where you see that violet glow, that moon-lick, without being able to say exactly where it starts or where it dies away."
>
> "No, don't touch it. The whole thing will vanish if you merely brush it."
>
> "But only just lightly! Perhaps this will be the time when I shall feel under this particular finger, my fourth, the most sensitive, the cold

blue flame and the way it vanishes into the skin of the wing..." A trace of lifeless ash on the tip of my finger, the wing dishonored, the tiny creature weakened. (*BD* 23-24)

["Ne touche pas du doigt l'aile de ce papillon.

—Non, certainement... Ou rien qu'un peu... Rien qu'à la place fauve-noir où glisse, sans que je puisse fixer le point précis où il naît, celui où il s'épuise, ce feu violet, cette léchure de lune...

—Non. Ne le touche pas. Tout va s'évanouir, si tu l'effleures seulement.

—Mais rien qu'un peu!... C'est peut-être cette fois-ci que je percevrai sous ce doigt-ci le plus sensible, le quatrième, la froide flamme bleue, et sa fuite dans le poil de l'aile... la plume de l'aile... la rosée de l'aile... Une trace de cendre, éteinte, sur le bout du doigt, l'aile déshonorée, la bestiole affaiblie..." (3: 289-90)]

Thus, as we see through the dichotomy set up between mother and daughter, a "great love" involves possessing through abstention. It also involves inconstancy, for a "great lover" gives of herself freely, rather than through constraint. Here, the obsessive and life-long love 'the Captain' has for 'Sido' is contrasted with love freely given and freely taken away, and thus with love for more than one love object.

In the letter opening the ninth chapter, 'Sido' speaks of her husband's love for her: When I returned from the two or three short trips I made to Paris to see you, before his death, I found my dear Colette a shadow of himself and hardly eating. Ah, what a child! What a pity he should have loved me so much! It was his love for me that destroyed, one after another, all those splendid abilities he had for literature and the sciences. He preferred to think only of me, to torment himself for me, and that was what I found inexcusable. So great a love! What frivolity! (*BD* 127)

[Les deux ou trois courts voyages que j'ai faits à Paris pour te voir, avant sa mort, quand j'en revenais je retrouvais mon cher Colette diminué, creusé, mangeant à peine... Ah! Quel enfant! Quel dommage qu'il m'ait autant aimée! C'est son amour pour moi qui a annihilé, une à une, toutes ses belles facultés qui l'auraient poussé vers la littérature et les sciences. Il a préféré ne songer qu'à moi, se tourmenter pour moi, et c'est cela que je trouvais inexcusable. Un si grand amour! Quelle légèreté! (3: 360)]

What social convention would consider serious—fidelity—is here called frivolity. It is inconstancy that is valorized.

The narrator then describes this same quality in 'Sido' in the following manner:

> Her form of inconstancy was to fly from the bee to the mouse, from a new-born child to a tree, from a poor person to a poorer, from laughter to torment. How pure are those who lavish themselves in this way! (*BD* 25)

> [Son inconstance, à elle, ce fut de voler de l'abeille à la souris, d'un nouveau-né à un arbre, d'un pauvre à un plus pauvre, d'un rire à un tourment. Pureté de ceux qui se prodiguent! (3: 290)]

While love for a single object does not consume 'Sido' to the point where she loses her ability to see and rejoice in any number of elements in the world around her, the father loses his ability not just to appreciate, but even to see, all that is not 'Sido.' In *Sido,* a scene is recounted in which the father is rendered jealous by a story 'Sido' tells about seeing a fox drowning its fleas, something she witnessed at the time of her first marriage. We see 'the Captain' respond thus:

> Delightful stories of which my father retained only the words "my first husband," at which he would bend on Sido that grey-blue gaze of his whose meaning no one could ever fathom. In any case, what did the fox and the lily of the valley, the ripe berry and the insect, matter to him? He liked them in books, and told us their learned names, but passed them by out of doors without recognizing them. (*Sido* 185)

> [Récits délicieux, dont mon père ne retenait qu'un mot: "mon premier mari...", et il appuyait sur 'Sido' ce regard bleu gris dans lequel personne n'a jamais pu lire... Que lui importaient d'ailleurs, le renard, le muguet, la baie mûre, l'insecte? Il les aimait dans les livres, nous disait

leurs noms scientifiques, et dehors les croisait sans les reconnaître... (3: 523)]

'Colette' reiterates the same valorization of inconstancy, and this time specifically in the domain of sexual love, in referring to her own behavior:

> Can it be that chance has made me one of those women so immersed in one man that, whether they are barren or not, they carry with them to the grave the shrivelled innocence of an old maid? At the thought of such a fate my plump double that I see in the sloping mirror, tanned by sun and sea, would tremble, if it could still tremble at a past danger. (*BD* 19)

> [Voyez-vous que le hasard ait fait de moi une de ces femmes cantonnées dans un homme unique, au point qu'elles en portent jusque sous terre, stériles ou non, une ingénuité confite de vieille fille?... D'imaginer un pareil sort, mon double charnu, tanné de soleil et d'eau, que je vois dans le miroir penché, en tremblerait, s'il pouvait trembler encore d'un péril rétrospectif. (3: 286)]

This inconstancy exists and is valorized because 'real' love is freely given. It arises and ends in a "cataclysm," it does not respond to a "contemptible regular hunger" (*BD* 30)). And thus a "great lover" takes on one last characteristic—the crucial one. She is able to be solitary, to be distinct and for herself, as well as to be with the other.

This is communicated again in the following passage, containing a part of another letter from 'Sido.' What also becomes clear here is the real nature of the treasure that 'Colette' had mistakenly sought to possess in a concrete way. She is struck by the joy expressed by 'Sido' while undertaking her everyday activities. 'Sido' writes:

> I'm better, and the proof is that at seven o'clock this morning I did the washing in my stream. I was enraptured. What a pleasure it is to dabble in clear water! I sawed wood, too, and made six little bundles of firewood. And I'm doing my housework myself again, which means it's being properly done. And after all, I'm only seventy-six!

You ['Colette' addresses her mother here] wrote to me that same day, a year before you died, and the loops of your capital B's, T's and J's, which have a kind of proud cap on the back of their heads, are radiant with gaiety. How rich you were that morning in your little house! At the end of the garden leapt a little stream, so swift that it immediately carried away everything that might have sullied it. You were rich with yet another morning, with a new victory over illness, rich with one more task, with the jewels of light glittering in the running water, with one more truce between you and all your pains. You were soaping linen in the stream, sighing because you could not get over the death of your beloved, you went "twee-e-e-e!" at the chaffinches, you were thinking that you would tell me about your morning, oh, you hoarder of treasure! (BD 33-34)

[Je vais mieux, et la preuve, c'est que j'ai savonné ce matin, à sept heures, dans ma rivière. J'étais enchantée. Barboter dans l'eau claire, quel plaisir! J'ai aussi scié du bois et fait six petits fagots. Et je refais moi-même mon ménage, c'est te dire s'il est bien fait. Et puis, en somme, je n'ai que soixante-seize ans!

Tu m'écris ce jour-là, un an avant de mourir, et les boucles de tes *b,* de tes *t,* tes *j* majuscules qui portent une sorte de fier chapeau en arrière, rayonnent de gaieté. Que tu étais riche, ce matin-là, dans ta petite maison! Au bout du jardin sautelait une étroite rivière, si vive qu'elle emportait, d'un bond, tout ce qui l'eût pu déshonorer... Riche d'un matin de plus, d'une nouvelle victoire sur la maladie, riche d'une tâche de plus, d'une joaillerie de reflets dans l'eau courante, d'une trêve de plus entre toi et tous tes maux... Tu savonnais du linge dans la rivière, tu soupirais, inconsolable de la mort de ton bien-aimé, tu faisais '*Uiii!*' aux pinsons, tu pensais que tu me conterais ta matinée... 0 thésauriseuse!... (3: 296)]

This wealth is contrasted with love as "compulsive giving,"[17] a giving characterized as an "egotistical frenzy" (*BD* 32), motivated in fact by a desire to retain and possess the loved one—thus another version of the same misguided treasure hunt that had tempted the young 'Colette.'

Instead, 'Colette' suggests that:

> [A]n age comes for a woman when, instead of clinging to beautiful feet that are impatient to roam the world, expressing herself in soothing words, boring tears and burning, ever-shorter sighs—an age comes when the only thing that is left for her is to enrich her own self. (*BD* 34)
>
> [[U]n âge vient où au lieu de s'exprimer toute en baumes, en pleurs mortels, en souffle embrasé et décroissant, sur les beaux pieds qu'elle embrassait, impatients de courir le monde,—un âge vient où il n'est plus donné à une femme que de s'enrichir.(3: 296-97)]

Thus we see a movement in Colette towards renunciation of a possessive love, as well as of an all-consuming need for love—the two are in fact only different manifestations of the same need—which are limitations of the real treasures, self and life.

Certainly the renunciation of passion is central and at first glance unambiguous in the novel. For, significantly, while the mother is idealized as a "great lover," she does not appear, as does the daughter, as an agent of sexual desire. This opposition between mother and daughter is set up at the beginning of the novel. The short opening section sets up a contrast between the mother and daughter around the symbol of the pink cactus. 'Sido' will not visit her daughter because her pink cactus may flower—a rare occurrence—and at age seventy-six she may not live to see it flower again.[18]

The pink cactus is thus established here as the object of desire for the mother. It is obviously not a sexual one—but the object of her desire for participation and pleasure in all aspects of life. 'Colette,' who is beginning to resemble her mother by virtue of her advancing age, cannot however, fully resemble her unless it might be at dawn. And even then, she would, unlike her mother, be "half-naked in a fluttering wrap hastily slipped on." Her feeling of distance from the mother's model is expressed in the continuation of the description. I would be found, the narrator confesses, "my arms trembling with passion and shielding—let me hide myself for shame!—the shadow, the thin shadow of a man" (*BD* 7).

Thus while the mother has renounced sexual passion, the daughter has not. Moreover, a first glance leads the reader to conclude that the mother is a source of pressure on the daughter to follow her example. She returns, a "ghost," to find her daughter holding in her arms the shadow of a man.

> "Stand aside and let me see," my beloved ghost would say. "Why, isn't what you're embracing my pink cactus, that has survived me? How amazingly it's grown and changed! But now that I look into your face, my child, I recognize it. I recognize it by your agitation, by your air of waiting, by the devotion in your outspread hands, by the beating of your heart and your surpressed cry, by the growing daylight all about you, yes, I recognize, I lay claim to all of that. Stay where you are, don't hide, and may you both be left in peace, you and the man you're embracing, for I see that he is in truth my pink cactus, that has at last consented to flower." (*BD* 7)

> ["Ecarte-toi, laisse que je voie, me dirait ma très chère revenante... Ah! n'est-ce pas mon cactus rose qui me survit, et que tu embrasses? Qu'il a singulièrement grandi et changé!... Mais, en interrogeant ton visage, ma fille, je le reconnais. Je le reconnais à ta fièvre, à ton attente, au dévouement de tes mains ouvertes, au battement de ton cœur et au cri que tu retiens, au jour levant qui t'entoure, oui, je reconnais, je revendique tout cela. Demeure, ne te cache pas, et qu'on vous laisse tous deux en repos, toi et lui que tu embrasses, car il est bien, en vérité, mon cactus rose, qui veut enfin fleurir." (3: 278)]

The reading that presents itself first is that the mother mistakes the man for her pink cactus, and validates her daughter mistakenly for something she is not doing. Thinking that the daughter is renouncing sexual desire, she approves her, thus spurring the daughter to try to achieve that renunciation. On second reading, however, another interpretation presents itself. In this second interpretation, the mother sees the man, and validates the daughter for what she *is* doing, that is, for her sexual passion, but on the understanding that that passion is felt in the way it should be. In fact, love of the right sort does seem to be the final goal, what the mother ultimately, as a ghost, most valorizes, for the pink cactus that she sees with her daughter, she qualifies as blooming *at last* (my emphasis), leading us to suppose that the one that she waited to see bloom in life never did. Thus

I argue that the passage, and the novel, do not posit the renunciation of love, but rather a new relationship of the female subject to love—a transformation that will take place at dawn.

In fact, the image of dawn is crucial to the story of the subject and her changing relationship to desire. It is only in examining this image of the dawn, and the way it functions in the text, that we can fully appreciate this story. Since the issue of the relationship of the self to desire is associated with the image of dawn, the importance of the image argues for the importance of the issue to this text. In fact the dawn as an image recurs incessantly, and is privileged to the extent of constituting the title of the work.

The mother is characterized as having always wanted to attain the dawn. We read:

> She pursued her innocent ends with increasing anxiety. She rose early, then earlier, then earlier still. She wanted to have the world to herself, deserted, in the form of a little enclosure with a trellis and a sloping roof.... She got up at six, then at five, and at the end of her life a little red lamp wakened her, in winter, long before the angelus smote the black air. In those moments while it was still night my mother used to sing, falling silent as soon as anyone was able to hear. The lark also sings while it is mounting towards the palest, least inhabited part of the sky. My mother climbed, too, mounting ceaselessly up the ladder of the hours, trying to possess the beginning of all beginning. (BD 25-26)
>
> [Elle alla vers ses fins innocentes avec une croissante anxiété. Elle se levait tôt, puis encore plus tôt. Elle voulait le monde à elle, sous la forme d'un petit enclos, d'une treille et d'un toit incliné. . . . Elle quitta son lit à six heures, puis à cinq heures, et, à la fin de sa vie, une petite lampe rouge s'éveilla, l'hiver, bien avant que l'angélus battît l'air noir. En ces instants encore nocturnes ma mère chantait, pour se taire dès qu'on pouvait l'entendre. L'alouette, aussi, tant qu'elle monte vers le plus clair, vers le moins habité du ciel. Ma mère montait, et montait sans cesse l'échelle des heures, tâchant à posséder le commencement du commencement... (3: 291)]

She is the model, to which 'Colette' aspires, but which she feels she will never be able to attain:

> When, as a little girl, I used to get up at about seven o'clock, astonished to find the sun still low, the swallows still perched in a line on the gutter and the nut-tree gathering its icy shadow beneath it, I would hear my mother cry: "Seven o'clock! My goodness, how late it is!" Shall I never catch her up, then? Free, and flying high, she says of constant, exclusive love, "What frivolity!" and then scorns to explain herself at length. It's for me to understand. (*BD* 132)
>
> [Quand je me levais, petite fille, vers sept heures, éblouie que le soleil fût bas, que les hirondelles se tinssent encore en file sur la gouttière et que le noyer ramassât sous lui son ombre glaciale, j'entendais ma mère s'écrier : "Sept heures! mon Dieu, qu'il est tard!" Je ne la rejoindrai donc jamais? Libre, volant haut, elle nomme l'amour constant, exclusif : "Quelle légèreté!" et puis dédaigne de s'expliquer longuement. A moi de comprendre. (3: 363-64)]

The mother, by arriving closer to dawn, is arriving closer to perfection. This is the case because arriving at dawn means arriving at rebirth into a state where there exists a balance between separation and connection, where one can experience 'real' love.

We see this in the last quotation where the mother's perfection, symbolized by her greater success in attaining the dawn, is accompanied by her privileged knowledge of love. Dawn as associated with knowledge of love is thus proposed; that this knowledge will be gained through a radical transformation is made clear by the images that liken the dawn to death and rebirth, as we see in the subsequent passages.

The last letter from 'Sido' causes 'Colette' to deduce that "[n]o doubt my mother wrote that last letter to assure me that she no longer felt any obligation to use our language" (*BD* 142), for it is not readable in the ordinary sense of the word. 'Colette' continues on the subject of this letter:

> Two pencilled sheets have on them nothing more than apparently joyful signs, arrows emerging from an embryo word, little rays, "yes, yes" together, and a single "she danced," very clear. Lower down she had written "my treasure"—her name for me when our separation had lasted a long time and she was longing to see me again. But this time I feel a scruple in claiming for myself so burning a word. It has a place

among strokes, swallow-like interweavings, plant-like convolutions—
all messages from a hand that was trying to transmit to me a new alphabet *or the sketch of some ground-plan envisaged at dawn under
rays that would never attain the sad zenith*. (*BD* 142, emphasis added).

[Deux feuillets crayonnés ne portent plus que des signes qui semblent
joyeux, des flèches partant d'un mot esquissé, de petits rayons, deux
'oui, oui' et un 'elle a dansé' très net. Elle a écrit aussi, plus bas, 'mon
amour'—elle m'appelait ainsi quand nos séparations se faisaient
longues et qu'elle s'ennuyait de moi. Mais j'ai scrupule cette fois de ré-
clamer pour moi seule un mot si brûlant. Il tient sa place parmi des
traits, des entrelacs d'hirondelle, des volutes végétales, parmi les messages d'une main qui tentait de me transmettre un alphabet nouveau, ou
*le croquis d'un site entrevu à l'aurore sous des rais qui n'attendraient
jamais le morne zénith*. (3: 371, emphasis added)]

What the mother's letter tries to communicate, through this new alphabet, is something glimpsed after she has already begun to make the transition from this life to what lies beyond it, and this is characterized as "some ground-plan envisaged *at dawn*."

Dawn is thus the hour of death, but it is also the hour of rebirth. The dual nature of the passage from one state to another is more clearly illustrated by another choice of words used at another point in the novel to describe the time at which it will take place. Earlier in the novel 'Colette' speaks of how at a certain point it was already too late to speak with her mother about love, for 'Sido' had already "attained her everlasting morning twilight" (*BD* 27). The words used to describe dawn here are significant—"morning twilight." While "twilight" means simply half-light, it is clearly meant to convey the idea of dawn in this passage, as it is the "morning twilight"; at the same time "twilight," although it can technically mean any half-light, is most commonly used to mean dusk. Thus 'Sido' has arrived at a death ("twilight"), but which at the same time has the characteristics of a rebirth ("morning," thus "dawn," thus "break of day," or, in the original French "*birth* of day," ["*naissance* du jour"]). The collapsing of dawn and dusk into one moment by this choice of wording, thus creating a moment outside of ordinary time, is again suggestive of the passage into something outside our ordinary experience that the mother will make at this moment.

Dawn is thus the moment of death and rebirth. However, as we have seen, it also functions as a symbol that differentiates between mother and daughter as far as progress goes, progress towards the state of perfection that will be achieved through this transformation. Let us return to the opening passage of the novel, and to the scene of the pink cactus. Again, as we have seen, in this scene 'Colette' first wonders whether her mother, if she were to return, would recognize her daughter who is now much aged. She decides finally that she might, if her mother were to return at dawn. However, the text then goes on to discuss the ambiguity of the resemblance, as discussed above, for rather than eager for the blooming of her pink cactus, 'Colette' would be at that hour "half-naked . . . arms trembling with passion and shielding . . . the thin shadow of a man" (*BD* 7).

This is the opening of the novel, setting up the problem, the need for the daughter to attain the example of the mother as regards love. It closes with 'Colette' welcoming this same dawn herself, having renounced love with Vial. It thus might seem, in line with the first possible reading of this passage mentioned above, in which the daughter strives to achieve the renunciation of sexual desire modeled by the mother, that the challenge set up at the beginning has been reached. And in fact I will argue that it has. However, I will argue this in consonance not with the first, but with the second reading of this passage mentioned earlier, in which the mother *does* validate the daughter's sexual desire. However, before returning to the significance of this scene of recognition at dawn, I will first examine other aspects of the novel's discussion of love, which will allow a greater appreciation of the complexity of the novel's problematic and its resolution. I will begin by examining further the question of the pink cactus.

'Colette' is embracing a man at the beginning of the work, at dawn, as her mother returns, rather than bending over a flower about to bloom, which had been the example of the mother. At the end of the novel, this same man is told to flee, and to come back only in such a form that he can be called her pink cactus or by the name of any other sort of flower as long as it is "flame-shaped" and "uncloses painfully." (*BD* 140). These are the characteristics of what man must become before he can return. It is difficult not to associate the image of the "flame" ["flamme"] with sexual passion; the literary language of the French seventeenth century inhabits the word whether we will it or no. And so we deduce that we are still talking about sexual passion or love. However, this passion will be one that "uncloses painfully"—not an easy one to attain. It is only as exorcised in the form in which he exists at present, as object of the wrong type of love, and having the form of the new type of love object, that he can return.

We see a similar passage at the very end of the novel. In the last paragraph, the transformation of this love object—man—is again mentioned. 'Colette,' who is looking forward to the harvest of the grapes—in other words, to the completion of *her* transformation, to the moment when it will achieve its fruition, must first wait. For

> the ambiguous friend who leapt through the window is still wandering about. He did not put off his shape as he touched the ground. He has not had time enough to perfect himself. But I have only to help him and lo! he will turn into a quickset hedge, spindrift, meteors, an open and unending book, a cluster of grapes, a ship, an oasis... (*BD* 143)
>
> [l'ami ambigu qui sauta la fenêtre erre encore. Il n'a pas, en touchant le sol, abdiqué sa forme. Le temps lui a manqué pour se parfaire. Mais que je l'assiste seulement et le voici halliers, embruns, météores, livre sans bornes ouvert, grappe, navire, oasis... (3: 371).]

Here, man's transformation is more radical, and seems to remove the protagonist further from the realm of love and sexual desire. In fact, in this passage it seems that 'Colette,' upon leaving life, will leave it alone, and that the one element allowed in a woman's life, love for man, is to be exorcised, and replaced by forms of creativity and ways of being much more diverse.

However, this in the end reveals itself not as an irreversible final move, but as a necessary step towards a changed relationship of the self to desire. For the dawn or moment of transformation that at last arrives, is blue, the color of purity, cold and virginal, but dragging with it "a very faint tinge of flesh colour that clouds it." (*BD* 143). Dawn, the moment of death and rebirth, does not herald rebirth into a world devoid of passion, but rather into a world in which passion and renunciation coexist, in which there is a balance of separation and connection. Most significantly, my reading of the text as portraying a preparation for death and rebirth through renunciation, viewed through the lens of Benjamin's theory, receives a final support in the fact that it is in her *room*—from within that security given concrete form in a spatial metaphor—that 'Colette' experiences, not total renunciation of desire, but the ability to envision a new relationship to desire. We have thus arrived at the conclusion that the novel is about renunciation, but not of all love. Rather it is the renunciation of a particular approach to love—an obsessive, grasping love, entered into through a "contemptible regular hunger," rather than freely, on the part of an independent individual existing prior to the love. It is the renunciation of this type of love, and the solitude achieved through this renunciation, that allow the welcoming of a new type of love, a new relationship of the self to desire. However, we will see that the novel proposes a circular argument as its solution, for if this solitude is necessary for the right approach to love, love is also seen as necessary for solitude.

At a particular stage of life 'Colette' has arrived at a solid enough identity to be able to achieve solitude. Yet this solid and single identity, symbolized by a single name, has been achieved through having lived under a succession of many names, and this as a result, seemingly, of having lived through many loves. In speaking of how, in writing novels about love, she gave herself many names, she writes:

> In them I called myself Renée Néré or else, prophetically, I introduced a Léa. So it came about that both legally and familiarly, as well as in my books, I now have only one name, which is my own. Did it take only thirty years of my life to reach that point, or rather to get back to it? I shall end by thinking it wasn't too high a price to pay. (*BD* 19)
>
> [Je m'y nommais Renée Néré, ou bien, prémonitoire, j'agençais une Léa. Voilà que, légalement, littérairement et familièrement, je n'ai plus qu'un nom, qui est le mien. Ne fallait-il, pour en arriver, pour en revenir là, que trente ans de ma vie? Je finirai par croire que ce n'était pas payer trop cher. (3: 286)]

And again, as we have seen earlier, she continues:

> Can it be that chance has made me one of those women so immersed in one man that, whether they are barren or not, they carry with them to the grave the shrivelled innocence of an old maid? (*BD* 19)
>
> [Voyez-vous que le hasard ait fait de moi une de ces femmes cantonnées dans un homme unique, au point qu'elles portent jusque sous terre, stériles ou non, une ingénuité confite de jeune fille? (3: 286)]

It is thus the many names, and the many loves, that enable her to arrive at the one name and the one identity. And it is this strong and stable identity that in turn allows her to achieve the solitude and the renunciation of the end, with its importance that I have already discussed. Solitude or renunciation, and love, are therefore set up as circular, each one needing the other. Thus I conclude once again that the novel is about the balance between separation and connection, rather than about renunciation alone. Neither end of the pole can be seen to be the final one, the absolute last word in this circular movement.

And if we see circularity in the refusal of a final meaning as far as separation and connection are concerned, we also see it, upon closer examination, in the construction of the mother figure as symbol of perfection. We have seen the reinstating of the mother figure in Colette's work, and the valorization of this figure. We have also seen its importance for Colette's work theoretically: the reinstating of this figure allows us to read the novel as expressing a specifically feminine voice. However, just as we note a reappearance of the tremendously important mother figure in these texts, we note as well in these later works a reappearance of the father figure. He is present in *Break of Day* as well as in the section of *Sido* entitled "The Captain," and while the space devoted to this figure does not compare with the space devoted to 'Sido,' the father here nevertheless has an importance of a different sort than that of the father of Claudine, for example, who was little more than a cardboard figure. The character of the father in these later works is not only more fully developed as an individual, but also plays in his turn a role in the daughter's apprenticeship as a writer. Colette's adoption of the patronymic as her signature leads Flieger to interpret the work of 'Colette' as a realization of the father's unfinished ambitions through an act of ghostwriting.[19] In short, all of this suggests that once 'Colette' in contrast to Claudine has reestablished herself as mothered, it is possible to envision a return to the father.

The father's reappearance in *Break of Day* is connected precisely with 'Colette' arriving finally at a single identity, for the single name which is at last hers, after all the names she has gone through, is, as I have said, her father's. Furthermore, the narrator says early on in the text, that in the place where she is now living, and in the life she is leading that "[she] recognize[s] the road back" (*BD* 9). While there are many indications that one important figure from childhood that she finds here, on this "road back," is the mother, there are other indications that the father is also present. The story is set in Provence, and this is her father's country, not her mother's. The ghosts that visit her here are the father's as well as the mother's (*BD* 132). And in the following work, *Sido,* the father for the first time constitutes the sole object of the daughter's discussion, in the middle section of that work entitled "The Captain." All of this lends substantiation to claims for the importance of the father as well as of the mother in the accession of 'Colette' to selfhood through writing; claims already made in Colette criticism, as I have mentioned above.

The father/daughter relationship is complex and cannot be entered into here in detail. However, what interests me here especially is the fact of its reappearance in a more flesh and blood form than in earlier works, and at the same time the rather marginal way in which it reappears. This is suggestive, for it brings us back to the question of the centrality of the mother, and not only what that reveals but also what that hides.[20] If the mother seems overwhelmingly the most visible and important figure to 'Colette' in her childhood world, this eventually leads us to search for that which, through this spotlighting, is being left out and unilluminated. The "dazzling" central presence of 'Sido' (74), as holder, nurturer, linguistic and literary source, and model, can blind the reader, and protagonist, not just to other characters such as the father (74), but to other aspects of 'Sido' as well.

Another look at Benjamin's theory proves enlightening here. We have seen that 'Colette' reinstates the "holding other" in her textual search for a feminine voice, and that this "holding other" takes the form of the mother, as is in fact usually the case in real life. However, while this figure and the role it plays are imbued with many positive connotations, they also carry certain negative ones. In particular, Benjamin's comments on the mother as a profoundly desexualized figure, and the effect this has on girls, are important here.

Numerous passages describing, indeed eulogizing 'Sido,' could be pulled from either *Break of Day* or *Sido* and used almost as illustrations of what Benjamin describes as the mother figure as she exists in patriarchal society—as altruistic, caring, and profoundly desexualized and de-eroticized. The opening passage from *Break of Day* presents just one example. 'Colette' voices the following eulogy of her mother as an example to follow:

> Whenever I feel myself inferior to everything about me . . . I can still hold up my head and say to myself: "I am the daughter of the woman who wrote that letter—that letter and so many more that I have kept. This one tells me in ten lines that at the age of seventy-six she was planning journeys and undertaking them, but that waiting for the possible bursting into bloom of a tropical flower held everything up and silenced even her heart, made for love. I am the daughter of a woman who, in a mean, close-fisted, confined little place, opened her village home to stray cats, tramps, and pregnant servant-girls. I am the daughter of a woman who many a time, when she was in despair at not having enough money for others, ran through the wind-whipped snow to cry from door to door, at the houses of the rich, that a child had just been born in a poverty-stricken home to parents whose feeble, empty hands had no swaddling clothes for it. Let me not forget that I am the daughter of a woman who bent her head, trembling, between the blades of a cactus, her wrinkled face full of ecstasy over the promise of a flower, a woman who herself never ceased to flower, unceasingly, during three quarters of a century." (*BD* 5-6)

> [Au cours des heures où je me sens inférieure à tout ce qui m'entoure . . . je puis pourtant me redresser et me dire : "je suis la fille de celle qui m'écrivit cette lettre,—cette lettre et tant d'autres, que j'ai gardées. Celle-ci, en dix lignes, m'enseigne qu'à soixante-seize ans elle projetait et entreprenait des voyages, mais que l'éclosion possible, l'attente d'une fleure tropicale suspendait tout et faisait silence même dans son cœur destiné à l'amour. Je suis la fille d'une femme qui, dans un petit pays honteux, avare et resserré, ouvrit sa maison villageoise

> aux chats errants, aux cheminaux et aux servantes enceintes. Je suis la fille d'une femme qui, vingt fois désespérée de manquer d'argent pour autrui, courut sous la neige fouettée de vent crier de porte en porte, chez des riches, qu'un enfant, près d'un âtre indigent, venait de naître sans langes, nu sur de défaillantes mains nues... puissé-je n'oublier jamais que je suis la fille d'une telle femme qui penchait, tremblante, toutes ses rides éblouies entre les sabres d'un cactus sur une promesse de fleur, une telle femme qui ne cessa elle-même d'éclore, infatigablement, pendant trois quarts de siècles..." (3: 277-78)]

It is to this same eulogized figure that she then addresses herself, calling her "my *chaste*, serene ghost"[21] (*BD* 6, emphasis added).

I return at this point to Benjamin's argument that woman lacks a desire of her own because of inability to identify with the mother as a desiring subject. Again, to recall Benjamin's argument, this is a situation that leads her to idealize this in the father, but that inevitably then puts her into a submissive position. These remarks reveal another aspect of the complex mother/daughter relationship created by these texts. In fact, the restraint and abstention that 'Sido' teaches her daughter, while proving a model in the daughter's search for the solitude necessary to selfhood and desire, participate, as well, in other stories. In *Sido*, the mother who condemns the daughter's desire to impose destruction on that which wants to live (the cotyledon), in fact approves this destruction in both the behavior of a boy child and of animals, both free from the necessity to restrain their desire:

> But she gladly sacrificed a very beautiful flower to a very small child, a child not yet able to speak, like the little boy whom a neighbor to the East proudly brought into the garden one day, to show him off to her. My mother found fault with the infant's swaddling clothes, for being too tight, untied his three-piece bonnet and his unnecessary woollen shawl, and then gazed to her heart's content on his bronze ringlets, his cheeks, and the enormous, stern black eyes of a ten months' old baby boy, really so much more beautiful than any other boy of ten months! She gave him a *cuisse-de-nymphe-émue* rose, and he accepted it with delight, put it in his mouth, and sucked it; then he kneaded it with his powerful little hands and tore off the petals, as curved and carmine as his own lips. (*Sido* 164)

[Mais elle sacrifiait volontiers une très belle fleur à un enfant très petit, un enfant encore sans parole, comme le petit qu'une mitoyenne de l'Est lui apporta par orgueil, un jour, dans notre jardin. Ma mère blâma le maillot trop serré du nourisson, dénoua le bonnet à trois pièces, l'inutile fichu de laine, et contempla à l'aise les cheveux en anneaux de bronze, les joues, les yeux noirs sévères et vastes d'un garçon de dix mois, plus beau vraiment que tous les autres garçons de dix mois. Elle lui donna une rose cuisse-de-nymphe-émue qu'il accepta avec emportement, qu'il porta à sa bouche et suça, puis il pétrit la fleur dans ses puissantes petites mains, lui arracha des pétales, rebordés et sanguins à l'image de ses propres lèvres... (3: 508)]

The flower here, as in the man/pink cactus conflation of the end of *Break of Day,* has sexual connotations, and in this case, connotations of female nubility: the flower is a *"cuisse-de-nymphe-émue* rose" (emphasis added), and the petals are likened to the child's own lips, in that they are "curved and carmine." Significantly, the child's desire towards this flower, which is even a destructive one, is not rebuked by the mother, but applauded.

"Stop it, you naughty boy!" cried his young mother.
But mine, with looks and words, applauded his massacre of the rose, and *in my jealousy I said nothing.* (*Sido* 164, emphasis added)

["Attends, vilain!"dit sa jeune mère.
Mais la mienne applaudissait, des yeux et de la voix, au massacre de la rose, *et je me taisais, jalouse...* (3: 508, emphasis added)]

And in a similar scene, the mother, in the garden with 'Colette,' remains arrested before the sight of a blackbird who is eating the family's cherries from the tree.

"How beautiful he is!" whispered my mother. "D'you see how he uses his claw? And the movements of his head, and that arrogance of his? See how he twists his beak to dig out the stone! And you notice that he only goes for the ripest ones." (*Sido* 166)

[—Qu'il est beau!... chuchotait ma mère. Et tu vois comme il se sert de sa patte? Et tu vois les mouvements de sa tête et cette arrogance? Et ce tour de bec pour vider le noyau? Et remarque bien qu'il n'attrape que les plus mûres... (3: 509)]

The daughter has to cry out more than once before the mother comes out of her transfixed admiration of the animal's uncomplicated and "arrogan[t]" pursuit of its desire, to protect the family's food:

"The cherries? Yes, of course, the cherries."
    In those eyes there flickered a sort of wild gaiety, a contempt for the whole world, a light-hearted disdain which cheerfully spurned me along with everything else. It was only momentary, and it was not the first time I had seen it. Now that I know her better I can interpret those sudden gleams in her face. They were, I feel, kindled by an urge to escape from everyone and everything, to soar to some high place where only her own writ ran. If I am mistaken, leave me to my delusion.
    But there, under the cherry-tree, she returned to earth once more among us, weighed down with anxieties, and love, and a husband and children who clung to her. Faced with the common round of life, she became good and comforting and humble again.
    "Yes, of course, the cherries... you must have cherries, too."
    The blackbird, gorged, had flown off, and the scarecrow waggled his empty opera-hat in the breeze. (*Sido* 166)

[– Les cerises?... Ah! Oui, les cerises... Dans ses yeux passa une sorte de frénésie riante, un universel mépris, un dédain qui me foulait avec le reste, allègrement... Ce ne fut qu'un moment,—non pas un moment unique. Maintenant que je la connais mieux, j'interprète ces éclairs de son visage. Il me semble qu'un besoin d'échapper à tout et à tous, un bond vers le haut, vers une loi écrite par elle seule, pour elle seule, les allumait. Si je me trompe, laissez-moi errer.
    Sous le cerisier, elle retomba encore une fois parmi nous, lestée de soucis, d'amour, d'enfants et de mari suspendus, elle redevint bonne, ronde, humble devant l'ordinaire de sa vie :
    – C'est vrai, les cerises... Il te faut aussi les cerises...

La merle était parti, gavé, et l'épouvantail hochait au vent son gibus vide. (3: 509)]

We see that the mother on these occasions occupies the position of the idealizing other in relation to the desiring subject, who in the case of the child, at any rate, is definitely identified as male. However, when in this last scene she is recalled to her duties as mother, as one who sacrifices herself for others, we see two reactions—first "a wild gaiety, a contempt for the whole world," and a "soar[ing] to some high place where only her own writ ran," that is, a defiance of law, of constriction, of the gender roles of patriarchy. It is only later that this law in the end wins out. Through it she again becomes, once "[f]aced with the common round of life, good and comfortable and humble again" and this by reason of the fact that she is "weighed down by anxieties, and love, and a husband and children who clung to her."[22]

Thus 'Sido' is complex. First, she occupies the role of "holding other," a figure that is portrayed as part of the childhood world recollected by 'Colette,' and is also a figure crucial in a theoretical sense for the building of a female textual self and voice. Second, the model for the renunciation of a clinging, dependent love that the mother provides is elaborated into a state of perfection to be achieved. This, however, is ultimately a prerequisite for a new relationship of the self to desire, for a new experience of love, rather than a renunciation of love entirely. And in fact, third, the "chaste" and self-sacrificing side of 'Sido' reveals itself to have both positive and negative connotations. In line with Benjamin's argument, because of the fact that the role of "holding other" is held exclusively by the mother, and because of this mother's consequent desexualized, deeroticized nature, the mother in the end is capable of becoming the mouthpiece of patriarchal law. She must in the end uphold it, since she cannot be independent of it. Significant, however, is the fact that 'Sido' also at times transcends it, and by this very act reveals the possibility of doing so. It is this challenge that the daughter takes up, to transcend this law.

In fact, *Break of Day* in the end operates the reversal of the very hierarchy it sets up, between "pure," "chaste," and superior mother, and "impure," daughter. The narrator herself hints at the constructed nature of the mother's purity: "my very dear mother, whom I liked to think untouched by my ordinary crimes," (*BD* 32) she writes; the word in the original French is literally "pure" (3: 295). While this purity serves a purpose for the narrator's construction of the story of renunciation and subsequent rebirth into a new state of balance between separation and connection, in the end, upon close examination, the construction of perfect purity is undermined. In fact, in the following passage, already quoted in part, we see the purity and impurity, of mother and daughter respectively, reversed.

> My mother climbed too, mounting ceaselessly up the ladder of the hours, trying to possess the beginning of the beginning. *I know what that particular intoxication is like.* But what she sought was a *red*, horizontal ray, and the pale sulphur that comes before the red ray; she wanted *the damp wing that the first bee stretches out like an arm.* (*BD* 26, emphasis added)

> [Mais ma mère montait, et montait sans cesse l'échelle des heures, tâchant à posséder le commencement du commencement... *Je sais ce que c'est que cette ivresse-là.* Mais elle quêta, elle, un rayon horizontal et *rouge*, et le pâle soufre qui vient avant le rayon rouge; elle voulut *l'aile humide que la première abeille étire comme un bras.* (3: 291, emphasis added)]

Here it is the daughter who owns the desire to possess the "beginning of the beginning," and it is the mother who is searching for the color red, which is the color of passion. The mention of the moist wing of the first bee recalls the butterfly wing that tempted 'Colette,' and that she rebuked herself for touching and spoiling—here it is the mother who seems tempted. The stable categories of purity and impurity that have been set up contaminate each other. The daughter searches for "purity," as the mother is pulled towards the pole of "impurity." Just as the mother is constructed as the daughter's model, by virtue of her purity, and therefore guides her to the necessary renunciation of the wrong type of love, so the daughter, through her textual impurity, brings about the restitution to the mother of the final object of that renunciation, the experience of desire—that very experience that according to Benjamin's description of patriarchy she had lost.

And so, once again, the two poles of an opposition are dissolved. Neither the one—the mother's purity, nor the other—the daughter's impurity, can definitively be seen as superior. Instead, we return to the final image of dawn in the last pages, as it at last arrives. "The cold blue has crept into my bedroom, trailing after it a very faint tinge of flesh colour that clouds it" (*BD* 142-43). Purity—the blue —does not triumph completely over passion—the red—the two will always continue in circular movement, one contaminating the other.²³

At the end, this refusal of a final meaning is reinforced as we are reminded one last time of the untamable nature of the text we are reading. However, before coming to this, let us look at one more of the novel's explicit statements about the nature of books. We are told the many diverse forms that the man, or "favori," who has been sent away, will take on. The exact form of this new "pink cactus" cannot be defined, but is suggested by a series of words: "quickset hedge, spindrift, meteors, an open and unending book, a cluster of grapes, a ship, an oasis..." (*BD* 143). The lived experience—the lover—will become a book, and a book, as we are warned elsewhere in the novel, is something other than the faithful realistic reflection of lived experience.

We are made aware of this as the trap of referentiality is presented to us one last time with one final twist. As this novel of renunciation reaches its conclusion, the narrator makes the following unexpected statement:

> I said to myself that, as far as the décor was concerned—the black night, the solitude, the friendly animals, a great circle of fields and sea all around—I should be thenceforward like the woman I have described so many a time, that solitary upright woman like a sad rose which carries itself the more proudly for having been stripped of its leaves. But I no longer trust in what I look like, having known the time when, while I was painting this lonely creature, I would go to show my lie, page by page, to a man, asking him, "Have I lied well?" And I would laugh, as my forehead sought that man's shoulder, and his ear that I nibbled, for I could never get over the belief that I lied. (*BD* 134)
>
> [[J]e me disais que, si je me fiais au décor,—la nuit noire, la solitude, les bêtes amies, un grand cercle de champs et de mer tout autour—

> j'étais désormais pareille à celle que je décrivis maintes fois, vous savez, cette femme solitaire et droite, comme une rose triste qui d'être défeuillée a le port plus fier. Mais je ne me fie plus aux apparences, ayant connu le temps où, tandis que je peignais cette isolée, j'allais page à page montrer mon mensonge à un homme en lui demandant: "Est-ce bien menti?" Et je riais, en cherchant du front l'épaule de l'homme, sous son oreille que je mordillais, car incurablement je croyais avoir menti... (3: 365)]

Thus the very story we have just read, of renunciation and the search for solitude, may be nothing but a lie, we are told. And yet, we are given the hint that perhaps not, for the narrator tells us that "I could never get over *the belief* that I had lied" (emphasis added); is the lie she believes she is telling, therefore, not one after all? Books, or texts—one of the forms that the "favored one" ["favori"] becomes, are "open and unending." They will not propose a final solution to any of the questions they raise. Instead, they are both "ship," means of exploration, and "oasis," that safe space, that haven of security and well-being, from which exploration may depart and to which it may return, allowing us to reenvision and reinvent the world.

4

Love and Self: *Chéri*

In the two previous chapters I traced Colette's development as a writer from the production of the initial *Claudine* novels to that of her masterpieces, the mature semiautobiographical works. This is more than a simple change in style or genre, and there is more to the development this progression of works represents than simple maturation as a craftswoman of words. The mature works are not so much fictionalized reminiscences alone as the construction of a feminine voice, and with it, the expression of a feminine selfhood and desire. In this sense, *Break of Day* does indeed constitute the "code for life as a couple" that 'Colette' suggests it is, and the cycle of works centered on the mother lays the groundwork for a return to novels about love written from the perspective of maturity.

That these later novels form a separate corpus from her earliest works is underscored by the remarks of 'Colette' herself. In *My Apprenticeships* she recalls the need she felt to write on aspects of life other than love as she neared the end of her life with 'Willy.' This need, moreover, is expressed in terms of honor and duty towards the self. In *My Apprenticeships,* she writes:

> I had become vaguely aware of a duty towards myself, which was to write something other than the *Claudines*. And so, drop by drop, I squeezed out the *Dialogues des Bêtes*. In it I enjoyed the moderate but honourable satisfaction of not talking about love.... All my novels, after that, dwelt most persistently upon love, and I have not grown tired

of the subject. But I brought it back into my books and found pleasure in it when I had recovered respect for love—and for myself. (*MA* 85)

[Je m'éveillais vaguement à un devoir envers moi-même, celui d'écrire autre chose que les *Claudine*. Et, goutte à goutte, j'exsudais les *Dialogues de bêtes*, où je me donnais le plaisir, non point vif, mais honorable, de ne pas parler d'amour. . . . Tous mes romans, après, ressassent pourtant l'amour, et je ne m'en suis pas lassée. Mais je ne me suis reprise à mettre l'amour en romans, et à m'y plaire, que lorsque j'eus recouvré de l'estime pour lui—et pour moi. (3: 1041)]

Thus her later novels treat many of the same themes as the *Claudines*, but the self-imposed exercise of writing on other aspects of life than women's stereotypical theme of love allows her to return to that subject matter later with profundity and distance. It is the most significant of these later novels—*Chéri*—and its investigation of love and self, that will be the subject of this chapter.

It is useful to place *Chéri* within the context of Colette's mature fiction taken as an ensemble. The same decades that saw the publication of Colette's major semiautobiographical works, the 1920s and 1930s, are those in which she produced most of the works of fiction of her maturity.[1] From 1919 to 1941 Colette produced nine fictional works of sufficient length to be called novels. These are *Mitsou* (1919), *Chéri* (1920), *The Ripening Seed* (1923), *The Last of Chéri* (1926), *The Other One* (1929), *The Cat* (1933), *Duo* (1934), *The Toutounier* (1939), and *Julie de Carneilhan* (1941).

As 'Colette' herself remarks, these are all, at first glance, love stories. Love is central to all these fictional scenarios. But these novels move considerably beyond the simple reiteration of a formulaic literary trope. In these later novels, love is not so much an emotional experience in and of itself but rather a means by which the mettle of the individual is tried. In this sense, then, all of this corpus rewrites the *Claudines*. Love here is the battlefield on which Colette chooses to portray the struggle for the maturity, integrity, and indeed survival of the individual.

Thus this corpus of love stories puts on center stage the issue of self. At the same time, because love is the backdrop to this drama, gender is also integral to these works. In Colette's fictional world, gender is presented in realistic fashion, but also constantly problematized. These love stories provide no escape from the constraints placed on human beings in a gendered, and indeed a hierarchically gendered society. But through tales of survival or of failure of the self, they do provide telling insights into the workings of gender, and gender as it is constructed by society is invariably put into question.

This questioning of conventional gender is most immediately apparent in the overwhelmingly consistent attributes of Colette's male and female characters in these works, and this brings us to an examination in detail of this corpus of novels. In fact we are faced with two categories of novels in these works, those that end with the failure of the protagonist—almost invariably male—in the face of life's various challenges, and those that chronicle the survival and strengthening of the individual—almost always a woman. These latter novels are tales of heroism.[2] Within a world that is not of their own making, Colette's heroic female protagonists give proof of lucidity, strength, and dignity as they deal with the vicissitudes of life and love. Furthermore, the resolution of these novels is not blissful love, but an increased awareness or equilibrium on the part of the individual. Examples of this group of novels are *Mitsou, Chéri* in the case of Léa, *The Ripening Seed, The Other One, The Cat* in the case of Camille, *Duo* in the case of Alice, *The Toutounier,* and *Julie de Carneilhan.*

In contrast to these, a smaller number of novels explore a contrary set of experiences that tend to be lived by male characters. Here we witness an inability to persevere and find sustenance in life, to reach maturity, or to sustain loss. These characters display regressive behavior or commit suicide. Examples include *Chéri* in the case of Chéri, *The Last of Chéri, The Cat* in the case of Alain, and *Duo* in the case of Michel. Thus the characters of the major novels fall into two different categories—those who exhibit an inability to achieve selfhood, and those who demonstrate survival and adaptation of the self, and these categories are themselves, to a large extent, gendered.

This gendering of heroes and victims gives rise to some questions. Does Colette attribute an essential nature to males and females? The core of the problem actually lies elsewhere. Rather than essential gender, it is a question of real strength of character as opposed to socially sanctioned dominance. In all the novels, the characters are part of the world of patriarchy. In Colette's fictional world, as in the 'real world' outside, men enjoy access to powerful roles more easily than women. Yet Colette's novels typically undercut the strength of men when that authority has its sole origin in their more powerful social position. It is women, typically less powerful socially, who develop the strength of realism, resilience, and practical wisdom that in Colette's world typifies not only heroism, but selfhood itself.

As we come to *Chéri,* however, we begin to note characteristics that set it apart. While *Chéri* can to a certain extent be categorized with the other novels, it nonetheless presents a more complex fictional situation than a number of the other works, such as *The Other One, The Cat,* and *Duo.* In all of these other novels the setting is the home of a bourgeois married couple, albeit in some cases within a bohemian milieu. Thus in all of these novels the wife is, still, in the 1920s and 1930s, legally subservient to her husband in a number of ways. We note the scene of domestic violence in *The Cat*—that tale of the brief months of marriage between two ill-assorted personalities. Alain, threatened by Camille's energy and vitality, and by the fact that she is not sufficiently impressed by his membership in an elite class, which is, however, on the decline, slaps her for what he considers her lack of respect—calling him "[s]illy boy" in a moment of disagreement and tweaking his nose (*Cat* 76). To take the example of another of the novels, *The Other One* from its opening pages makes us aware that Farou's womanizing is something that Fanny has simply learned to accept.[3] *Duo* explores the more radical fictional scenario of an affair on the part of the woman, yet rather than indicating a move towards greater equality in Colette's fictional world, it simply illustrates the inequality in a different way. Too accustomed to his privileged position to survive the blow of his wife's infidelity, Michel commits suicide, thus underscoring paradoxically his dominant position in society and within marriage, and his consequent lack of strength, courage, and adaptability in the face of difficulties.[4]

In certain ways *Chéri* fits in with the corpus of Colette's later novels, most obviously in the weakness displayed by Chéri and the survival of Léa. Yet this novel has its own complexities. The relationship between Chéri and Léa is not that of a bourgeois married couple, and within this relationship, from the beginning, it is the man, Chéri, who occupies the subservient role. Unlike the female characters of the other novels, however, he does not adapt, survive, and rise above this initial position. Certain elements therefore set this novel apart, and it is of particular interest, not just for its mastery of the novelistic form, but also for the unusually rich and complex tale, not only of gender, but also of selfhood and love, that it relates.

One of the first things to strike the reader of *Chéri* is the mixture of conventional and unconventional in the milieu it depicts and in the workings of gender within this world. To begin with, this novel operates a neat reversal of gender roles in its two main characters. Instead of a relationship between a wealthy older man and a much younger 'kept' woman (as in *Mitsou*), we encounter in *Chéri* a wealthy older woman and her young lover. Moreover, Léa is authoritative, decisive, ultimately independent, while Chéri is weak, vacillating, and unable to live without love. It is as if the set, preestablished script for innumerable love stories had been reversed.

However, while Colette's forceful portraits of Léa and Chéri may undermine the reader's expectations, their many subversions of conventional gender roles do not spell happiness. *Chéri* offers the example of androgynous characters whose unconventional relation to gender is an impediment to selfhood. The reasons for this are to be found in the socio-economic realities of the world these characters inhabit. The subversion of gender that we see in this novel is a result of an institution—prostitution—created by patriarchy. Although this world of the *demi-monde* is to a certain extent cut off from the mainstream, it is not independent of it. It reproduces in exaggerated, concentrated form the inequalities of the larger society. For this reason, the gender roles we see here, while unconventional, remain nonetheless unequal and oppressive. Let us note that the "feminine" characteristics Chéri displays are not those that are typically construed as positive—sensitivity, or gentleness, for example—but rather a true lack of inner strength and an unhealthy dependence. At the same time, Léa's "masculine" characteristics—her overpowering strength and domineering authority—also contain negative overtones. Androgyny here does not have to do with growth, but with having been stifled and oppressed. Chéri is neither an adult woman nor man, nor an androgynous being through strength and struggle, but rather through the realities of an institution created by patriarchal oppression; in the end he is "inhuman."

Thus, the very neatness of the reversal of gender in *Chéri* redistributes the roles, but does not change the pattern of domination. This will be acknowledged by the two characters only at the end of the story, when it is too late. For this reason, *Chéri* is reminiscent of a classical tragedy. While the lovers' destinies are linked from the beginning, human weakness as well as circumstance combine to prevent their union, and truth, which provides a cathartic dénouement, replaces the romance's traditional happy ending.

Most readers of Colette are familiar with the basic elements of the plot of *Chéri:* the love relationship between the forty-nine-year-old "courtisane," Léa, and the twenty-five-year-old Chéri, child of another "courtisane" and member of Léa's set, Charlotte Peloux. Equally familiar is the knowledge that this love is one in which elements of an erotic relationship and a maternal/filial relationship are inextricably intertwined, and that as the novel opens this relationship is jeopardized, due to the impending marriage of Chéri to the daughter, Edmée, of another aging courtisane, Marie-Laure. Familiar to most readers of Colette as well is the problematic of aging, loss, and acceptance for Léa. However, paradoxically, in spite of the title, most criticism has focused on Léa, rather than on Chéri, who faces another problematic, that of subjugation and rebellion. The acceptance of age is indeed a major theme not only in *Chéri* but also in *The Last of Chéri,* where it will be Chéri's turn to confront this fear. But equally important in *Chéri* are the questions of separation, maturity, and selfhood. This is true for Léa as well as Chéri, and it is the itinerary of the two characters in this domain that I will trace in the following pages.

The first lines of the novel allow the reader to begin tracing these intersecting itineraries.

"Give it me, Léa, give me your pearl necklace! Do you hear me, Léa? Give me your pearls!"

No answer came from the huge brass-bedecked wrought-iron bedstead that glimmered in the shadows like a coat of mail.

"Why won't you let me have your necklace? It looks every bit as well on me as on you—even better!"

At the snap of the clasp, ripples spread over the lace frilled sheets, and from their midst rose two magnificent thin-wristed arms, lifting on high two lovely lazy hands.

"Leave it alone, Chéri! You've been playing long enough with that necklace."

"It amuses me... Are you frightened I'll steal it?" (*Chéri* 3)

["Léa! Donne-le-moi, ton collier de perles! Tu m'entends, Léa? Donne-moi ton collier!"

Aucune réponse ne vint du grand lit de fer forgé et de cuivre ciselé, qui brillait dans l'ombre comme une armure.

"Pourquoi ne me le donnerais-tu pas, ton collier? Il me va aussi bien qu'à toi, et même mieux!"

Au claquement du fermoir, les dentelles du lit s'agitèrent, deux bras nus, magnifiques, fins au poignet, élevèrent deux belles mains paresseuses.

"Laisse ça, Chéri, tu as assez joué avec ce collier.

—Je m'amuse.... Tu as peur que je te le vole?" (2: 719)]

Colette opens this novel with a conflictual dialog, a scene of negotiation centered on Léa's pearl necklace. The pearl necklace reappears throughout *Chéri,* as well as throughout its sequel *The Last of Chéri,* and is indeed symbolic of both the setting of the novel and the issues at stake for not only Léa but also Chéri. Throughout the novel, Léa is described in terms of a very small number of colors. While her eyes and much of her clothing are blue, her body and her rooms are consistently described in terms of two colors: white, and especially pink. At the beginning of the novel we read, "[s]he could still afford to show her body, pink and white." In the next paragraph we encounter the following description of her room: "The noonday sun poured into the gay, rosy, over-decorated room. Its luxury dated: double lace curtains, rose-bud watered silk on the walls, gilded woodwork, and antique furniture upholstered in modern silks" (*Chéri* 8). These descriptions insisting on pink and white recur continuously. Considering that she is no longer young, Léa remarks that now "I have to wear something white near my face, and very pale pink underclothes and tea-gowns" (*Chéri* 13). On page 36 she is "dressed in white, the color flaming in her cheeks" (36). A bit later, Léa pulls closer around herself her "pink dressing-gown . . . the pink that she called 'indispensable'" (*Chéri* 42). Further on: "The coloured lining of the white gandoura she put on was suffused with a vague pink" (*Chéri* 126). After her shock at Charlotte's where she encounters "old Lili" and her young lover, her pink bedroom is a comfort (*Chéri* 60). Towards the end of the novel she is described as "[n]aked, and brick-pink from the reflection of her Pompeian bathroom" (*Chéri* 126). Even her chambermaid is named Rose. White and especially pink recur constantly in descriptions of both Léa and her rooms. And these are also the colors of her pearls.

Thus the pearls evoke, first of all, Léa, and particularly the pink and white flesh of Léa, and their roundness is also suggestive of her voluptuousness. With their perfection, they are also symbols of beauty. This is in turn an instrument of money and power in a world in which beauty is an object of exchange. The pearls are, in fact, the gift of one of Léa's former lovers. Thus they are also evocative of the prestige of a beautiful and successful courtesan such as Léa. Moreover, in addition to their beautiful color and form, the pearls are also shimmery and reflective. In this way they suggest mirrors and the narcissism associated with the love of mirrors and reflections.

Thus the qualities of the pearls, their *pearliness,* is evocative of qualities such as beauty, and its attendant prestige and narcissism, which are central to the novel. These qualities constitute not just the background to the story but the very arena in which the characters' stories necessarily evolve. In this world, beauty is the conduit to all prestige and power. And this in turn arises directly from the socioeconomic world in which the story is set. A look at some of the characteristics of the *demi-monde* will allow us to understand this socio-economic world, and the psychological consequences for its inhabitants.

The world of the *demi-mondaines* and their children is a closed one (*Chéri* 25). The women socialize amongst each other; their contact with the rest of society is limited to their liaisons with wealthy men. Yet this world, if it is closed to most contact with the rest of society, reproduces the characteristics of that society in many ways. The *demi-monde*, for example, is also a highly conventional world. Chéri protests that he is above social conventions (*Chéri* 4), but this amounts to little more than a conventional and ultimately empty stance in itself. In fact, the *demi-monde* exhibits many of the narrow-minded prejudices and conventions of the petite bourgeoisie.[5] As the novel opens, there is no question of any of the central characters in the novel living in defiance of the values of the group. The young will get married according to the wishes of their elders, within an institution of marriage in which social class and financial interest are the decisive factors. Charlotte Peloux's repetitive trumpeting aloud of clichés and axioms is the clearest illustration of the narrow and conventional horizons of this world.

This closed, conventional nature of the *demi-monde* is due to the courtesans' role in the socioeconomic order. For the *demi-mondaines* and gigolos who people the world of *Chéri* occupy a particular place in, or rather outside of, economic productivity. In spite of the luxury in which they live, they experience "the wearing and difficult duties of a parasite" (*Chéri* 88). In fact, a parasite is, by definition, dependent, and this has consequences.[6] In the case of the characters that people *Chéri,* the parasitic nature of their work curbs their freedom. This becomes particularly clear when we contrast Colette's portrayal of the *demi-monde* in *Chéri* with her portrayal of music hall artists in other works, and especially what distinguishes the two groups: the relationship of the characters to their work.

Colette's tales of the music halls also portray a life on the fringes of society. However, the characters who make their living in this manner, while poor, do nonetheless achieve a high level of selfhood, and this because they maintain a certain degree of independence vis-à-vis their work. They sell their labor as artists, and, while grossly undercompensated, they nonetheless remain free agents once work hours are over. The duties of music-hall performer, while placing them outside the realm of bourgeois respectability, does not place them outside a code of individual morality. They do not enjoy the benefits of acceptance into bourgeois society, but they are their own masters, and demonstrate qualities of integrity, independence, self-reliance, and generosity.[7]

This is for the most part not true in the world of *Chéri,* and it is the characters' work as parasites that is the key to the difference. The relationship in *Chéri* of the characters to their work is not one of independence. Work is not separate from their private lives; rather their very private lives *are* their work. It is in this way that their freedom is curbed. There is no separation from work, and no place outside of one's functionality, of one's being useful to another, in which the self can assert itself. Thus assertion of the self has no arena in which to appear. It is replaced by rivalry among the members of this particular social group, a rivalry based on beauty and appearance. Significantly, neither Léa nor Chéri has any inclination towards reading and writing, those acts that provide the privileged arena for a contestation of discourse and an assertion of self in other works of Colette. Yet both are at ease with figures and calculations. On the eve of her renunciation, as a substitute for love and for Chéri for which she clearly has no real inclination, Léa makes an attempt to settle down to reading: "without much hope, [she] picked a detective story from the shelf of a dark closet. She had no taste for fine bindings and had never lost the habit of relegating books to the bottom of a cupboard, along with cardboard boxes and empty medicine bottles" (*Chéri* 126). However, the following morning, when she believes she will be leaving soon to begin a new life with Chéri, we observe, with Chéri, the following scene: "He saw her open a railway time-table and run her finger down the columns; then she seemed absorbed in some calculation" (*Chéri* 141). Descriptions of Chéri are similar: "His calculations were quick and accurate, and the figures he jotted down on slips of paper—dashed off rapidly, round and regular—were in marked contrast to his rather slow and childish handwriting" (*Chéri* 23-24). Reading and writing—those signs of selfhood—are undeveloped in both Léa and Chéri, but their calculations, in other words, their ability to negotiate and survive in the money-oriented *demi-monde*, are good.

Thus the characters demonstrate well-developed survival skills, but not the independence and moral stature of selfhood. This dependence also has consequences for the 'love' relationships of the novel. The nonexistence of such relationships, indeed the very impossibility of their existence, is linked to the economic and social structures already discussed, as well. The lack of space in which to assert the self also closes off the possibility of love. This may seem paradoxical, as it is a commonplace that this is a love story. However, a close reading of the text confirms that love in *Chéri* ultimately exists in spite, and not because, of the world it is set in.

Love can mean widely different things; a look at some of its distinct meanings will help us to clarify this issue in *Chéri*. Three definitions of this emotion are given by *Le Petit Robert*. The first is as follows: "Disposition to desiring the good of someone other than oneself and to devoting oneself towards that person." The next reads: "Affection between members of a family." The third is: "Inclination towards a person, most often of a passionate nature, based on the sexual instinct, but which carries with it varied behaviors" (my translation).

The one variant of love that we encounter as we begin the novel is the third one. Yet when we recall Benjamin's analysis of self and love, we see that relationships of erotic love in *Chéri* know certain limitations. In particular, as we have seen, Benjamin quotes D. W. Winnicott who asserts that the "moment . . . of really recognizing the other as existing outside the self . . . is the decisive aspect of differentiation," and she contends that this same experience, that is, "the reciprocal recognition that intensifies the self's freedom of expression, is actually the goal of erotic union."[8] This selfhood that is strong enough to recognize the other's selfhood is not achieved by Chéri, or indeed in general by the characters in this novel. For this reason, without the accession to selfhood that permits the experience of erotic union as described by Benjamin, the relationships of erotic love tend to appear as mere dalliances or relationships of expedience.

If relationships of erotic love thus take only a limited form in *Chéri*, this is true in the end for all kinds of love. Moreover, the limitations placed on love in one area have consequences for love in another area. This becomes clear when the love between family members—the second dictionary definition—is examined. The world of *Chéri* is characterized by a very limited range of interpersonal relationships, and family relationships are no exception. There are very few family ties in evidence, and what few there are—always mother/child ties—are relationships of neglect, in the case of Charlotte and Chéri, or hostility and rivalry, in the case of Marie-Laure and Edmée. We do not encounter any fathers. Significantly, both Chéri and Edmée consider themselves orphans, although both have mothers living (*Chéri* 74; 82). Finally, the first definition of love, that of altruistic love, is the least in evidence of all. If selfhood is precluded by the socioeconomic structure of this world, then love is, as well.

Thus the pearliness of the pearls, their pink and whiteness, their roundness, their perfection, their glistening, reflective qualities, serve to evoke the multiple aspects of beauty, which, upon close analysis, prove to be the center of this world and the arena within which the characters move, interact, and evolve. Yet that evolution is truncated. The intrinsically dependent nature of the work of a parasite has consequences, and its greatest consequence is the lack of freedom that it imposes. Despite the reputation of the *demi-monde* as bohemian and outside the norms, this world is more closed and highly conventional than the mainstream, and proves more stifling to the development of selfhood than does the world of the bourgeois middle class. And so, finally, for this reason, it is also a world that excludes love.

Having seen the qualities evoked by the central symbol of the pearls, and how with close analysis these prove the key to understanding the socioeconomic and psychological world of the novel, I will now move to a reading of the pearls as a means of figuring the issues, itineraries and development of the two main characters. To do so, I return to the opening scene of the novel, one revolving around the negotiation of Léa's string of pearls. In order to understand what is being negotiated, let us look at what the pearls mean in particular for both protagonists.

While the pearls are suggestive of beauty, and the power, money and prestige that accompany it, they are also, significantly, symbols of an *indestructible* beauty, for these precious stones remain unchanged through time. The beauty of the pearls enjoys a permanence that the beauty of the woman who wears them does not. And this brings us to the final semantic field in which the pearls participate—age. For although the pearls themselves are impervious to time, the string contains exactly the same number of pearls as years that Léa has lived. They are a string of forty-nine, and in this way, at the same time that they suggest unchanging beauty, they also evoke the passing of time. Their role as an indicator of age and the process of aging is supported by a further element in the text, one not dependent on the qualities of the pearls themselves, but which comes out of the place the pearls adorn—Léa's neck. It is her neck that is showing signs of age. For this reason Léa no longer wears them at night, for fear that in the early morning, before she has time to do her toilette, Chéri, who loves to play with them, will notice the deterioration of her body and specifically her neck.

Thus for Léa the pearls remain symbols of beauty and all its attendant qualities, but they also serve to highlight the contrast between the unchanging beauty of the stones, and the mortal, ephemeral beauty of human beings, and especially, Léa herself. And this is the very crux of her story. The values that stem from the privileging of beauty are the foundation of Léa's world. At the beginning of the novel she fingers her pearls "[a]s if telling the beads of a rosary" (*Chéri* 7). If she loses her beauty, she loses her entire identity. Moreover, and most importantly, she will also lose

Chéri. And yet this loss is imminent. The need for its acceptance is hinted at from the beginning in images of Chéri as a winged figure, always on the point of flight, and in the image of the doorway.

In fact, the novel is structured by Chéri's arrivals, departures, and returns. The very first chapter sets up the tension between departure and the status quo. In this first chapter we encounter Chéri living at Léa's apartment, yet it is known that this relationship is destined to end, and this knowledge figures in Léa's thoughts. For example, in examining her aging body, she finds that it is nonetheless still beautiful, and that "the high-slung breasts, 'would last . . . till well after Chéri's wedding' " (*Chéri* 8).

Thus from the beginning we know that Chéri is destined to depart. Moreover, this chapter ends with Chéri's actual departure from the apartment, although only to lunch at his mother's. This foreshadowing of the definitive departure of the final chapter is also echoed by the foreshadowing of Léa's acceptance, for we read that "[w]ith Chéri out of the house, Léa became herself again, very much alive, cheerful, and on the spot" (*Chéri* 12). Yet she is not yet ready to let go. She follows Chéri, and it is with "battle written on her face" that she gives the order to her chauffeur: "To Madame Peloux's" (*Chéri* 14).

Other arrivals, departures, and returns continue to prepare us for the end. Through a flashback, we learn of the beginning of Léa and Chéri's liaison in Normandy, where Léa has taken Chéri to help him recover strength and well-being after a period of dissipation and ennui. Both expect their return to Paris to be the end of the affair, but the separation that takes place upon their return does not last. We read:

> "Ouf!" Léa sighed, as she entered her house in the Avenue Bugeaud, alone. "How wonderful!—a bed to myself!"
>
> But at ten o'clock the following night, she was sipping coffee and trying not to find the evening too long or the dining-room too large, when a nervous cry was forced from her lips. Chéri had suddenly appeared, framed in the doorway—Chéri, wafted on silent, winged feet. (*Chéri* 40)
>
> ["Ouf, soupirait Léa en rentrant seule dans sa maison de l'avenue Bugeaud. Que c'est bon, un lit vide!"

> Mais le lendemain soir, pendant qu'elle savourait son café de dix heures en se défendant de trouver la soirée longue et vaste la salle à manger, l'apparition soudaine de Chéri, debout dans le cadre de la porte, Chéri venu sur ses pieds ailés et muets, lui arrachait un cri nerveux. (2: 745)]

This precedent having been set, we are prepared for Léa's reactions as she struggles to accept what is next expected to furnish the final break—Chéri's marriage. Once again, she is at Charlotte's—the scene is reminiscent of the earlier one, except that Chéri and Edmée are on their honeymoon in Italy. As she returns to this familiar setting, she cannot but hope for Chéri's return. She sits outside a moment, away from the others, and indulges in a moment of reverie.

> She picked a tea rose, which shed its petals. She listened to the breeze in the birch, to the trams in the Avenue, to the whistle of the local train. The bench she sat on was warm, and she closed her eyes, letting her shoulders enjoy the warmth of the sun. When she opened her eyes again, she hurriedly turned her head in the direction of the house, feeling positive that she was going to see Chéri standing in the garden entrance with his shoulder against the doorway. (*Chéri* 55)

> [Elle cueillit une rose de Bengale qui s'effeuilla, écouta le vent dans le bouleau, les tramways de l'avenue, le sifflet d'un train de Ceinture. Le banc où elle s'assit était tiède et elle ferma les yeux, laissant le soleil lui chauffer les épaules. Quand elle rouvrit les yeux, elle tourna la tête précipitamment vers la maison, avec la certitude qu'elle allait voir Chéri debout sur le seuil du hall, appuyé de l'épaule à la porte... (2: 756)]

The text here is very ironic, for the people who end up passing through the door to Charlotte's house that afternoon are not destined to allow Léa to fulfill her fantasy or return to the past, but rather are destined to remind her brutally of reality and the future. They are "old Lili" whose affectations and denial of age render her truly ridiculous, and Lili's young lover, Guido, who looks as if he were caught in a trap. The age difference here being even greater than between Léa and Chéri (Lili is seventy to Guido's seventeen), this couple is a caricature of possibilities Léa does not yet want to face. Significantly, one of the horrors that the spectacle of "old Lili" presents is that she is wearing a pearl necklace. The contrast between the pearls' unchanging beauty and the extraordinarily decrepit and aged state of Lili's body is truly grotesque, providing Léa with a forceful warning of what will happen if she does not take care and accept reality. The shock she feels at this encounter sends her back to her apartment shaken and afraid she is falling ill.

Once home, she takes measures to be sure she will not catch cold, but even after she has had dinner and is safe in bed, she cannot stop thinking about what she has seen. One image persists, although she attempts to brush it from her mind. "She was obsessed by the vision of an empty doorway, with clumps of red salvia on either side." And a few paragraphs further: "She let her mind wander from one incident of her past life to another, from this scene to that, trying to rid her thoughts of the empty doorway framed by red salvia." It is this image—the doorway that should frame Chéri, which is framed by red flowers but is itself empty— that precipitates her anguish. "Suddenly she jumped as though shot, racked by a pain so deep that at first she thought it must be physical, a pain that twisted her lips and dragged from them, in a raucous sob, a single name: 'Chéri!' " (*Chéri* 61-62).

Finally, at the very end, after she has left and come back, and considers herself exorcised of her passion, after Chéri himself has observed her return, yet can also consider himself exorcised, and return, not to Léa, but to Edmée, we have a final return of Chéri, a final apparition in the doorway (*Chéri* 127). Yet this, although it does precipitate the mutual recognition and declaration of their love, does not signal the beginning of a new life together, as both, at first, are sure that it will. Rather, it precipitates, at long last, the realistic appraisal of their situation for both parties. Léa at last recognizes that she has become an old woman. And Chéri, at last, voices the reality that their love masks—that being with Léa "is likely to keep [him] twelve for half a century" (*Chéri* 144).

Having traced Léa's story, let us now return to the initial scene of negotiation and examine it from the perspective of Chéri. While for Léa the cluster of meanings associated with the pearls has to do with decline, for Chéri, it has to do with growth. Chéri, to an even greater extent than Léa, is fascinated by the sight of strings of pearls. Consistently throughout the novel and its sequel he toys with pearls worn not just by Léa but by other female characters as well. His fascination with the pearls is often read as a symbol of his love for Léa—its endurance, and the fact that it cannot be replaced.[9] And while love is certainly central to the picture formed by Chéri and the pearls, another reading restores its necessary and compelling complement. The pearls symbolize for Chéri the maturity and authority—envied in Léa—that constitute selfhood, and allow access to an erotic union between equals.

A closer look at Chéri will clarify this. To begin with, and of primary importance, Chéri is "rebellious only to become submissive, enchained lightly but powerless to free himself." A bit further on we read: "[Léa] put a hand on his young head, which impatiently shook off the yoke" (*Chéri* 5). He is dominated, yet desires to free himself of this domination. But he is in a difficult situation not shared by anyone else in the novel. Chéri is alone in making his struggle from the child position.[10] And while on the one hand Chéri is at ease in this role—his love relationship with Léa is to a large extent a mother/child relationship—on the other hand it proves at times intolerably constraining.

Thus Chéri's case is a particularly difficult one, and it is his struggle against domination and for selfhood that we see in his relationship to the pearl necklace. At the same time, love is not absent from his desires. In fact, love takes two forms in this novel. It is both a negative force, which works at cross-purposes with independence and the integrity of the self, and also a positive ideal that remains unrealized. It is the desire for this second type of love, between equals, made possible by accession to selfhood, that ultimately motivates much of Chéri's behavior around the pearls. However, it is love as a negative force, the cause of weakness and suffering, that provides the battleground on which he struggles to assert himself and on which he fails. To speak of a battle is not an exaggeration, and the scene of negotiation that opens *Chéri* is indeed furnished with battle imagery. It has already been noted that Léa's bed is described in military terms, as an "armure," or suit of arms (2: 719, my translation).[11] This preparation for battle is echoed by a similar piece of defensive equipment associated with Chéri, the "shield" (*Chéri* 4). The battle that will ensue, however, in spite of preparation on both sides, will be unequal. Léa has achieved a degree of selfhood that Chéri can in no way match. Selfhood, that is to say, strength, maturity, and authority as a courtesan. She has been successful, she is wealthy enough to retire. Léa also dominates the group of which she is a member through moral qualities—her intelligence, her lucidity, and her realism, although this last quality, until the end, remains only latent.

It is this strength and maturity in Léa that allow us to begin to interpret Chéri's actions with the pearls. However, further dimensions to Chéri's story yet again reveal themselves as the pearls are further examined. The shimmery, mirror-like quality of the pearls has already been noted, and the image of the mirror as reflector of beauty is of prime relevance to this novel. In *Chéri,* beauty, while not the conduit to selfhood, is the prerequisite for advancement and power and so the function of the mirror as reflector of beauty recurs frequently. Both Chéri and Léa gaze into a mirror during the course of the first chapter to judge their beauty. Later, as Léa attempts to prepare herself to retire, and to renounce Chéri, she considers redecorating her apartment with paintings, and thus taking down the mirrors (*Chéri* 125). Mirrors can play tricks, however, and are not always the docile servants of those who use them. It is through an unintentional glance in the mirror, one in which she does not even recognize herself, that Léa is ultimately confronted with the reality of her age, and in this way, when least expected, the mirror also plays the role of the revealer of truth. However, mirrors in Léa's world play yet a third role, one that does not place the subject in relation with him or herself, but places the subject in relation to another subject. Specifically, mirrors play the third role in this novel of framing Chéri. In imagining himself reunited with Léa, he imagines himself *in the mirror.*

> He whistled softly, arranging himself in front of the pier-glass so that it framed his figure exactly like the one between the two windows in Léa's room—the one which would soon frame in its heavy gold, against a sunny pink background, the reflection of his naked body— naked or loosely draped in silk—the magnificent picture of a young man, handsome, loved, happy, and pampered, playing with the rings and necklaces of his mistress. (*Chéri* 99-100)
>
> [Il sifflotait en carrant son reflet dans le miroir oblong, juste à sa taille comme celui de la chambre de Léa, entre les deux fenêtres. Tout à l'heure, dans l'autre miroir, un cadre d'or lourd sertirait, sur un fond rose ensoleillé, son image nue ou drapée d'une soierie lâche, sa fas-

tueuse image de beau jeune homme aimé, heureux, choyé, qui joue avec les colliers et les bagues de sa maîtresse..." (2: 788)]

Chéri exists as a *reflected* being in Léa's rosy world, playing, moreover, with her necklaces. In the case of Chéri, the shimmeriness, the reflectiveness of the pearls, their mirror-like qualities suggest not only narcissism—a trait he certainly exhibits—but also the dependent nature of his being, dependent on Léa for its secondary, reflected existence. And indeed, Chéri's initiatives towards self are in fact bound up with Léa. His attempts to assert do not confront her, but rather remain fixated on her, taking the form either of imitation and adulation, or rivalry.

We see this in the first scene. When Chéri attempts to "try on" Léa's strength and authority in toying with her pearl necklace, the rivalry between the two is clear. "Are you frightened I'll steal it?" he asks her (*Chéri* 3). And as far as rivalry in beauty goes, Chéri is in a position to threaten Léa, with his youth and his extraordinary good looks. Significantly, Chéri who goes to the mirror to see what the pearls look like on him judges himself "good-looking." A few pages later, after his departure, Léa puts them on, and in her turn, judges herself in them in the mirror. Her reaction is decided and uncompromising—she is ugly. Yet if the victory in this superficial battle goes to Chéri, his ultimate fate remains shadowy. Significantly, his chest, as he tries on Léa's pearls before the mirror, is "curved *like a shield*" (*Chéri* 4, emphasis added). The battle image associated with Chéri is a particularly defensive image. And this is a portent, for although attempts to challenge her are frequent, a genuine assertion of self on the part of Chéri in relation to Léa will not take place until too late.

Incidents involving pearls continue to give insights into Chéri's story of subjugation and rebellion. The episode at the end of section four offers further evidence of Chéri's domination by Léa, and his inability to extricate himself from this situation. After one of the several scenes in the novel in which Léa and Chéri spar, and during which one manages to convince the other—always to the other's displeasure—that the love between them is a mere dalliance—Chéri appears, for the first time that Léa can remember, discouraged. She is saddened by it, and to cheer him up offers to buy him a pearl. His reaction is telling. He cries:

"Top-hole! A pearl for my shirt-front! A pale pink pearl. I know the very one!" (*Chéri* 46)

["Chouette! Oh, chic, une perle pour la chemise! une un peu rosée, je sais laquelle!" (2: 749)]

Here he no longer threatens to steal her pearls; rather, she offers him one. And his choice falls upon the one that most resembles her pearls, and herself—"a pale pink one." His attempts at growth still do not challenge her domination. Rather than confronting her, he wants to *be* her. Her reaction to his request is equally telling. She replies:

"Not on your life! A white one, something masculine, for pity's sake! Don't tell me, I know which one just as well as you." (*Chéri* 46)

[– Jamais de la vie, une blanche, quelque chose de mâle, voyons! Moi aussi, je sais laquelle. (2: 749)]

She communicates here her belief that she is not an appropriate model for him, but the manliness, the gendered adult strength, maturity and independence she identifies as the appropriate qualities for him, are precisely precluded by her domination, exemplified by her authoritative correction of his choice. As already noted, Chéri presents a rare case in Colette's work in which androgyny is presented as negative, for in him 'male' qualities—the "something masculine" Léa refers to, which would allow him to structure himself as an adult member of society—are not sufficiently developed and strengthened to support later modifications. Moreover, at the very end of the novel, Léa voices her recognition of this, and her role in bringing it about:

"Had I really been the finest, I should have made a man of you, and not thought only of the pleasures of your body, and my own happiness. The finest! Oh no, my darling, I certainly wasn't that, since I kept you to myself. And now it's almost certainly too late..." (*Chéri* 151)

[Si j'avais été la plus chic, j'aurais fait de toi un homme, au lieu de ne penser qu'au plaisir de ton corps, et au mien. La plus chic, non, non, je ne l'étais pas, mon chéri, parce que je te gardais. Et c'est bien tard.... (2: 826)]

Léa has been an obstacle to Chéri's growth, and this is related to the reversal of gender seen in the two main characters. Nonetheless, the relationship between Léa and Chéri is the tie that is central to Chéri's being, and to the novel's structure. His return to her is felt as inevitable, and it is the final exchange that takes place upon this return that acknowledges Chéri's truth, and precipitates both characters towards a new and different awareness.

Before Chéri's final return, however, the novel prolongs his search through his relationship with two other female characters. If the pearls are a prism through which we are able to see and analyze Chéri's relationship with Léa, they perform the same function for Chéri's relationship with Edmée and The Pal. These two alternate endings serve, as did that of 'Juliette' in the matter of books, as "means of warding off the danger of short-circuit ['the wrong solution to the problems'], assuring that the main plot will continue through to the right end."[12] These 'wrong solutions' shed further light on Chéri, and from the point of view of the novel's structure, reinforce the strength of the tie between him and Léa, since neither 'solution' succeeds in displacing the importance to this young man of his relationship with her. From a gender theory point of view, these two relationships are also interesting, for both women are representative of a particular female social role under patriarchy, the essence of which, in both cases, is to be of service to the male. Edmée is Chéri's wife, and The Pal is associated with prostitution, not that of chic courtesans such as Léa, but of brothels.[13]

In relating with both these women, Chéri encounters two new situations in which his selfhood is potentially tried. Authority and maturity, as well as the love they make possible, continue to be the issues that the pearls evoke. However, neither one of these 'wrong solutions' provides an adequate challenge. And thus, although in the case of both Edmée and The Pal, strings of pearls again fascinate, it is only as a reflection of the pearls worn by Léa.

Like Chéri's relationship with Léa, his bond with Edmée is signified by his attraction to her pearl necklace: "[s]itting close beside her, Chéri put one arm round her shoulders and with his free hand began to finger the small, evenly matched, very round and very beautiful, pearls of her necklace" (*Chéri* 70). Shortly afterwards, when she has spoken to him, he reacts in the following way: "[h]e seemed not to have heard. He was staring at the pearls with obsessed anxiety" (*Chéri* 70). The tracing of the pearls is fascinating for the reader, as well, for Chéri's relationship to Edmée revealed through these stones represents the other side of the coin of the unwillingly submissive Chéri we see with Léa.

In fact, the relationship between Chéri and Edmée, at times verging on one of solidarity between "orphans" (*Chéri* 74), but more often stilted and even hostile, nearly comes to an end in a heated quarrel precipitated by Edmée's jealous rifling of Chéri's affairs in search of old love letters. Countering her accusation that he never loved her, in a rhetorical move in which bad faith and a genuine lack of understanding of emotions are hard to distinguish, Chéri demands: "Do I have a separate room? Don't I make love to you well?" Her hesitations in answering this last question in the affirmative, her tentative suggestion that what he calls "love" can sometimes be "a... kind... of alibi" (*Chéri* 79-80), precipitate a violent reaction on the part of Chéri, and he immediately goes about putting her in her place. While the scene involves no physical violence, it does entail verbal violence, for his language relegates Edmée to the status of so contemptible an inferior as to be an object:

> "Ugh!" he repeated, "Look what's talking!"
> "What are you saying?"
> "Look what's talking, and what it says. Upon my word, it actually has the cheek to..." (*Chéri* 80)
>
> ["Peuh!... répéta-t-il. Ça parle.
> —Comment?
> —Ça parle, et pour dire quoi? Ça se permet, ma parole...." (2: 774)]

It is important to note that Edmée is not passive in the exchanges that take place between herself and her husband. For example, in reaction to Chéri's remarks quoted above, we read:

> She jumped up in a rage. "Fred," she said, "don't dare to speak to me again in that tone! What do you take me for?" (*Chéri* 80)
>
> [Elle se leva avec rage : 'Fred, cria-t-elle, tu ne me parleras pas deux fois sur ce ton-là! Pour qui me prends-tu? (2: 774)]

She gives proof of spirited intelligence in her interactions, but this does not alter the fact that she occupies a role—that of wife—which imposes restrictions on her behavior. Moreover, she falls victim to the same force that pulls at Chéri. Although she proposes a divorce as an answer to their quarrels, she recognizes that she will not follow through on it, because of love. "In her heart of hearts she acquiesced: 'It's true, I love him. At the moment, there's no remedy'" (*Chéri* 82).

The pearls that Edmée wears are associated with the same questions we have seen since the beginning.[14] The possibility of selfhood, of the equal relationship with the other, that they symbolize, continues to fascinate Chéri. This selfhood and this relationship are again unattainable, however, for here Chéri is able to dominate too easily. In fact, in the socially sanctioned dominance of the husband role in late nineteenth-century France he is able to dominate sadistically, almost without effort. This sadistic behavior is moreover seconded by Charlotte—there exists a patriarchal complicity between mother and son. We read:

> Charlotte Peloux, over-excited at the proximity of so tender a victim, was inclined to lose her head and squander her barbs, using her claws indiscriminately.
>
> "Keep calm, Madame Peloux," Chéri would throw out from time to time. "What bones will there be left for you to pick next winter, if I don't stop you now?" (*Chéri* 72)
>
> [Charlotte Peloux, exaltée par la proximité d'une victime si tendre, perdait un peu la tête et gaspillait les flèches, mordant à tort et à travers...
>
> 'Du sang-froid, Madame Peloux, jetait de temps en temps Chéri. Qui boufferez-vous l'hiver prochain, si je ne vous arrête pas?' (2: 768)]

Yet the crucial question of authority for Chéri is not resolved by this easy and socially sanctioned domination. He practices an exaggerated, sadistic authority with Edmée, but it is no more an expression of real strength than his inability to confront Léa. This is made quite clear by an incident that takes place during the time when, unable to bear existence in his new home with his wife, he is living at Desmond's. He speaks to his friend about Edmée in the following fashion:

"Really, that young thing's too sweet! Did you ever see such a dream of a wife? Never a word, never a complaint! I'll treat her to one of those bracelets, when I get back... Upbringing, that's what does it! Give me Marie-Laure every time for bringing up a daughter!"

["Elle est trop gentille, aussi, cette petite! A-t-on jamais vu un amour de femme comme celle-là? Pas un mot, pas une plainte! Je vais lui coller un de ces bracelets, quand je rentrerai... Ah! l'éducation... parlez-moi de Marie-Laure pour élever une jeune fille!"]

Yet his macho bravado is shown for what it is worth immediately afterwards, as we read:

But one day in the grill-room at the Morris, abject terror was written on his face when he caught sight of a green dress with a chinchilla collar just like one of Edmée's dresses. (*Chéri* 91)

[Mais un jour, dans le grill-room du Morris, l'apparition d'une robe verte à col de chinchilla, qui ressemblait à une robe d'Edmée, avait peint sur le visage de Chéri toutes les marques d'une basse terreur. (2: 782)]

If with Léa Chéri is unable to assert authority and self, and if with Edmée he exerts an exaggerated, cruel authority, but which hides fear, the relationship with The Pal provides yet a third case. Edmée as wife provides too easy a sport, while at the same time giving proof of a strength, nascent but promising, that frightens him. The Pal, however, presents no challenge at all. She exists only to facilitate things for others, she provides no presence of her own. This is dictated by the nature of her work, and this quality is in turn reinforced by her name, which identifies her solely in relation to another—"The Pal" is the translation of "La Copine," which means "the girlfriend." These elements give clues to her function in the novel, and her pearls confirm it.

While he is living at Desmond's, a period during which he is frequently out with The Pal, Chéri is once more fascinated by the string of pearls she wears. However, while those of Edmée are "small," and "evenly matched"—beautiful, but as yet small and undeveloped—those of The Pal are "false" (*Chéri* 92). She will provide no solution to what Chéri seeks, although she facilitates for him the fixation on the pearls, and hence what they symbolize—an elusive goal that Chéri will never attain.

Thus the pearl necklaces of two other women distract Chéri temporarily with reflected images of the love he seeks. But nothing can prevent him from ultimately returning to the wearer of those pearls, which he truly envies and desires to wear, and whose wearer he loves. And this leads to a revelation of truth, but not to Chéri's growth. It is too late. Chéri is able to ape authority, but he is unable to exert real authority.

Thus the drama of *Chéri* is twofold—one of love and one of self. Chéri's final assertion of self with Léa lifts him at last out of the two poles of either childish, ineffectual petulance or cruel domination; his voice at last emerges. As for Léa, by relinquishing Chéri she attains that dimension of love that was most conspicuous for its absence in their relationship—altruism. But *Chéri* is tinged with sadness, for the title character comes to voice too late, and only to express the impossibility of the two lovers' union. And, as he leaves, Chéri is characterized by one last image of weakness. Although the image of Chéri leaving, viewed through Léa's eyes, is one of Chéri moving towards youth and life ("Chéri look[ed] up at the spring sky and the chestnut trees in flower"), in the last words of the novel he is described as filling his lungs with air "like a man escaping from prison" (*Chéri* 154). Thus the final image of Chéri suggests a certain weakness and passivity. Instead of freeing himself he has *escaped;* the image suggests an importance or power conferred on that which he is leaving and the past. In spite of his ability in the end to voice his situation, Chéri cannot rise above it. From the defensive image of the shield, from rivalry in beauty and his character lightly "enchained" to his evasion at the end, he is never in a position of strength. On the battlefield of negative love, Chéri has not been strong enough. The suicide of *The Last of Chéri* is the only logical conclusion to his itinerary.

Thus gender, although unconventional, does not provide a truly happy resolution for either character. Chéri never achieves the manliness, the adult strength and maturity of the "something masculine" that Léa desires for him, and thus is unable to incorporate androgynous qualities into his being from a position of strength. Léa's subversion of gender is certainly more positive, for her authority does permit her to survive. Even more radical is a further subversion of gender that Colette includes at the end of *The Last of Chéri*. Here, while Chéri has taken to worrying about his wrinkles and his advancing age, Léa has moved beyond some of the stereotypic attributes of femininity such as beauty, and has become a fat, yet contented, old woman. Yet the dimension of love that she had hoped for with Chéri is lost. The exaggerated traits of the "other gender"—Chéri's assertion that comes too late, Léa's overpowering authority—work against them. For this subversion of gender is in the end simply the other side of a coin, rather than a real challenge to gender as hierarchy. In this sense, self ultimately fails in the case of both Léa and Chéri, as the references to reading and writing suggest. But the truth revealed in the last scene, as well as the gentleness and generosity with which the two lovers say good-bye, impart to the characters a dignity that lifts the story out of the banal and imparts to it the quality of tragedy. To their double monstrosity—Chéri as "inhuman," Léa as that particular monster, "an old woman" (*Chéri* 111)—is opposed their nobility. Léa reflects:

> "My poor Chéri! It's a strange thought that the two of us—you by losing your worn old mistress, and I by losing my scandalous young lover—have each been deprived of the most honourable possession we had upon this earth!" (*Chéri* 121)
>
> ["Mon pauvre Chéri.... Est-ce drôle de penser qu'en perdant, toi ta vieille maîtresse usée, moi mon scandaleux jeune amant, nous avons perdu ce que nous possédions de plus honorable sur la terre...." (2: 804).]

Their love story, which in the socioeconomic world they inhabit ought not to exist, but which they experience and to which they give voice, rewrites the script within which their lives had been confined, and leaves its mark, albeit imperfect and unfinished, on the world that had formed them and that they will both soon leave behind.

5

Androgynous Selfhood as Resistance

The mother and daughter figures throughout Colette's work, and in *Break of Day* in particular, allow for an exploration and articulation of a feminine selfhood, voice, and desire, through the interplay of the notions of purity and impurity. These same notions are the means through which another question is explored in the 1932 work *The Pure and the Impure*.[1] This work undertakes the textual exploration of selfhood within the realms of gender and sexuality. While the "maternal cycle"[2] takes the protagonist beyond the constraints of a voice that is explicitly other and allows the construction of the protagonist's own, and gendered, voice, and while the novels of Colette's maturity re-examine love and self through this voice, *The Pure and the Impure* steps back, as it were, to pose the question from the beginning, within a broadened framework. The nature of gender in a general sense is the subject of this later novel's exploration.

The Pure and the Impure consists of vignettes, mostly conversations between 'Colette' and a variety of individuals who all bring a different light to bear on the question of "the Inexorable" (*PI* 24)—"the dominant force that directs and controls human sensual behavior in all its manifestations."[3] This dominant force at times moves the various characters to behaviors that are in line with the conventionally scripted versions of their gender, and at times moves them to behaviors in conflict with these conventional scripts. In this way the novel and its investigation of "the Inexorable" pose at the same time, of necessity, the question of gender. How to express one's being in a world that imposes gender, and how to destabilize and transcend the traditional notions of gender and sexuality, are the questions to which the vignettes bring different answers. The encounters with various individuals who through their behavior cause the traditional notions of gender and sexuality[4] to crack and to reveal their limitations are the means through which 'Colette' makes her journey to understanding in this realm, and to the acquisition of wisdom. This novel therefore explores once again, in a different domain, the notion of selfhood as acquired in resistance to discourse. Two models of individuals thus in conflict emerge, that of the "monster,"[5] who fails to achieve selfhood, and that of the "androgynous being," who successfully contests discourses and constructions. 'Colette' journeys in search of the element that distinguishes them, and this wisdom eventually acquired is the subject of the last section of the book. I will argue that it is the persistence in the pursuit of one's desire, in conflict with discourse, and in conflict with the desire of others, that constitutes this differentiating element. Consequently selfhood in this last novel examined is ultimately posited, quite simply, to be acquired through the pursuit of one's desire—the road to selfhood is through "the Inexorable." In addition, this selfhood acquired is that of a being who remains gendered. 'Colette,' in the here and now of patriarchal culture, does not propose a being capable of stepping outside of gender. However, the person who achieves selfhood remains linked with her or his original "bi-, or supra-, or non-gendered" self.[6] This is the nature of that privileged being, that self, that 'Colette' calls the androgynous being.

Already in the vignette "The Mirror" from *Tendrils of the Vine* (1908), 'Colette' speaks of this androgynous nature, which—as part of the general state of grace that had been hers at that time—she had known as a child. In speaking to Claudine, whom she declares to be her nondouble, 'Colette' says, to distinguish herself from her:

> I've grown up, but I was never little. I have not changed. I remember myself with a clearness, a melancholy, that do not deceive me. The same obscure and chaste heart, the same passionate taste for everything that breathes freely and far from people—trees, flowers, gentle and fearful animals, the furtive water of unused springs—the same serious-

ness quickly transformed for no reason into exaltation... That is I, as a child, and now... But what I've lost, Claudine, is my fine pride, my secret certainty of being a precious child, of feeling in myself the extraordinary soul of an intelligent man, of a woman in love, a soul too big for my little body... Alas, Claudine, I've lost all of that, and have become after all but a woman.... (1: 1032, my translation).

[J'ai grandi, mais je n'ai pas été petite. Je n'ai jamais changé. Je me souviens de moi avec une netteté, une mélancolie qui ne m'abusent point. Le même cœur obscur et pudique, le même goût passionné pour tout ce qui respire à l'air libre et loin de l'homme—arbre, fleur, animal peureux et doux, eau furtive des sources inutiles,—la même gravité vite muée en exaltation sans cause... Tout cela, c'est moi enfant et moi à présent... Mais ce que j'ai perdu, Claudine, c'est mon bel orgueil, la secrète certitude d'être une enfant précieuse, de sentir en moi une âme extraordinaire d'homme intelligent, de femme amoureuse, une âme à faire éclater mon petit corps... Hélas, Claudine, j'ai perdu tout cela, à ne devenir après tout qu'une femme... (1: 1032)]

The childhood world that has been lost, the magical space and time of security and well-being, is one in which 'Colette' existed as a gendered being. This is clear in the French, where she describes herself as having been "*une* enfant précieuse," (emphasis added), but retaining at the same time a bi-gendered nature, having the soul both of "[un] homme intelligent" and of "[une] femme amoureuse." Just as the end of childhood marks the end of a state of grace, so adult existence, as no more than a conventionally scripted form of 'woman' after the childhood state as an androgynous being, is felt to be a form of exile and a loss.

Finding one's way in the world of gender after having suffered this loss is at the heart of the problematic of *The Pure and the Impure*. The novel uses the central metaphor of sight in its elucidation of this problematic. The text's main issue, of selfhood as opposed to loss of self, is illustrated through images of muddiness and clarity, legibility and illegibility—all metaphors stemming from the general organizing principle of light and seeing. The protagonist's quest, itself illustrating the text's main issue, is therefore also articulated through metaphors stemming from this same source.

The need to see is highlighted in a concrete and humorous manner in the vignette concerning Renée Vivien.[7] Into Renée's stifling, closed and shadowy house 'Colette' brings a lamp, an "offending, an inadmissible big oil lamp," which she puts down on the dinner table in front of her plate (*PI* 85). This is symbolic of the project of the entire novel.[8] For the problem for 'Colette,' as we have seen, is the unraveling of a mystery, shrouded in darkness.[9] From the opening scene in the opium den, with its "shaded lights" (*PI* 4), taking place at night, to Renée's close, overfurnished, and dimly lit house, to the very image of "the Inexorable" itself as a "cavern" (*PI* 24), 'Colette' is groping her way in the dark.[10] It is, however, not only the unraveling of a mystery that needs to be accomplished. Before this can be attempted, 'Colette' must first distinguish between what is really worthy of investigation, and what is not; she must separate between the "real and phony mysteries," in Janet Whatley's phrase.[11] It is here that the image of the veil is revelatory. The illusory creature, the secrets of whom she seeks, the "androgynous being," is characterized as "veiled, never naked" (3: 596, my translation). However, the veil covering this "real" mystery is not the same as the ostentatious veils worn by those calling attention to a "phony" mystery. Moreover, the "androgynous being," for all that he or she is veiled, will in the end be readable and provide 'Colette' with illumination. The ostentatious veils not only call attention to a phony mystery, they fail in the end to provide a clue to the real one.[12] In the protagonist's quest, those who aid her are also characterized by an exceptional sight. From Boldini, the "old demon of painting" (*PI* 65), a practitioner of the visual arts, to Amalia X, looking for truth in her tarot cards, she receives wisdom from those who see. This exceptional sight is one which 'Colette' herself will master little by little in the course of her journey, and this is what will allow her to arrive at its end. For in this text, as in the case of the older 'Colette' of *My Apprenticeships* who looks back on her younger self, 'Colette' in *The Pure and the Impure* is learning to read. She is acquiring the skill of interpreting signs whose meaning escaped her at a younger age.

As we shadow the protagonist in her journey, and follow her in her reading, let us take up first the question of veils. In this text, as we have remarked, the ostentatious veil functions in two ways, to draw attention to a mystery where there is none, and to prevent understanding of the real one. Charlotte of the first vignette provides the first example.

She is the opening figure of the work. The reasons for this are given in the following passage.

> The veiled face of a woman, refined, disillusioned, knowledgeable in deception, in delicacy, is a suitable opening to this book which will speak sadly of pleasure. (*PI* 25, translation modified)
>
> La figure voilée d'une femme fine, désabusée, savante en tromperie, en délicatesse, convient au seuil de ce livre qui tristement parlera du plaisir. (3: 566)

Thus this woman whom 'Colette' encounters in the opium den is characterized as "knowledgeable in deception"; we assume that this is because, as we have learned, she simulates orgasm with her young lover. In this context, 'Colette' speaks thus of Charlotte:

> O intractable, lordly senses, as intractable and ignorant as the princes of bygone days who learned only what was indispensable: to dissimulate, to hate, to command! Yet it is you that Charlotte held in check, couched beneath the quiet night soothed by opium, assigning arbitrary limits to your empire... (*PI* 24-25)
>
> [Sens, seigneurs intraitables, ignorants comme les princes d'autrefois qui n'apprenaient que l'indispensable: dissimuler, haïr, commander... C'est vous pourtant que Charlotte, couchée sous la paisible nuit assagie par l'opium, tenait en échec, assignant des limites arbitraires à votre empire.... (3: 566).]

Yet Charlotte is "deceptive" on another level as well—that of the signs 'Colette' is learning to interpret, and it is the veil that signals this. Rather than hiding a 'scandalous' sexuality and a contestation of received discourses, Charlotte's veil in fact covers some of the same old scripts. Whatley writes:

> As Charlotte, a native informant, explains the accounts of the opium den, the price of sandwiches, the tonic qualities of maté, the dealings with the concierge, the narrator Colette muses: "Une aussi claire

> ordonnance de ce qu'il faut appeler la débauche eût désolé, sans doute, un autre que moi."
>
> ["A regulation as clear as this in what must be called debauchery would no doubt have distressed anyone else" (*PI* 20)][13]

As Whatley demonstrates, Charlotte, for all her frequenting of the opium den, and semipublic simulation of sexual pleasure, appears as bourgeoise, and this most especially as concerns her conventionally feminine attitude towards her younger lover. In fact, as we read:

> This substantial Charlotte was a female genius, indulging in tender subterfuge, consideration, and self-denial. And here she was, this woman who knew how to reassure men. . . ." (*PI* 18)
>
> [Un génie femelle, occupée de tendre imposture, de ménagement, d'abnégation, habitait donc cette tangible Charlotte, rassurante amie des hommes... (3: 562)]

Her behavior recalls Benjamin's description of the mother in patriarchal society—caring, nurturing, and profoundly deeroticized. She practices a "deferential lie, the passionately maintained dupery, the unrecognized feat of valor that expects no reward" (*PI* 18). In fact, what seems scandalous in Charlotte—the frequenting of the opium den, the affair with the younger lover, the sex act practiced semipublicly, all seem to point to something that has broken free of the constraints of bourgeois order, and we might expect, by that token, of conventional gender constraints, especially as concerns sexuality. But instead, as Whatley demonstrates, what is revealed in the story of Charlotte are the "hidden, unsuspected depths of bourgeois order, of motherly protection" (19) contained within her. The journalist that 'Colette' meets upon first entering the den, and whom she despises for being unable to understand the real motive for her visit, assumes she is there for the exoticism, the falsely scandalous scripts. While the incident concerning Charlotte might satisfy a "reader" looking for such a text, the encounter of 'Colette' with this enigmatic figure leaves her pondering, and without a solution.

> How many shadows still conceal her... It is not for me to dispel them. When I think of Charlotte, I embark upon a drifting souvenir of nights graced neither by sleep nor by certitude. (*PI* 25)
>
> [Sur elle que de ténèbres encore... Il ne m'appartient pas de les dissiper. Je m'embarque, quand je pense à Charlotte, sur un voguant souvenir de nuits que ni le sommeil, ni la certitude n'ont couronnées. (3: 566)]

Charlotte remains for her unreadable.

Renée Vivien (the *nom de plume* of the Englishwoman Pauline Tarn) is another ostentatiously veiled character, but who in the end fails to provide a clue to the mystery. She and her house are described thus:

> Among the unstable marvels, Renée wandered, not so much clad as veiled in purple or in black, almost invisible in the scented darkness of the immense rooms barricaded with leaded windows, the air heavy with curtains and incense. (*PI* 81)
>
> [Parmi des merveilles instables, voilée, mieux que vêtue, de noir ou de violet, à travers la nuit odorante des salons barricadés de vitraux, dans un air épaissi de rideaux, de fumées d'encens, Renée errait. (3: 599)]

This is another veil leading first to a phony mystery. Whatley discusses the childishly 'haunted house' tone of Renée's environment (19), and how 'Colette,' rather than feeling the "shiver of intoxicated fear" that this décor is supposed to evoke, wishes only that she could "be younger, so [she] could be a little fearful" (*PI* 85). Renée's lifestyle, similarly, fails to inspire 'Colette' with the awe one normally feels for the uncanny, or that which lies entirely outside the bounds of the conventional or the known. Instead, 'Colette' muses: "The alcohol... the thinness... the poetry, the daily Buddha... And that's not all. Where is the dark origin of all this nonsense?" (*PI* 91).

Once again, we see in Renée a Juliette figure, a reader of texts, someone who seeks her definition in them, rather than having the ability to maintain distance from them, and in this way to retain integrity of self.[14] 'Colette' recounts how more than once:

> I caught her curled up in a corner of a divan, scribbling with a pencil on a writing pad propped up on her knees. On these occasions she always sprang up guiltily, excusing herself, murmuring, "It's nothing, I've finished now..." (*PI* 81)
>
> [Je la surpris accotée dans un coin de divan et crayonnant sur ses genoux. Elle se levait d'un air coupable et s'excusait: "Ce n'est rien...J'ai fini thout de suithe..." (3: 599)]

As discussed in chapter 3, writing in Colette's work functions as an image of the expression of selfhood. In this light, the guilt demonstrated by Renée in connection with writing is suggestive. Without a conviction of her right to selfhood, she instead elaborates a highly sensational text to live by, a substitute thrill or excitement. In the end, it is she who is swallowed up by it. In fact, the 'haunted house' she lives in seems to command Renée more than she does it. Already we have seen her described as someone who "drifts" through the house—"Renée wandered" (*PI* 81). 'Colette' remarks on the strangely clandestine feel of the dinner parties she attends there (*PI* 94). Moreover, here in this space that is supposedly hers, Renée is subject to the whims of an arbitrary "master." The dangerous, uncertain air that life under this "master" takes on is described thus:

> This "master" was never referred to by her feminine name. We seemed to be waiting for a catastrophe to project him among us, or for an exorcism to dissipate him. But he only dispatched to Renée invisible messengers, bearing lacquer, jade, enamels, cloth... A collection of ancient Persian gold coins came, glittered, disappeared, leaving its place to cases of butterflies and exotic insects. . . . From one of these marvels to another, Renée came and went, uncertain, already detached, and exhibiting the modest indifference of a museum guard. (*PI* 85-86, translation modified.)
>
> [Ce "maître" de qui personne ne prononçait le nom de femme, nous avions vaguement l'air d'attendre qu'une catastrophe le projetât au milieu de nous, où qu'un exorcisme le dissipât. Mais il ne faisait que dépêcher à Renée des messagers invisibles et chargés, porteurs de laques, de jades, d'émaux, d'étoffes... Une collection de monnaies d'or

> anciennes de la Perse vint, brilla, disparut, laissant la place à des vitrines de papillons et d'insectes exotiques. . . . D'une à l'autre, Renée allait, incertaine, déjà détachée, et témoignait d'une modestie indifférente de gardienne. (3: 601-02)]

Not only does the "master" inspire fear and uncertainty, her gifts have the effect of effacing her lover. Renée has no relation to these things except to take care of them—the things have primacy over her, not the other way around. Love on the part of the other person is for her *as affiliated* with these objects, rather than with her as such. She is displaced by them, to the extent that she ends up nothing more than their guardian.

Most curiously, this "master," whose love displaces and effaces Renée, actually seems in the end a text she has created. At one point, after Renée has confided to 'Colette' that she fears for her life at the hands of this lover, 'Colette' muses that the details and the 'danger' in Renée's situation seem "borrowed from P. J. Toulet's Monsieur du Paur" and as if conceived under the influence of alcohol. "Perhaps, even, the exhausting lover never existed," 'Colette' continues, wondering if this "lover" might owe her "quasi-tangibility to the last effort [. . .] of an imagination which, losing its way, brought forth ghouls instead of nymphs" (*PI* 96, translation modified).

Renée nearly starves herself to be able to embody on stage her idea of Lady Jane Grey (*PI* 88-89). In a similar fashion the text she creates and within which she lives, playing the roles it gives her, dispossesses her of her self, and eventually, of her life.

In the end, the word that summarizes her best is "impoverished," as 'Colette' discovers when her ability to "read" Renée becomes stronger. The opposite of the "rich" who acquire, Renée holds on to nothing. 'Colette' confides:

> When I recall the changes that gradually rendered Renée more understandable, I believe I can link these with certain gestures at first, then with some words that threw a different light on her. Some people become transformed by riches, others acquire a real life only by impoverishment, their very destitution giving them life. (*PI* 86)

> [Si je me reporte aux changements qui peu à peu me rendirent Renée plus intelligible, je crois que quelques gestes, quelques mots, d'abord, me l'éclairèrent d'une lumière différente. Il y des êtres qui se transforment par enrichissement, d'autres n'acquièrent une vie réelle qu'en se dépouillant, et leur misère seule les crée. (3: 602)]

If she nearly starves herself away, physical objects also lend her little presence. Nothing sticks to her: "[s]he was constantly giving things away: the bracelets on her arms opened up, the necklace slipped from her martyr's throat" (*PI* 82). The pagan philosophy that informs her poetry slips from her at death in the same fashion: "Enfeebled, she became humble and was converted. Her paganism was so little rooted in her" (*PI* 96-97). The setting, stage props, and scripts she adopts allow her to play at an identity, but at death desert her, leaving her to seek definition in other, more stable and socially sanctioned discourses such as that of Christianity.

Thus Renée Vivien seeks self-definition, but she does so by creating a ready-made stage set and text through which to do it. Not only does it fail to impress its reader except with its childishness, it seems in the end to have little to do with Renée herself, as it eventually slips from her. The elaboration of identity here is in fact not that; this identity is a mask behind which Renée hides.

And if the script she adopts to provide her with her lifestyle fails to carry conviction, for her or others, her sexuality seems no more revelatory of selfhood in her. 'Colette' speaks of an attitude oriented towards counting up pleasure in her description of " 'Madame How-many-times,' counting on her fingers, mentioning by name things and gestures" (*PI* 93) that she glimpses behind Renée's poses. 'Colette' continues:

> She carried off with her more than one secret, and beneath her purple veil, Renée Vivien, the poet, led away—her throat encircled in moonstones, beryls, aquamarines and other anemic gems—the immodest child, the excited little girl who taught me, with unembarrassed competence: "There are fewer ways of making love than they say, and more than one believes...." (*PI* 97)
>
> [Elle emporta plus d'un secret et sous son voile violet Renée Vivien, le poète, emmena—col ceint de pierres de lune, de béryls, d'aigues-

> marines et autres joyaux anémiques—l'immodeste enfant, la petite fille intempérante qui m'enseignait, avec une compétence désinvolte: "Il y a moins de manières de faire l'amour qu'on ne dit, mais plus qu'on ne croit..." (3: 609)]

What 'Colette' views in a negative light here is not "immodesty," but the fact that Renée does not achieve selfhood through this. Whatley (20) discusses the importance of the financial metaphor for sexuality in this book, as regards Damien the "creditor" (*PI* 51), for example, who cannot forgive women for having taken from him more pleasure than he got from them. In the case of Renée, sexuality is a means of collecting, or a miserly hoarding up, as unrelated to her accession to an independent or adult selfhood as are her alcoholism and anorexia. In fact, beneath her ostentatious veils, covering her phony mystery—an 'exotic' or 'shocking' sexuality, but that actually has more to do with fear and immaturity than with independence or the contestation of received discourses—Renée remains a mystery, and precisely for her sexuality.

> [S]he was . . . drawn down beneath the earth, toward everything that is of no concern to the living. Drawn down by what hand? I would have very much liked to know to what extent the Inexorable aided those forces which pulled towards the depths this ephemeral, this formless creature. (*PI* 97, translation modified.)
>
> [(E)lle fut . . . tirée vers le dessous de la terre, vers tout ce qui n'est pas l'affaire des vivants. Par quelle main tirée? J'aurais bien voulu savoir dans quelle mesure l'Inexorable aida les forces qui halèrent en bas l'éphémère, la fondante créature. (3: 609)]

Thus Renée Vivien is another example of a seeming shaking off of conventional gender and sexuality, but that is little more than a pose or an "alibi" (*PI* 97). The mystery of sexuality and female selfhood remains a mystery with her. The same will prove to be the case with the seemingly revolutionary "Ladies of Llangollen."

Jerry Flieger presents an insightful analysis of the vignette devoted to these "Ladies" in *The Pure and the Impure*. Specifically, she speaks of the "delusion"[15] cultivated by the two aristocratic Welsh lovers who escaped from their homes in romantic fashion in 1778, to spend the rest of their lives together. Living in a rural setting, they enjoyed what the journal of Eleanor Butler, the older of the two, describes as "an infinite series of days 'of the most perfect and sweet retirement' " (129). However, in Flieger's argument, what appears to be an unending idyll of perfect harmony and bliss between the two women, with which no foreign or unlike element was ever allowed to interfere, was in fact a "despotic dream" on the part of Eleanor, and a "monstrous illusion of closed symmetry" (133). This relationship ends up the opposite of Eleanor Butler's idea of it, Flieger's argument runs, because of the denial—at least on the part of Eleanor, who left the written account through which we know their story— of difference. By retiring from the world that is inhabited by both sexes, this couple aspires to live a life into which no conflict, precisely because there will be no difference, will ever appear. "Impure heterogeneity is counterpoised to an Imaginary parade of mirror likenesses," Flieger writes (129). She quotes Colette's novel in continuing her argument: "The pudicity that separates two lovers during the hours of repose, of ablutions, of illness never insinuates itself between two twin bodies that have similar afflictions, are subject to the same cares, the same predictable periods of chastity... A woman marvels at herself, is thrilled by her resemblance to the woman she loves and pities" (*PI* 111, qtd. in Flieger 129-30). However, in Flieger's reading, as 'Colette' analyzes the journal of Eleanor Butler, what emerges is not just the similarity of the two bodies, but the melding of two selves into one. 'Colette' continues in the same vein:

> When could they lay hold of a sense of the future, those two enamored women who, at every moment, demolish and deny it, who envisage neither beginning nor end nor change nor solitude, who breathe the air only à *deux*, and, arm in arm, walk only in perfect step with each other? (*PI* 110)
>
> [Où prendraient-elles le sens de l'avenir, ces deux qui, à tout instant, le défont et le nient, qui n'envisagent ni commencement ni fin, ni changement ni solitude, ne respirent l'air qu'à deux, ne vont, le bras sur le bras, que d'un pas bien accordé?... (3: 616)]

The outside world simply fades away, and even the world of Llangollen, as Flieger notes, takes on an unreal quality. 'Colette' describes the "turf" here as "buoyant as a cloud and as green as the green in our dreams" (*PI* 119). "Above the cottage and its hill, did there even exist a season of fine weather or a season of bad weather?" she wonders, and concludes, "[t]here was only Llangollen weather" (*PI* 123).

Yet paradoxically, as Flieger argues, this very flight from the outside world with its difference, particularly in socially constructed gender, and the denial as well of difference between the two women, leads to nothing so much as a reproduction of difference, and precisely the restitution of traditional, hierarchized gender roles. Flieger quotes the following passage, which I reproduce:

> See here, stout-hearted Eleanor, you who were responsible for all the daily decisions, you who were so profoundly submerged in your Well-Beloved, were you unaware that two women cannot achieve a perfect union? You were the prudent warden—the masculine element. It was you who measured the distance at which the real world must be kept, who gave to some parts of a few miles of rolling countryside a pastoral aspect. Your urbanity, which opened wide the cottage door to the well-born passerby, knew still better how to shut it. (*PI* 126)
>
> [Robuste lady Eleanor, responsable de toutes les décisions quotidiennes, si sincèrement abîmée dans votre Bien-Aimée, ignoriez-vous que deux femmes ne peuvent réaliser un couple entièrement femelle? Vous étiez le prudent geôlier—le mâle. C'est vous qui mesuriez la distance nécessaire entre vous et le monde réel, qui disposiez, çà et là, sur quelques milles de paysage accidenté, une figuration bucolique. Votre urbanité, qui ouvrait grande à des passants bien nés la porte du cottage, savait encore mieux la refermer. (3: 625)]

While this denial of difference leads to a reproduction of that same difference, this state hardens into fixedness, and makes the characters blind. At this point we are again reminded of Renée Vivien for several reasons. First, the two women, at their flight, take their cues from the romanesque. "Infatuated with romance, they had leaped from a window rather than leave by way of the open door" (*PI* 117) 'Colette' writes.

"There were complications, legal processes, tragedies, childish tears... but from all this a unique sentiment sprang, straight and firm and flowering like the iris nestling against its green stem" (*PI* 117). The adventure that begins commanded by the romanesque is never questioned. The two place complete trust in this; in this way they end up "loyal," 'Colette' writes, to a "delusion" (*PI* 127). Like Renée, who, compared to a blind child, "play[s] without the help of light" (*PI* 82), these women also fail to see.

In like manner, and again as in the case of Renée, the radical sexuality that seems to be their story is again not really what that story reveals. What seems to be a radical subversion of received discourses of sexuality and of gender and power relations, which the "ordinary reader" (*PI* 126) might be tempted to read as liberating, is instead a reproduction of those power relations. Most surprisingly, sexual passion, the supposed *raison d'être* of the relationship and living arrangement, is what is in the end least present here.

> I want to speak with dignity, that is, with warmth, of what I call the noble season of feminine passion. I write "noble season" and not "season of noble love," for even if it has lost its purity I can only compare it to the burningly passionate and chaste season of betrothals.
>
> The noble season of love, condemned by most people, shows its nobility by *disdaining unambiguous sensual pleasure*. . . . (*PI* 110)
>
> [(J)e voudrais parler dignement, c'est-à-dire avec feu, de ce que je nomme la saison noble d'une passion féminine. J'écris saison noble, et non saison de noble amour; saison telle que je ne puis la comparer, même si elle a cessé d'être pure, qu'à celles des fiançailles enflammées et chastes.
>
> La saison noble des amours que le commun condamne place sa noblesse dans *son dédain de la volupté précise*. . . . (3: 615-16, my emphasis)]

And thus, in this vignette as well as in the others already studied, what seems radical is actually conservative. To Charlotte's maternity and self-abnegation, and Renée's immaturity and flight, is added the enforced bliss of these two women frozen in time and living out the chimera of a fairy tale.

Thus we have seen three examples of what seem to be cases of unaccepted female sexuality, yet all of them fail in their promise to the reader of subversion of received discourses and of liberation. Let us now turn to a strand that can be traced throughout this text that does, in contrast, lead the reader to an unsettling of dominant discourse, and to a change from these patterns of failure and flight.

It is the Ladies of Llangollen who provide the clearest clue to this new strand, for their story illustrates most clearly what, in all the vignettes studied up till now, leads to failure. For it is the denial of difference that Flieger notes in the relationship between the two Ladies of Llangollen that is key. The denial of the existence of an outside world with its two genders, which is implicit in their lifestyle of "retirement," and the denial of the difference between the two women lead most neatly to a reproduction of those very differences between them. Not only are they different, in spite of the "delusion" of complete unity, but that difference manifests itself as a difference in power. 'Colette' proposes in her text a more profound unsettling of gender than an overly facile denial of its here-and-now existence. It is this observation that will lead us to 'Colette' unraveling a "real mystery," that of the road traveled by those who neither deny difference, nor, in consequence, repeat the set patterns of power associated with the particular difference of sex and gender.

At this point 'Colette' addresses the question of androgyny. This question is central to the text, highlighted by vignettes involving the character 'Colette' grappling with the issue herself towards the beginning of the book.

This grappling is set off by a remark to 'Colette' by Damien, in the second section of the book. He refuses the idea of traveling with 'Colette,' giving as his reason that "[he] only like[s] to travel with women" (*PI* 58).[16] This exclusion of her from her gender leads 'Colette' to meditate on gender and androgyny explicitly in the following section of the novel. Yet if we look more closely, androgyny emerges as even more clearly highlighted. It is the culmination, the logical end point, as a question, of the first two sections of the book, and indeed the mystery that the text as a whole sets itself to investigate, and which it explores in all the vignettes that follow.

We recall how in the vignette entitled "The Mirror" from *Tendrils of the Vine* 'Colette' speaks of the "precious child" that she once was, convinced of feeling in herself the "extraordinary soul of an intelligent man, of a woman in love" (1: 1032, my translation). This dual nature is in fact reflected in the two opening sections of *The Pure and the Impure*. As other critics have already persuasively argued, the "Charlotte" of the first section and the narrator 'Colette' are two forms of one and the same character.[17] The "Charlotte" of the first section thus suggests that aspect of herself that 'Colette' qualifies as a "woman in love." In the second section of the novel, the character 'Colette,' here no longer disguised or veiled by the name "Charlotte," is taken for a man by Damien, and is thus quite obviously incarnating the "intelligent man" that forms, ideally, the other part of herself. Yet quite obviously these two initial vignettes set up a problem, rather than point the way to a solution. As the veiling of one aspect of the self by a different name suggests, this is not the glorious childhood androgyny lamented by the adult narrator of "The Mirror." Rather, this is a split experienced by the self, which can express itself, in schizophrenic fashion, only through the creation of more than one name and identity. It is in later vignettes that a resolution of the problem of an androgynous self is sketched out.

This grappling with the question of androgyny in which 'Colette' engages is introduced by the following scene. An acquaintance, Damien, refuses her invitation to travel together, giving as his reason that "[he] only like[s] to travel with women . . ." (*PI* 58). 'Colette' confides that his words hurt her, and that secretly she would have liked to be a woman. Then, she goes on to clarify the real nature of her androgynous self. In speaking of androgyny, she writes:

> I am not alluding to a former self, a public and legendary figure that I had ostentatiously cultivated and arranged as to costume and external details. I am alluding to a genuine mental hermaphroditism which burdens certain highly complex human beings. And if Damien's pronouncement vexed me, it was because I happened to be making a particular effort at the time to rid myself of this ambiguity, along with all the flaws and privileges, and to offer them up, still warm, at the feet of a certain man to whom I offered a healthy and quite female body and its perhaps fallacious vocation of servant. But as for the man, he was not taken in; he had detected the masculine streak in my character by some trait of mine I could not identify, and, though tempted, had fled.

Later he returned, full of grudges and mistrust. And I did not yet think to put to use the warning Damien had given me.

Of what avail is it to warn the blind? The blind trust only their own well-known infallibility and are determined to assume the full responsibility of hurting themselves. Thus I hurt myself in my own stupid and forthright way. *(PI 60)*

[Je ne fais pas allusion à un ancien aspect de moi-même, aspect public, dont j'ordonnais, avec ostentation, la légende, les détails extérieurs, le costume. Je vise le véridique hermaphrodisme mental, qui charge certains êtres fortement organisés. Si la parole de Damien me fâcha, c'est que j'espérais alors dépouiller cette ambiguïté, ses tares et ses prérogatives, et les jeter chaudes aux pieds d'un homme, à qui j'offrais un brave corps bien femelle et sa vocation, peut-être fallacieuse, de servante. Mais l'homme, lui, ne s'y trompait pas. Il me savait virile par quelque point que j'étais incapable de situer, et fuyait, bien qu'il fût tenté. Puis il revenait, plein de griefs et de méfiance. Et je n'eus pas, alors, l'idée d'utiliser l'avertissement que Damien m'avait donné.

Que sert d'avertir l'aveugle? Il ne se fie qu'à son infaillibilité bien connue d'aveugle et tient à se meurtrir en toute responsabilité. Je me meurtrissais donc d'une manière obtuse et loyale... (3: 586-87)]

This incident with Damien and the passage that follows tell us a lot already about what is going on. First of all, an androgynous nature as it is first pointed out to her by Damien is actually not androgynous. It is an either/or thing, which excludes her from her gender. A refusal of the truncated, confined "femininely" gendered self allows her only one other possibility—exclusion from her gender, and the possibility of inhabiting only a non-gendered limbo. We note that at this juncture the character 'Colette' longs to take on that conventional gender (the "perhaps fallacious vocation of servant") in order to escape that limbo.

And, since she longs to become a woman, she clearly does not at this point consider herself to be one, at least a conventionally scripted form of woman. However, the reason for her not being a woman, she continues, does not lie in costume, in dressing like a man. The reason she accepts for not being a woman is her androgynous nature, which is "mental," and not dependent on clothes or manner. What leads her to want to reject that nature is that that nature is the reason for her rejection by Damien, who was tempted, but fled. She finished by confiding that she was unable, at the time of this interchange with Damien, to make positive use of his remark and the revelation it could have given her. Thus we assume that she will do that later. She confides that she was at that time "blind."

Clearly, the narrator at the time of narrating is no longer blind, and has been able to put the "warning" to use. She has ceased to be blind and now sees. What we also see through her eyes is the androgynous nature not only of herself, but also of others. It is significant that a description revealing just this nature, in herself and in her friend Marguerite Moreno, is what we find immediately following the "warning" from Damien. While the youthful character 'Colette' discusses this question that she does not yet understand with Marguerite Moreno, the older narrator describes. And here, in this description on the part of the mature narrator, what we see is not the either/or type of nature that was all Damien (himself also blind, we assume) could see. Rather it is the existence within one gendered being of both "masculine" and "feminine."

This becomes clear after the discussion between 'Colette' and Marguerite Moreno is completed, and Marguerite Moreno has fallen asleep. First we read that it is in sleep that one recuperates one's strength:

> Then she yawned and succumbed to sleep, leaning her head against the high-backed armchair. Her strong, sexless features softened a little as she sank into the sleep of all trained workers, who know how to recoup their strength by taking a ten-minute nap in the bus or in the Métro.... (*PI* 63)
>
> [Puis elle bâilla et céda au sommeil. Son regard puissant et sans sexe s'amollit à peine au moment où elle appuya la tête sur le dossier du fauteuil, en sombrant dans le prompt sommeil des travailleurs entraînés, qui savent récupérer leurs forces et totalisent dix minutes d'assoupissement en autobus et en métro.... (3: 588)]

Sleep thus allows one to recover one's strength. This is because it is a means of return to one's androgynous nature, as we see as the passage continues:

> Asleep, she rather resembled Dante, or a refined hidalgo, or Leonardo da Vinci's Saint John the Baptist. Now that our woman's wealth of hair is shorn, when our breasts and hands and stomach are hidden, what remains of our feminine exteriors? Sleep brings an incalculable number of women to assume the form they would no doubt have chosen if their waking state did not keep them in ignorance of themselves. The same applies to men... Oh, the charm of a sleeping man, how vividly I recall it! From forehead to mouth he was, behind his closed eyelids, all smiles, with the arch nonchalance of a sultana behind a barred window. And I who would willingly have been completely woman, completely and stupidly female, with what male wistfulness did I gaze at that man who had such a delightful laugh and who could respond to a beautiful poem or landscape... (*PI* 63)

> [Elle ressemblait, en dormant, un peu au Dante, un peu à un hidalgo fin, un peu au saint Jean-Baptiste vu par Léonard de Vinci. Coupé le foin précieux de la chevelure, la main, le ventre, que reste-t-il de nos dehors femelles? Le sommeil remporte un nombre incalculable de femmes vers la forme qu'elles auraient sans doute choisie, si l'état de veille ne les entretenait pas dans l'ignorance d'elles-mêmes. Pareillement pour l'homme... O grâces d'un homme endormi, je vous revois encore! Du front à la bouche, il n'était derrière ses paupières fermées que sourire, nonchalance et malice de sultane au moucharabieh... Et moi qui aurais "bien voulu," sotte, être tout entière une femme, je le contemplais avec un mâle regret, celui qui avait un si joli rire et s'émouvait d'un beau vers, d'un paysage... (3: 588-89)]

Gender is entirely confused here, and sexual desire, as well, no longer depends for its direction upon the falsely constricting categories of the waking state. Marguerite is characterized here as male, and yet it would seem that 'Colette' who describes herself here as desiring her, is male as well. While sleep renders Marguerite masculine, men are feminized by this state. Yet ultimately, what the sleeping state reveals, is the human being's androgynous nature, as we see in the passage that sums up this scene:

But Marguerite Moreno was sleeping, her conquistador nose turned toward adventure. Her deep sleep gave to her mouth, small and firm in her waking state, a plaintive look of submission.

Cautiously I reached for a light coverlet and laid it over *Chimène and Le Cid, closely united in the sleep of a single body*. Then I resumed my post at the side of a worktable, where my *woman's eyes* followed, on the pale blue bonded paper, the hard and stubby *hand of a gardener* ["*jardinier*" in the original French—thus the masculine form] writing. (*PI* 64, emphasis added)

[Mais Marguerite Moreno dormait, son nez de conquistador tourné vers l'aventure. Son repos profound rendait à sa bouche, petite et ferme, l'expression plaintive, l'acquiescement que lui refuse toujours une veille en armes.

Avec précaution, j'atteignis une couverture légère, et je couvris *Chimène et le Cid, étroitement unis dans le sommeil d'un seul corps*. Puis j'allai reprendre mon poste au bord d'une table-bureau, d'où mes *yeux de femme* suivirent, sur le velin turquoise, une courte et dure *main de jardinier*, qui écrivait. (3: 589, emphasis added)]

With the insight of the mature narrator, looking back on her earlier self, we can see this reality of androgyny. But the 'Colette' of the vignettes that follow has not yet reached this point. We continue to follow her in her search for the truth. This quest takes her through several false paths, but is also illuminated at various points by seers and givers of wisdom.

The first seer to guide her towards truth is the painter Boldini. 'Colette' tells of her encounter with him directly after recounting the conversation between herself and Marguerite Moreno. Again, this encounter is introduced by 'Colette' herself musing in the abstract on the subject that the encounter will illuminate. She reflects that "[a] woman needs a fine and rare sincerity and a rather noble modesty to determine what it is in her that trips up and that allows some of her official sex to seep into her clandestine one" (*PI* 64-65, translation modified). Later she continues:

I was not long deluded by those photographs that show me wearing a stiff mannish collar, necktie, short jacket over a straight skirt, a lighted cigarette between two fingers. Certainly I turned on them a less penetrating look than did that arrant old demon of painting, Boldini. (*PI* 65)

[Elles ne m'abusèrent pas longtemps, ces images photographiques où je porte col droit, régate, un petit veston sur une jupe plate, une cigarette fumante entre deux doigts. Je pose sur elles un regard moins perçant, à coup sûr, que ne fut celui de l'insigne vieux démon de la peinture, Boldini. (3: 589-90)]

Here we notice several interesting things. 'Colette' admits openly that moving into a "clandestine sex" (through cross-dressing) does not mean necessarily eliminating from oneself the "official sex." Thus dressing as a man does not eliminate femininity.

In addition, and most importantly for the scene that follows, this passage talks about the way in which she eventually loses her illusions that one can be liberated from one's self or gender by changing one's costume. She loses these illusions in part by looking at old photographs of herself, but her ability to see is less perceptive than that of Boldini.

It is an insight gained through a visit to his painting studio that eventually allows her to gain understanding on this question. Here she will be given a message from someone with special powers to see. She herself will only later become aware of Boldini's powers, but writes that "I remember that my dog Toby trembled against my legs; he already knew more than I did, certainly, about the misshapen divinity who was leaping about there in front of us" (*PI* 66).

Boldini provides a clue on the subject of dress. His first remarks addressed to her are on the subject of her relationships to masculinity and to femininity through costume. He asks her if she, on the one hand, wears a "dinner jacket" in the evening, and later, if she dances on stage "quite naked." While she struggles to set him right on the exact details of her doings, he returns to his painting, calling her "proper young lady" (*PI* 65-66). His dismissal of her seeming radicalness comes after his questions on her relationship to *both* genders through costume. It is not just the elaborate refusal of feminine modesty that he sees through as being unconvincing (she remains in spite of her seemingly daring nudity or seminudity a "proper young lady"). It is also the seeming radicalness of her easily acquired masculinity that fails to impress him. What 'Colette' does learn, through her encounter with him, is that liberation from constricting gender roles comes not through an overly simplistic attempt to throw it off—which, as we have seen, often leads paradoxically to nothing so easily as a reproduction of traditional gender and power relations. Rather, liberation from constricting gender comes from assuming one's gender, but enlarging it, so that it may contain infinite possibilities. This is the message of the visit to Boldini.

For what Boldini is painting, when she arrives, is the white of a woman's dress. "[T]he gown of a big unfinished portrait of a woman, a satin gown of blinding white—peppermint-lozenge white—caught and flashed back all the light in the room," (*PI* 65) 'Colette' writes of the situation upon her entrance into the studio. And later:

> He paid no more attention to me. An empty gown, lackluster, not quite white, was posing for him on an armchair. It was from that dull gown that he was creating on the canvas, stroke by stroke, the whites of cream, of snow, of glazed paper, of new metal, the white of the unfathomable, and the white of bonbons, a tour de force of whites... (*PI* 66)
>
> [Il ne s'occupa plus de moi. Une robe vide, éteinte, à peu près blanche, posait pour lui sur un fauteuil. C'est de ce blanc terni, que naîssaient sur la toile, touche à touche, les blancs de crème, de neige, de papier glacé, de métal neuf, les blancs d'abîme et de bonbon, les blancs de tour de force... (3: 590)]

While a traditional feminine costume, under the touch of the seer Boldini, is seen to be capable of containing anything, from "bonbons" to "new metal" to "the unfathomable," the 'Colette' of the vignette does not yet understand. The narrator states that:

> The "proper young lady," offended, took dignified leave, adjusted the knot of a mannish necktie that had been imported from London, and went away, looking as much as possible like a bad boy, to rejoin a strange company of women who led a marginal and timorous life, sustained by an out-of-date form of snobbishness. (*PI* 66-67)
>
> [La "bonne petite bourgeoise", offensée, sortit dignement, en rectifiant le nœud d'une régate qui venait de Londres, et s'en alla, de son air

le plus mauvais garçon, retrouver une compagnie étrange, qui ne vivait plus que d'un reste de vie craintive et de son snobisme épuisé. (3: 590)]

The older narrator continues to relate: "How timid I was, at that period when I was trying to look like a boy, and how feminine I was beneath my disguise of cropped hair" (*PI* 67). She will need the help of other seers before she acquires the wisdom to abandon her false paths.

The next guide makes Boldini's point more explicitly. 'Colette' recounts a conversation she had with Amalia X, a "former companion . . . on theatrical tours" (*PI* 99). "[T]he worthy Amalia" speaks to 'Colette' while "shuffling [a] pack of tarot cards on a small galvanized table in a dingy café at Tarbes or Valenciennes" (*PI* 101). Conversing as she reads her cards, she first brings up the false path of switching gender in her recollections of "Lucienne de __" whom she characterizes as having been "a pseudo-man" (*PI* 102). Lucienne thus, like Renée and the Ladies of Llangollen, lived out her existence through an adopted script and role: "Strange, that a woman like this who rivaled and defrauded men should have as her single ambition to look and act the part of a dashing young man about town" (*PI* 100-01) 'Colette' writes.

This attempt at switching gender carries unambiguously negative connotations. 'Colette' herself recalls Lucienne as someone who played a dilettante's game, "the trifling of someone who enjoyed inflicting mental cruelties" (*PI* 100). This is contrasted with Amalia's own life: " 'I had everything,' she asserted, 'beauty, happiness, misery, men, and women... You can call it a life!' " (*PI* 101). She then points the way to the crucial difference between her behavior and that of Lucienne's, which to many might not seem at first glance to be so different. Amalia's life, while it included many of the same diverse experiences as that of Lucienne, never took on the same characteristics of dilettantism and cruelty, for Amalia knew that "[w]e never have to stop being a woman" (*PI* 102). She elaborates on this:

"You see, when a woman remains a woman, she is a complete human being. She lacks nothing, even insofar as her *amie* is concerned. But if she ever gets it into her head to try to be a man, then she's grotesque. . . . La Lucienne, from the time she adopted men's clothes, well!... Do you imagine her life wasn't poisoned from then on?" (*PI* 102-03)

> ["Tu comprends, une femme qui reste une femme, c'est un être complet. Il ne lui manque rien, même auprès de son 'amie.' Mais si elle se met en tête de vouloir être un homme, elle est grotesque. . . . La Lucienne de ***, à partir du jour où elle a adopté le costume d'homme, est-ce que tu crois que sa vie n'a pas été empoisonnée?" (3: 611-12)]

Thus changing costume does not free one from the constraints of gender's conventional scripts. Amalia X joins Boldini in pointing this out as a false solution. Rather, both enlighten 'Colette' as to the nature of the real solution—subverting the dimensions of gender and enlarging its possibilities from within.

'Colette' leaves Amalia looking at her "Knave of Swords." She is further along in her search, but not yet satisfied. Amalia, she realizes, will never be able to explain anything except by saying "[m]e, I went through it" (*PI* 108). 'Colette' seeks a knowledge beyond the empirical. It is in the enigmatic last section of the book that 'Colette' initiates us into the secrets of what she has learned. This last section does not resemble the earlier ones, in which 'Colette' converses with, reads about, or remembers, a person or persons at length, and through which those persons become known to us as well-rounded individuals. This last section has the characteristics of a dream, in which seemingly unrelated fragments succeed each other, in a manner that at first glance reveals no obvious meaning.

'Colette' thus leads us into the world of the sleeping. It is the same world in which, as we saw in the earlier scene centering around 'Colette' and Marguerite Moreno, people leave the falseness of the waking life and recover their androgynous nature.

At the beginning of this final section, 'Colette' first talks about the monopoly of youth on success at pretending—what she calls "dissimulation" (*PI* 155). She likes to puncture their artifice, she takes pleasure in doing so: "[i]nsight, the voluptuous gift of wounding!" (3: 643, my translation). We note that 'Colette' is given an androgynous nature here. This is certainly a masculine side to her that is portrayed, and, moreover, a distinctly sadistic one.

From there, she goes on to a discussion of who is more needy of whom. Those she dominates, are they perhaps more "givers of life" after all than "mendicants"? (*PI* 157). All these relationships of domination and dependence carry a danger, expressed in the following manner: "To receive from someone happiness—there's no avoiding that word that I do not comprehend—is it not to choose the sauce in which we want to be served up?" (*PI* 157).

Another model of interaction is proposed—that which exists between herself and a four-year-old child she calls "the All-Powerful," or "my rival, the All-Powerful." "Whether one has to do with an animal or a child, to convince is to conquer and to subdue," she writes. She continues:

> I know, just two hundred steps from this table, a little four-year-old girl who fears neither spanking nor thunder and lightning nor wasps, assured of her power and of her seduction, and more or less uncoercible. (*PI* 158, translation modified)
>
> [Je connais à deux cents pas de cette table une petite fille de quatre ans admirable, qui ne craint ni la fessée, ni le feu du ciel, ni les guêpes, assurée dans sa puissance et dans sa séduction, et à peu près incoercible. (3: 643)]

The All-Powerful and 'Colette' have similar powers over each other, for each one can make the other sleep. 'Colette' recounts that the child's nurse comes at times to seek her aid in this matter:

> Sometimes, toward the end of the day, when the father is yawning with nervous exhaustion, when the violet shadows that ring the large eyes of her young mother make them seem larger, the child's nurse, white-faced, comes to fetch me: "*She* is terrible. *She* did not want to take her nap this afternoon. We are worn out, but *she* is fresh as a daisy..." (*PI* 158)
>
> [Parfois, vers la fin du jour, quand son père épuisé baille d'énervement, quand un cerne lilas élargit les grands yeux de sa jeune mère, sa nurse palie vient me chercher: "*Elle* est terrible... *Elle* n'a pas voulu dormir cet après-midi... Nous sommes recrus, et *Elle* est fraîche comme un piment..." (3: 643-44)]

For the first time, here, with this incoercible child, reading another, or trying to read another—what 'Colette' has been doing throughout the novel—is felt to be negative. It is what will make the child sleep, but

'Colette' does not want to thus domesticate her. She says, in speaking of her role in helping the parents:

> My role is to act indifferent and to read beneath the changing features of the All-Powerful her real thoughts. Shameful métier, in which I succeed all too well. Why is it that, without means other than my eyes and words, I leave the All-Powerful mollified and overcome with sleep? (*PI* 159)
>
> [Mon rôle est d'être insensible, et de lire, sous le front changeant de la Puissance, ses pensers véritables. Honteux métier, où je réussis trop bien. Pourquoi, sans autres moyens que le regard, les paroles, laissé-je la Puissance amollie, livrée aux assauts du sommeil? (3: 644)]

However, she recounts that in this case, power is mutual.

> But my rival, the All-Powerful, will have her turn, when I become enfeebled. Hovering above me like a dragonfly, she will murmur, "There, there... Rest, go to sleep," and to my astonishment I shall sleep. (*PI* 160)
>
> [Mais la Puissance rivale aura son tour. Penchée comme une libellule au-dessus de ma faiblesse neuve, elle murmurera : "Là... Reposez-vous... Dormez," et je m'étonnerai de dormir. (3: 644)]

After this exposition of her relationship with this rival power, 'Colette' goes on to discuss in a general manner the question of relationships with people who are her "equals" (*PI* 160). She is glad of them, she writes, for otherwise she would be tired of relationships in which she would be two things—giver and taker. These words sum up the manner in which many of the characters discussed earlier—from Charlotte the "donatrice"[18] to Damien the creditor to Renée the miser—do relate to others.

This element of economic exchange is absent in the relationships between herself and those she describes as her equals. These people also differ from those described earlier in that they "secrete" an identity. Unlike the "monsters," who remain mysteries, who are unreadable, the androgynous equals "secrete from one day to the next their own ethics, which makes them even more understandable to me and colors them variously" (*PI* 161).

This question of readability becomes clearer as she discusses in particular her friend who is simply referred to as "D." What counts for her in listening to D., she writes, is his "reverence for [her] personal conception of D." (3: 646, my translation). Thus she appreciates what seems to be a particularly subtle form of courtesy, his reverence for the text she is reading in him—"[a] figure, an ideogram" (3: 646, my translation). However, she then speaks of how such a text, such a figure, such an ideogram, "is comprised of heavy and light strokes," and that "one must often press down hard when tracing a pattern, must use in a decorative way the dark stain in the background" (*PI* 163). In this way he, as he presents himself to her, is a text. However, at the same time, such texts are constantly and necessarily modified, to the ends of *aesthetics* rather than truth—"in a decorative way." Moreover, what is suggested here is that modification is occurring on the part of 'Colette,' as interpreter of D., as well as on D.'s part. Thus one creates a text, which is one's identity, but this is an ongoing aesthetic project, and the text created is not a stable artifact, but part of an ongoing process and also, in part, the creation of others. 'Colette' speaks even more explicitly a bit further on of the role of this text in personality.

> Instinct and unbridled Herculean strength do not alone impel my friend D. to settle a public row by knocking two crazed heads together.[19] Not in one day or spontaneously is a thoughtful "Polynesian" like D. fashioned, or a "child of nature" such as I. (*PI* 163)
>
> [L'instinct, une force herculéenne débridée, ne poussent pas seuls mon ami D *** à mettre la paix dans une bagarre publique, en blettissant l'une contre l'autre têtes folles. Ce n'est pas en un jour, ni de primesaut, que se façonnent un 'Polynésien' réfléchi comme D *** , ni une 'enfant de la nature' telle que moi. (3: 646)]

The text quoted by 'Colette' is very suggestive—identity is a literary creation. The difference between that of D. or 'Colette,' and the texts through which Renée and the Ladies of Llangollen for example sought their identity, is in the 'ready-made' nature of the texts that the latter characters leaned on. Here, 'Colette' suggests that she and her "equals" live according to a text, but that they create it, modify it, and recognize its constructed—aesthetic, "decorative"— nature. Moreover, like Bakhtin's heteroglossia and Kristeva's intertextual language, this text is the site of a convergence of meanings. This is Kristeva's "literary word" as "an intersection of textual surfaces . . . a dialog among several writings: that of the author, the addressee (or the character), and the contemporary or earlier cultural context."[20] The text that D. presents to 'Colette,' which 'Colette' reads and then presents to us, is exactly such "an intersection of textual surfaces"—a place of negotiation of meaning between D., 'Colette,' we readers, and the cultural context. What makes this particular example of negotiation of meaning not only healthy, but efficacious and satisfying, is the fact that, as was the case with the reading mother as narratee, all parties involved assume the power inherent in their roles.

Thus identity, 'Colette' posits, is a text: decorative, but at the same time necessary, for it is what allows her to read others and therefore to know them. Here we note that if 'Colette' hesitated to "read" the All-Powerful it is perhaps because the All-Powerful, as a child, had not consciously created her "text" in the way an adult would, and did not therefore have the defenses of an adult, or at any rate the degree of conscious participation in deciding what would be read, that an adult would have. The All-Powerful in this way recalls the Little One of *My Mother's House*, in other words, 'Colette' herself as a child. The Little One, who had not yet found her own language, found herself in a similar way vulnerable to becoming the instrument of adult speech rather than its conscious manipulator. With the adult characters in Colette, however, readability is desirable. 'Colette' then goes on to another question, that of the senses. This will provide the clue to the nature of the difference between "the androgynous being"—a readable text, and the "monsters" with their ultimate unreadability. What is essential is not "identity." Rather, it is essential, but what makes it possible, is passion—following the senses rather than holding them in check. She continues, still in speaking of herself and D.:

> He and I and others like us come from the distant past and are inclined to cherish the arbitrary,[21] to prefer passion to goodness, to prefer combat to discussion. (*PI* 163-64)

[Nous venons de loin, lui, moi, d'autres, entraînés à chérir l'arbitraire, à pencher vers la passion plutôt que la bonté, préférer le combat à la discussion. (3: 646)]

It is thus the pursuit of their desire that is crucial. It is in this way that they are able to create the texts that allow them to live, rather than those that stifle them.

At the same time, even as she speaks about these similarities with her friends, she warns of their danger. "But scarcely have I praised these parallels and affinities when I cease to enjoy myself" (*PI* 164). Too much similitude is stifling, as was the case with the Ladies of Llangollen. "Remove from me everything that is too sweet! Arrange for me, in the last third of my life, a clear space where I can put my favorite crudity, love" (*PI* 164), she concludes.

Here, the focus of the dream-like series of images shifts, and from the figure of a little girl (the All-Powerful), we move, for an introduction to the discussion of the senses, to that of an old woman. If one cannot become bored with jealousy, one cannot become old either, 'Colette' writes, and she speaks of this being the case for one of her grandmothers—"the mean one" (*PI* 164), who at sixty still loved and still knew jealousy. For jealousy keeps the senses sharp. The jealous person is a detective (*PI* 165), whose senses are sharpened by the need to know.

Thus the discussion of jealousy returns us to the question of the senses, which starting with Charlotte had been displaced ("held in check") and—the "phony mystery"—greatly advertised but very little present. The discussion of jealousy also brings us to the question of equality. This emerges in the story of 'Colette' and Madame X, her rival in love for a man.

Inequality in their level of wishing each other ill was the cause of a series of misadventures for 'Colette.' She recounts that she was imprudent enough to give herself over entirely to her work as a writer, and to abandon her other work of antagonism. She lists the results of "such inequality."

> I began by falling into a ditch in the Place du Trocadéro, then I caught bronchitis. Then, in the Métro, on my way to the publisher, I lost the last part of a manuscript of which I had not kept a duplicate. A taxi-

driver short-changed me, leaving me on a rainy night without a sou. Then a mysterious epidemic bore off three of my angora kittens... (*PI* 169-70)

[Je commençai par tomber, place du Trocadéro, au fond d'une tranchée, puis je pris une bronchite. Puis je perdis dans le métropolitain, en le portant chez l'éditeur, la dernière partie d'un manuscrit duquel je n'avais pas gardé le double. Un chauffeur de taxi me vola le billet de cent francs que je lui demandais de changer et me laissa la nuit, sous la pluie, sans un sou. Une épidémie mystérieuse m'enleva trois chatons angora... (3: 650)]

It is necessary for her to come back to equality with Madame X. This permits, paradoxically, a positive outcome to their relationship, as 'Colette' relates in continuing.

And we lived on mutually bad terms until the bond between us was worn out and the space ceased to be a pathway of wicked beams of thought, a harp of resonant waves, a starry ether hung with signs and portents. I was not the only one to regret it, for we had quarreled without feeling any fundamental antipathy. Time recompenses honorable adversaries. Mine, as soon as she stopped being an adversary, had some delightful anecdotes to tell which could amuse only ourselves.

"One day when I was going to Rambouillet to murder you..." (*PI* 170)

[Et nous vécûmes en bonne inintelligence, jusqu'à ce que d'elle à moi le lien fût usé, et que l'espace cessât d'être un chemin de mauvais rayons, une harpe d'ondes résonnantes, un éther étoilé de signes suspendus... Je ne fus pas seule à le regretter, car nous nous combattions sans foncière antipathie. Le temps récompense les adversaires honorables. La mienne, dès qu'elle cessa de l'être, me conta d'une façon charmante les anecdotes qui n'amusaient que nous deux: "Un jour que j'allais à Rambouillet pour vous tuer..." (3: 650-51)]

Thus this ill-wishing, to the point of intentions of homicide, is very clearly given positive connotations here. The narrator makes an explicit statement in favor of her behavior here and that of her rival, and in so doing demonstrates its importance to the novel. For it is what sets 'Colette' and Madame X apart from Charlotte, whose example had opened it. 'Colette' writes:

> I committed only one real fault, but I repeated it and was duly punished. Which was only just. An old saying warns never to give either a boat or a bird. I would add: or a man. (*PI* 172)
>
> [Je ne commis qu'une faute véritable, je la répétai, et j'en fus punie. C'était justice. Il ne faut, dit-on, donner, ni un bateau, ni un oiseau. Je me permettrai d'ajouter: ni un homme. (3: 652)]

Self-abnegation—that which characterized Charlotte—is here construed as the single error, the error par excellence. And in fact, it is in refusing to give up the man they desire, it is in this incoercible steadfastness that had characterized "the All-Powerful rival," that two women in the end may come together, "honorable adversaries," detach themselves from their common male love object, and find themselves "face to face, in order not to say mouth to mouth" (3: 653, my translation).[22]

With this observation, reached on the last pages of the novel, we arrive at a conclusion as to the nature of the "androgynous being" who is being investigated by 'Colette.' The sexual love between women here does not depend, first of all, on an attempt at throwing off their gender on the part of the two women. It is arrived at instead by remaining within that gender, but enlarging its possibilities, and this through *the pursuit of their desire*. The steadfast pursuit of her desire leads woman first to heterosexual love, then to a sexual love for woman, as Colette implies in her closing lines. The relationship of the Ladies of Llangollen is a mirror image of the world the Ladies sought to leave behind, a mirror image of the constraints of conventional gender. They live within the same sorts of rigid limits and definitions as in the world they have fled. In contrast, in this last scene of the novel, woman goes beyond the world of fixed definitions and roles, and the power imbalance this inevitably creates. In this final scenario, woman's love object cannot be identified in a definitive manner. Heterosexual love leads her to love for another woman, yet in circular fashion; that love would not exist without the love for man that brought it about. Rather than reacting against the constraints of gender in a way that in fact further imprisons her within them, woman, at the end, through the pursuit of her desire, achieves within the realm of sexuality a possibility of being that refuses a final definition.[23]

Conclusion

This discussion has examined selfhood in language, and has taken as its starting point certain notions articulated by Kristeva and Bakhtin, namely, that within that language in which the subject necessarily comes into being and exists, one is always in struggle. Always made up of other language, language itself is in conflict, or rather *is* conflict. The subject within it must find her or his subjectivity in relation to, and in conflict with, the many voices, and the many discourses, that make up the neverendingly changing intertextual network that is language.

From this theoretical starting point, I have traced, in Colette's work, and particularly in her semiautobiographical works, the development of a gendered selfhood within language. I have paid particular attention to the development of an assumption of subjectivity within language, a subjectivity that is achieved through remaining in relation to and in resistance to discourse, within the multiple and conflictual nature of language. More specifically yet, I have concentrated on that subjectivity as gendered, through an examination of the intersection of the subject as female, with the language of society as patriarchal.

Learning to read as a child serves as a model for the activity that will continue to be key throughout the later stages of life, in both reading and writing—the contestation of discourses, and the powers that they represent and create. Colette's works themselves are analyzed as contestations of traditional and patriarchal discourses of female selfhood and desire, and as the creation of new ones.

Reading and writing are expanded in these texts to activities that one carries on continually. One reads and writes discourses within and into the society in which one lives. Individual identity is ultimately posited to be a text, as is seen in the culminating sequence of images in *The Pure and the Impure,* where the character D. takes care to facilitate his "readability" in his relationship with 'Colette.' Thus relating to others is a form of reading and writing as well, more, or in some cases less, successful, as in the case of Chéri. Through all of these areas, the common thread of the necessity of subjectivity is found to run, a subjectivity posited as resistance to discourse—the texts of others.

I further conclude that the path to this subjectivity is through the senses, what is called in *The Pure and the Impure* "the Inexorable." It is the steadfast pursuit of desire, by one who is coerced neither by discourse, nor by other individuals with their wishes and desires, that the subject makes his or her "mark" within the text—the network of language—within which she or he lives. In *The Pure and the Impure* the desire pursued, which brings this result, is that feminine desire least admissible in the patriarchal text—sexual love between women. This pursuit of desire, here this particular sexual desire, is what in *The Pure and the Impure* brings the subject to a recognition of herself and of others, in that moment of differentiation which Benjamin describes as the experience itself of selfhood within intersubjectivity, and which she posits to be the goal of erotic union.

This subjectivity, however, is not a stable, fixed thing achieved once and for all. It is mutable, and exists only in becoming. For if it is in the pursuit of one's desire that this type of subjectivity comes into being, the desire that is pursued is itself unstable. The possible lesbian desire of 'Colette' remains allusive, hinted at, in the final pages of *The Pure and the Impure,* rather than named. Moreover, the text does not posit the obtaining of the object of desire as a final end, as that which lifts the subject out of the text, the nonfiniteness of the neverending chain of language. Rather, desire as it is portrayed exists as mediated, and a final object of desire cannot be pinned down, for the attempt to do so brings one inevitably to another object of desire.

Thus this study concludes that subjectivity in Colette is writing, through desire. Through this subjectivity, one is not lifted out of the text. However, through this, one becomes an active participant in and modifier of the text, that web of society/language and its discourses in which the human subject necessarily exists.

Notes

Introduction

1. Elaine Marks, *Colette*, 201.
2. Charles Taylor, *Sources of the Self: The Making of the Modern Identity*, 3. Subsequent references to this work are indicated parenthetically in the text.
3. Nancy Chodorow establishes a similar, synthesized framework for her recent work in psychoanalytic theory. "I try to develop a theoretical understanding that can both recognize individual clinical uniqueness and make general claims about psychological life and the relations between psyche and culture," she writes. See Nancy Chodorow, *The Power of Feelings*, 3. Later she adds, "I argue that cultural meanings that matter to us are created and experienced psychodynamically as well as linguistically or in terms of a cultural or discursive lexicon." See *The Power of Feelings*, 130. A similarly synthesized conclusion to the question of feminine genius taken up by Julia Kristeva is expressed thus: "You are a genius to the extent that you are able to challenge the sociohistorical conditions of your reality." See "Is There a Feminine Genius?" 504.
4. Throughout this study I use the term gender to designate the cultural institutions of the masculine and the feminine. Judith Butler's work is helpful here, which sees gender as performative, as "the repeated stylization of the body, a set of repeated acts within a highly rigid regulatory frame that congeal over time to produce the appearance of substance, of a natural sort of being." See Judith Butler, *Gender Trouble*, 33. In the same way, I refer to notions coming from psychoanalytic criticism for their usefulness in illuminating the functioning of patriarchal culture in the socially constructed world of the here and now. I do not subscribe to a psychoanalytic notion of gender as an essential category.
5. See especially Donna Norell, "Colette and the Burden of a Legend," 301-18, for an excellent, extensively researched overview of the reception of Colette's work from the early years of her career until recent decades. Norell's recent annotated bibliography, *Colette: An Annotated Primary and Secondary Bibliography* is an invaluable aid to anyone wishing to explore the area of Colette's reception yet further.
6. Donna Norell, "Colette and the Burden of a Legend," 303. See also Lynne Huffer, *Another Colette: The Question of Gendered Writing*, 4-5 and 15, for another discussion

of the persistent refusal to see in Colette's semiautobiographical works anything other than, as Huffer asserts on page 15, "a window into the author's life."
7. For examples of early perspectives on Colette that diverged from the norm, see Léon Thoorens, "Grandeur et misère de Colette," 1917-24. Thoorens was among the first to evaluate her work with an appreciation of the oppression she experienced at the beginning of her career. Other examples include Elaine Marks, *Colette*, and Goudeket, quoted in Norell, "Colette and the Burden of a Legend," 303.
8. See Bernard Bray, "La manière épistolaire de Colette," 100-101. The issue of *Cahiers Colette* in which Bray's study appears contains the essays presented at the first scholarly conference held on Colette, the Dijon conference of 1979.
9. This notion is discussed in Norell, "Colette and the Burden of a Legend," 302.
10. I borrow the phrase from Huffer. See especially "Inscribing a Gendered *Auctoritas*: Colette's Maternal Model" in *Another Colette: The Question of Gendered Writing*, 15-44.
11. Paul John Eakin, foreword to *On Autobiography* by Philippe Lejeune, ed. Paul John Eakin, trans. Katherine Leary, viii.
12. Philippe Lejeune, "The Autobiographical Pact," in *On Autobiography*, ed. Paul John Eakin, trans. Katherine Leary, 22.
13. Laurie Corbin sheds valuable light on the entire field of women's autobiography and its divergences from the genre that Lejeune's pioneering work does so much to illuminate. Corbin writes:
> The writing of the self is a process which differs for women and for men for several reasons. Women are placed differently in relation to representation than men; lacking the same type of subject status as men, their ability to enunciate their subjectivity is problematized. Their relation to language can also be seen as more adversarial in that women have often been discouraged from expressing themselves, in speech but particularly in writing. The theorization of "feminine" identity that can be found in women's autobiographical writings is therefore duplicitous: both affirming and denying identity, both representing and questioning "femininity," autogynographies, as Domna Stanton calls them, have multiple, sometimes contradictory projects. It is a multi-faceted view of the self that challenges monolithic definitions of "Woman," showing differences between women as well as within them. See Laurie Corbin, *The Mother Mirror*, 5-6.
14. Senhouse, for example, reads *My Mother's House* and *Sido* uncritically as autobiography in his introduction to the English translation of these works. For example,

he assumes that the mention of " 'Sido' [the name both of Colette's real-life mother and of the mother character in the semiautobiographical works] in any other book by Colette, thinly disguised as fiction though it be, provides a clue to the authenticity of that passage as factual." Roger Senhouse, introduction to *My Mother's House* and *Sido,* by Colette, xii-xiii. The compilation of passages from Colette's works done by Robert Phelps in *Earthly Paradise* is even qualified outright as "an autobiography."

15. See in particular Lastinger's reading of *Break of Day* in Valérie Lastinger, "*La naissance du jour:* la désintégration du 'moi' dans un roman de Colette," 542-51. In general, the paradoxical nature of the relationship of these works to more classical genre categories is reflected in the formulations of critics: "fiction and autobiography," "reality and inventions"; in Gouaux-Coutrix's adoption of Doubrovsky's "the truthful lie" ("le 'mentir vrai' "). These expressions come from Bernard Bray, "La manière épistolaire de Colette: réalité et inventions," and Mireille Gouaux-Coutrix, "Fiction et autobiographie: le 'mentir vrai' chez Colette."

16. The issue of demonstrating the extent to which Colette's semiautobiographical works are at variance with the reality of her lived existence is of such importance in Claude Francis and Fernande Gontier's work that it justifies the title *Creating Colette* for the English translation of their work. This lively biography provides much valuable information on Colette's life, and on the creation of the national myth that her name came to evoke.

17. Dana Strand, *Colette: A Study of the Short Fiction*, 8.

18. As Flieger points out, Colette's "autobiographical fiction" is equally resistant to categorization according to classical definitions of genre. She asserts:

> Autobiographical fiction—represented by such works as *The Vagabond*, *Chéri* and the *Claudine* series, which make ample use of autobiographical material but do not identify the protagonist as author—is perhaps the more familiar of these two categories [fictional autobiography and autobiographical fiction], belonging to a long literary tradition in which the author draws from her own life experience to shape her work. But in Colette, even this relatively straightforward category is complicated: for actual people from Colette's own life often appear in these works of fiction *without* a change of name, in delightful entanglements of imagination and reality. To cite one particularly rich example: in *Claudine at School,* the heroine meets the most famous actress of the day, Polaire—who, in real life, has built her reputation on playing none other than the fictional "Claudine," the admirer she meets in the novel. This is a hall of mirrors: for we recall that the real Colette

and Polaire were alter egos of sorts, whom Colette's husband, Willy, paraded around dressed as twins, as a publicity stunt to promote the *Claudine* series. All costumes were straight out of the *Claudine* series, Colette's books, signed by Willy, who at first took credit for them. The whole *mise-en-abîme* is a text in itself, a tangle of cross-reflections and uncanny resemblance. Jerry Flieger, *Colette and the Fantom Subject of Autobiography*, 5.

19. Lastinger, "*La naissance du jour:* la désintégration du 'moi' dans un roman de Colette," 545.
20. Lejeune theorizes that the reader is not really concerned with whether the narration is entirely accurate (exhaustive, thorough), as long as the *intention* to uphold the autobiographical pact is there. Thus, in a sense, fidelity is more important for us, in the autobiographical mode, than accuracy. Colette thus breaks the autobiographical pact in its most important aspect. It is not that her memory is faulty due to psychological processes (repression, displacement, forgetting) that we might take as in some way a more faithful rendering of her psyche than a dry recital of facts. Rather Colette does not promise fidelity; she warns the reader, in fact, to be wary of the exact opposite. In fact, as we read Colette in the light of the autobiographical space outlined by Lejeune, we see that while authors such as Gide or Mauriac have invited readers to see their novels as more truly autobiographical than their autobiographical works, Colette provides an exact contrast. That move, in the case of Colette, had already been made *for* her by critics. What we notice from Colette herself is the opposite move—not an indication of the autobiographical space in which she desires that the reader read her works, in spite of their nonautobiographical, novelistic, form, but rather the nonautobiographical, fictional space in which she desires that the reader read them, in spite of their seeming autobiographical form (the presence of a narrator who is the main character, and who bears the same name as, and seems initially identical with, the author). For Lejeune's remarks on autobiographical space, see Philippe Lejeune, "The Autobiographical Pact," in *On Autobiography*, ed. Paul John Eakin, trans. Katherine Leary, 41.
21. Flieger, *Colette and the Fantom Subject of Autobiography*, 6. Subsequent references to this work are indicated parenthetically in the text.
22. In particular and as stated above, Lejeune's early formulations of autobiography excluded Colette from the French autobiographical canon. See Philippe Lejeune, *L'Autobiographie en France*, 22, 25, 26. I do not take exception with Lejeune's decision to do this, as it is in accordance with the criteria he drew up in his comprehensive and groundbreaking study. Nonetheless, the fact remains that as Colette is

situated in the gray area between genres, she is not examined within the context of most serious autobiographical genre study.

23. Danielle Deltel, "Le meccano du souvenir : les doublets autobiographiques chez Colette," 151.
24. Claude Pichois and Alain Brunet, *Colette*, 292.
25. Another tradition in Colette criticism is expressed by Michèle Sarde in her foreword to *Colette, Free and Fettered* (the translation of *Colette, libre et entravée*). Sarde writes that "[i]n the light of Colette's life, I have questioned my own existence as a woman" (7). Also a common thread amongst many of those (in this case women) who have been moved to read and study Colette, this relation between reader/critic and text can even be seen in popular music. See Rosanne Cash's song, "The Summer I Read Collette [*sic*]" on the compact sound disk *Ten Song Demo* (Capitol, 1996).
26. In Focault's words, I intend subjectivity not as "originator" but as "variable and complex function" of discourse. Michel Foucault, "What Is an Author?," in *The Foucault Reader*, ed. Paul Rabinow, 118.
27. Bernard Lecherbonnier, et. al., *XXe siècle*, in the collection *Littérature: Textes et Documents*, 713.
28. Paul Rabinow, introduction to *The Foucault Reader* by Michel Foucault, 4.
29. For a further discussion of these ideas, see Michel Foucault, "Truth and Power," in *The Foucault Reader*, ed. Paul Rabinow, 51-75.
30. Paul Rabinow, introduction to *The Foucault Reader* by Michel Foucault, 7. Subsequent references to this work are indicated parenthetically in the text.
31. Although Colette did not make a habit of speaking out on issues such as incest, abortion, and domestic violence, Norell has effectively demonstrated that she was not silent or indifferent on such questions, as is often presumed. See Norell's assessment of 'Colette as Feminist' in "Colette and the Burden of a Legend," 309-15.
32. Mikhail Bakhtin, "Epic and Novel," in *The Dialogic Imagination*, ed. Michael Holquist, 3-40.
33. Mikhail Bakhtin, "Discourse in the Novel," in *The Dialogic Imagination*, ed. Michael Holquist, 262-63.
34. Julia Kristeva, "Word, Dialogue and Novel," in *Desire in Language*, ed. Leon S. Roudiez, 64-65.
35. Bauer and McKinstry argue that, albeit in a different way, men are also effaced by society's dominant discourse, which they equate with Bakhtin's "authoritative voice. A "masculinized or rationalized public language" is no more the vehicle for men's personal expression than women's, although Bauer and McKinstry do not deny that within society's current configuration men enjoy a privileged access to the authority

that this discourse confers. See Dale Bauer and Susan McKinstry, eds., *Feminism, Bakhtin and the Dialogic*, 2. For further explorations of the potential for feminist theory and praxis of the Bakhtinian approach to literary texts, see Bauer and McKinstry in its entirety.

36. As this study is in English, I will use the term "narratee," the translation from the French of Gerald Prince's term "narrataire." I use it in Prince's sense, according to the following definition: "All narration . . . . presupposes not only (at least) one narrator but also (at least) one narratee, the narratee being someone whom the narrator addresses." Gerald Prince, "Introduction to the Study of the Narratee," in *Reader-Response Criticism*, ed. Jane Tompkins, 7.
37. Jessica Benjamin, "A Desire of One's Own: Psychoanalytic Feminism and Intersubjective Space," in *Feminist Studies/Critical Studies*, ed. Teresa de Lauretis, 78-101. Subsequent references to this work are made parenthetically in the text.
38. Janet Whatley, "Colette's *Le Pur et l'Impur:* On Real and Phony Mysteries," 16-26.
39. Sido, *Lettres à sa fille*, 259.
40. Colette's life has been well documented and is not the focus of my work; however, I will mention one last episode. During the Second World War Colette, along with other writers who are not associated with fascism such as Giraudoux, Cocteau, and Valéry, contributed work to publications that supported the Vichy government or the collaboration. See Bernard Lecherbonnier, et. al., XXe *Siècle*, in the collection *Littérature : Textes et Documents*, 435. During the war Colette published pieces, albeit with no political content, in collaborationist newspapers in Paris. I know of no evidence to suggest that Colette sympathized with fascism, nor do I detect fascist overtones in her writing. The question of Colette's motivation is addressed by Judith Thurman, who mentions both the possibility that she may have wished to acquire credit in order to ransom her husband should he be interned again, or that she may simply have believed that the Germans would win the war. See *Secrets of the Flesh*, 457. This episode is treated by Claude Pichois and Alain Brunet, as well. See "Les Années Grises de l'Occupation" in *Colette*, 425-62. Whatever Colette's motivations might have been, she was responsible for these acts, which lent her illustrious name to the collaboration, and which cannot be overlooked or dismissed. The study of Colette's relationship to the collaboration and the ramifications for our reception of her work are therefore an area to be explored by future research.

Chapter 1
1. Michel de Certeau, *The Practice of Everyday Life*, 166.
2. Roland Barthes, *The Pleasure of the Text*, 4.

3. Peter Brooks, *Reading for the Plot*, 13. Subsequent references to this work are indicated parenthetically in the text.

4. Ross Chambers, *Story and Situation*, 4. Hans Robert Jauss, Wolfgang Iser, and Philippe Lejeune have preceded Chambers in work from these angles, but Chambers's contribution lies in his concentration on the "implications of the contextual nature of meaning for the analysis of *narrative texts themselves*," as he argues on page 4. Thus Chambers stresses the need to read texts in situation and also to read "in the texts, the situation that they produce as giving them their 'point,' " again on page 4. For an overview of reader-response criticism in general, see Jane Tompkins, ed., *Reader-Response Criticism*. Another good overview focusing specifically on the female-gendered reader is provided by Sara Mills, *Gendering the Reader*, 1-20. Mills sees, as do I, the structuring of meaning by the text, and the process of interpretation on the part of the reader, as being "best . . . described using a notion of negotiation." See *Gendering the Reader*, 12.

5. Michel de Certeau, *The Practice of Everyday Life*, xviii. Subsequent references to this work are indicated parenthetically in the text.

6. The problematic of women, reading, and resistance has generated other, at times conflicting, theoretical views. Judith Fetterley was the first to posit a specifically feminine reader with her book *The Resisting Reader: A Feminist Approach to American Fiction*. She looks at ways in which the canon of American literature "neither leaves women alone nor allows them to participate"; ways in which it "insists on its universality at the same time that it defines that universality in specifically male terms," and "co-opt[s] [the female reader] into participation in an experience from which she is explicitly excluded," requiring her to "identify against herself." See *The Resisting Reader*, xii. Fetterley concludes in saying that "the first act of the feminist critic must be to become a resisting rather than an assenting reader and, by this refusal to assent, to begin the process of exorcising the male mind that has been implanted in us." See *The Resisting Reader*, xxii.

Shoshana Felman questions Fetterley's approach on two points, namely whether resistance of this sort is possible, and whether it is in the end even desirable. "[F]rom where," she asks first,

> should we exorcize this male mind, if we ourselves are possessed by it, if as educated products of our culture we have unwittingly been trained to . . . identify . . . with the dominating, male-centered perspective of the masculine protagonist, which always takes itself—misleadingly—to be a measure of the universal?

Felman thus questions the female reader's ability to effectively set herself outside culture in order to resist. Furthermore, in response to Fetterley's statement that she sees her book as a "self-defense survival manual for the woman reader" (see *The Resisting Reader*, viii), Felman poses her second objection.

> [C]an *reading* truly be subsumed by *self-defense*? . . . . Does not reading involve one risk that, precisely, cannot be resisted: that of finding in the text something one does not expect? The danger with becoming a "resisting reader" is that we end up, in effect, *resisting reading*.

She advocates not so much "'resist[ing]' the text from the outside but rather to seek[ing] to trace within each text *its own resistance to itself,* its own specific literary, inadvertent *textual transgression of its male assumptions and prescriptions.*" See Shoshana Felman, *What Does a Woman Want?: Reading and Sexual Difference* (Baltimore and London: Johns Hopkins University Press, 1993), 5.

In her turn, Sara Mills in *Gendering the Reader* adds another dimension to the subject of gender and reading. Almost twenty years after Fetterley's work, Mills considers her notion of the resisting reader "a useful concept"; she adds to it a precise, empirical consideration of the language of the text itself; of "the ways in which language elements may both determine the way that we read and be used in the process of resisting that dominant reading." See *Gendering the Reader*, 28. She elaborates on page 34:

> It is . . . possible to maintain the notion that the text constructs a dominant reading which the reader deciphers according to discourses which she has already encountered, and this dominant reading will construct gendered subject positions for the reader. However, it is clear . . . that the reader is not addressed in a unified way and that she has a range of options available to her: s/he is part of a negotiated process over the meanings of the text and about the range of subject positions which she will adopt or resist. It will be in the interest of readers to recognize some of the subject positions and reject them, whilst others will be adopted.

The ability to remain independent and negotiate with texts that Mills theorizes here is the closest to my own view of reading of the three discussed here. Nonetheless, while the aspect of reading that Mills studies—the adoption or rejection of subject positions generated by the text on the part of the reader—is an aspect that I also study in Colette, my study is also interested in a further step, the role of the reader in the actual *creation* of the subject positions and the text itself.

7. The characterization of Juliette as "asiatic" and "Kalmuk" (*MMH* 70-71) and her eyes as "Mongol" indicates the presence in this text of an Orientalist discourse, contributing to the creation of 'Juliette,' with her passive, fated role, as definitively "other." See Edward Said, *Orientalism*.
8. Brooks, *Reading for the Plot*, 104.
9. Chambers, *Story and Situation*, 15. Subsequent references to this work are indicated parenthetically in the text.
10. Rachel Blau DuPlessis, *Writing Beyond the Ending*, 66-67.
11. Throughout this study Colette's own ellipses are single-spaced, to distinguish them from mine.
12. The chapter devoted to the sister in *My Mother's House* is not the only place in Colette in which long hair is mentioned in conjunction with oppression and melancholy. In *My Apprenticeships* the narrator writes of the "insecure and useless life" (47) that she led with Willy during her first marriage; these first years of marriage are also lived under the oppressive sign of long hair.

> I let myself sink back, sink down into a half dream, a half light, a vagueness, the habit of silence, the dim pleasure of being pale and a little breathless, of spreading my long, heavy hair—long, long as myself—over a trailing Renaissance gown. (*MA* 35)
> ["Je m'enlisais dans le demi-songe, le demi-jour, le flottement, l'habitude de me taire, le vague plaisir d'être pâle, un peu essouflée, d'épandre sur une longue robe d'intérieur style Renaissance, mes longs, mes lourds cheveux aussi longs que moi-même..." (3: 1006).]

13. Susan Cohen, "An Onomastic Double Bind: Colette's *Gigi* and the Politics of Naming," 801.
14. This passage rewrites Baudelaire's poem "Tresses" ("la Chevelure"), and in rewriting it puts into question the discourses that inform it. In Baudelaire hair is fully invested with the mystique of woman as locus of sexuality for man, and through her sexuality, definitively other. This mystique remains unquestioned in Baudelaire where we read:

> Rapture! To fill tonight our secret lair
> With memories asleep within this hair;
> I long, in the air, to shake it like a veil!
> [Extase! Pour peupler ce soir l'alcôve obscure
> Des souvenirs dormant dans cette chevelure,
> Je la veux agiter dans l'air comme un mouchoir!]

We note the contrast with Colette's undoing of this mystique. She asserts, given the deadening effects of the relationship of women to sexuality symbolized by long hair, that in fact "[a]morous dalliance [the translation of "l'alcôve," the same word as in Baudelaire] sees no more of you [loose long hair] than the passerby." Her introduction of a predatory, destructive note (the mesh or "rets") in the description of hair and the constraints on feminine sexuality that are linked to it, is innovative in relation to Baudelaire's text.

15. Colette experimented with reading and desire in another much earlier novel, *The Innocent Libertine*. (This work, which dates from before Colette's break with Willy, was originally written as two separate works, *Minne* and *Les Egarements de Minne*, published in 1904 and 1905 respectively. They were abridged, fitted together to form one novel and published in French under the title *l'Ingénue libertine* in 1909.) Here the female reader who is called Minne attempts to escape, in part by reading, the constraints placed on her by her sex and her bourgeois status, and in this she resembles in some ways 'Juliette.' However, in contrast to the story of 'Juliette,' the emphasis in this earlier novel is on the transgressive aspects of reading as it relates to desire; its escapism is clearly linked to a desire that goes beyond the bounds of patriarchal convention. Moreover, Minne does not simply read, she also takes action, albeit very naively. There is a life and energy in Minne's story that is lacking in that of 'Juliette.' Furthermore, it is not the act of an unsympathetic character, but of the protagonist, whose name, often accompanied by the endearment 'chérie,' strongly resembles the pet name given to 'Colette' by her mother: 'Minet-Chéri.' For all that she is presented more sympathetically, however, Minne's attempt at achieving a certain liberation, stimulated in part by reading, does fail. In the following chapter I will discuss at length the constraining discourses of femininity and sexuality that inform Colette's earliest works, and that render this outcome predictable. For a convincing analysis of this early novel, see Annabelle Cone, "Misplaced Desire: The Female Urban Experience in Colette and Rohmer," 423-31.

16. De Certeau, *The Practice of Everyday Life*, 172. Subsequent references to this work are indicated parenthetically in the text.

17. Cohen, "An Onomastic Double Bind," 808.

18. Jacqueline Rose, Introduction—II, to *Jacques Lacan and the 'école freudienne,'* a collection of essays by Jacques Lacan, eds. Juliet Mitchell and Jacqueline Rose, 30. Subsequent references to this work are indicated parenthetically in the text.

19. This 'pushiness' of discourse exists on three levels. First, in the case of this particular discourse, the discourse of love is pushy—it is an all-consuming emotion, it pushes out all else. Then, on the level not of what the discourse says but of what it does, this discourse pushes out all else in the texts, it swallows up everything else ("[i]t's a great bore—all the love in these books," she used to say. "In life, my poor Minet-

Chéri, folk have other fish to fry."). On a third level this discourse is pushy, even outside texts, as we saw in the case of 'Juliette' as reader— it becomes a complete world, a substitute world, it pushes out any other, for the unresistant reader.

20. Michel Foucault, "What Is an Author?" in *The Foucault Reader*, ed. Paul Rabinow, 107.
21. Again, 'Colette' in the matter of books is a revisionist Eve: it is in the garden that she tastes her first forbidden fruit.
22. Chantal Bertrand-Jennings speaks of how in *L'Asommoir,* for example, "Gervaise's culpable laziness and indulgence seem responsible for her misery as well as for that of her class," which is certainly to be expected in Zola, where Gervaise is not unique in being destined in a determinist fashion for failure. See Bertrand-Jennings, *L'Eros et la Femme chez Zola,* 74. However, this pessimism—even *mauvaise foi*—weighs particularly heavily with the female characters in the Rougon-Macquart series, because of "a myth of woman [in the Naturalist school] conceived as the physiological being *par excellence,* the most likely prey for envelopment by her milieu, the privileged site of neuroses, sensuality experienced as an unmasterable force, mystical madness," thus particularly helpless in the face of a doom predetermined by biology. See Jacques Dubois, *L'Assommoir de Zola : société, discours, idéologie,* 10. Adrienne Rich, in her chapter "Hands of Flesh, Hands of Iron" fills in details on the consequences of this "myth of woman" for the practices and discourse surrounding childbirth in Europe. She describes some of the gynecological and obstetrical practices through European history that have led us to a stage where "the process of labor . . . becomes tinged with cultural reverberations of terror, and a peculiar resonance of punishment." See Rich, *Of Woman Born: Motherhood as Experience and Institution,* 133. She also speaks of how childbirth moved from an activity in which women assisted each other, to a male domain in which technology from which women were excluded, coupled with misogynist attitudes, rendered women children or objects in their own process of giving birth. Citations she provides from a 1760 treatise against male midwifery written by Elizabeth Nihell, a graduate of the Hôtel Dieu midwifery school, echo the reaction of 'Colette' to what she finds in the Zola novel to a surprising degree. Rich paraphrases Nihell thus, including a direct quote from her treatise: "Men have justified their intrusion into the profession by '*forging the phantom of incapacity in women*' " (*Of Woman Born,* 147), and we marvel at the closeness to Colette: "I recognised nothing of my quiet, country-bred experience," a closeness even more striking in the original French, where we read: "je ne reconnus rien de ma tranquille *compétence*" (emphasis added).

Chapter 2

1. See Suzanne Relyea for details on the oppressive nature, for women, of the institution of marriage in France at the time Colette wrote her first works. While Relyea does not distinguish between the narrator of *My Apprenticeships* and Colette, she does provide useful information on the legal and financial constraints Colette confronted as a married woman in the late nineteenth and early twentieth centuries. See "The Symbolic in the Family Factory: *My Apprenticeships*," 287-89.
2. Nicole Ward Jouve, *Colette*, 141.
3. I refer the reader to Adam and Goldenstein for a detailed analysis of the child's passage from manipulating words independently of their meaning, for them a "poetic state" dominated by "the most absolute freedom," to eventual acceptance of that meaning, as it is recounted in the anecdote of the "presbytery." See Jean-Michel Adam and Pierre Goldenstein, "Une poétique du signe : les choses par leur nom?...", 36.
4. Jean Baudrillard, "Simulacra and Simulations," in *Jean Baudrillard: Selected Writings*, ed. Mark Poster, 166. Subsequent references to this work are indicated parenthetically in the text.
5. Elaine Marks notes, for example, the participation of the *Claudine* texts in a well-established masculine literary tradition of the lesbian. While she observes an originality in Claudine's voyeurism in that it is "neither secret nor cerebral" but "related to her appetites," she notes that "what is less original are Claudine's insolence and impertinence, the marks of the titillated and titillating schoolgirl whose desire for Aimée and later for Rézi recalls the presence of the lesbian in many turn-of-the-century texts, a male creation, the summum of naughtiness." See Marks, "Lesbian Intertextuality," in *Homosexualities and French Literature*, eds. George Stambolian and Elaine Marks, 363.
6. 'Colette's' choice of the character Maugis as illustration of the perfection she achieved in reproducing the discourse of another is particularly revelatory. This character is described elsewhere in *My Apprenticeships* as Willy's particular creation, and furthermore, his self-portrait. Colette writes:

    In *Claudine à Paris* there appeared for the first time a figure that was henceforth to flourish in all the works of M. Willy—if I may so call them. Henry Maugis is, perhaps, the only disclosure M. Willy has ever made us about himself. And when I say 'us' it is that in my lack of knowledge about this exceptional man I am compelled to speak as a member of the crowd; to have worked for him and beside him taught me to dread, not to know him better. Maugis the woman-fancier, all lit up with fatherly vice, the lover of puns and foreign drinks, the scholarly man, learned in music, letters, Greek, who is fond of duelling, sentimental, unscrupulous, who mocks as he secretly wipes away a tear, who plumps out a bullfinch belly, calls little women in underclothes 'baby,' prefers the half-dressed to the naked and socks to silk stockings—that Maugis is no creation of mine.

I think that M. Willy yielded, on the day he invented 'fat Maugis,' to one of his chief manias, which was an obsession with self-portraiture, a passion for looking at himself in the glass. From then on, it did not leave him and took a vast quantity of forms that seemed, to the public at large, to be no more than an inordinate sense of self-advertisement. (MA 61)

[Dans *Claudine à Paris* éclôt un personnage qui se promènera désormais dans toute l'œuvre, si j'ose dire, de M. Willy. Henry Maugis est peut-être la seule confidence que M. Willy nous ait faite sur lui-même, et si je dis "nous", c'est que mon ignorance d'un homme aussi exceptional exige que je me range parmi la foule. D'avoir travaillé pour lui, près de lui, m'a donné de le redouter, non de le connaître mieux. Ce Maugis, "tout allumé de vice paternel," amateur de femmes, d'alcools étrangers et de jeux de mots, musicographe, hellénisant, lettré, bretteur, sensible, dénué de scrupules, qui gouaille en cachant une larme, bombe un ventre de bouvreuil, nomme "mon bébé" les petites femmes en chemise, préfère le déshabillé au nu et la chaussette au bas de soie—ce Maugis-là n'est pas de moi.

Je crois que M. Willy céda, en créant "le gros Maugis", à l'une de ses mégalomanies, l'obsession de se peindre, l'amour de se contempler. Elle ne le quitta plus guère, et prit des formes multiples, où le public ne vit qu'un sens débridé de la publicité. (3: 1024-25)]

7. As Joan Hinde Stewart points out, "Claudine seeks a sexual identity; in her day she was one of the rare female protagonists in fiction to embark on such a search." See "The School and the Home," 264.
8. Sigmund Freud, "Instincts and Their Vicissitudes," in *A General Selection from the Works of Sigmund Freud*, ed. John Rickman, M.D., 78.
9. Jessica Benjamin, "Master and Slave: The Fantasy of Erotic Domination," in *Powers of Desire*, ed. Ann Snitow, 281. Subsequent references to this work are indicated parenthetically in the text.

Chapter 3

1. Jessica Benjamin, "A Desire of One's Own: Psychoanalytic Feminism and Intersubjective Space," in *Feminist Studies/Critical Studies*, ed. Teresa de Lauretis, 79. Subsequent references to this work are indicated parenthetically in the text.
2. Chodorow accounts for the reproduction of mothering in a similarly circular fashion. "The social organization of gender," she argues, "has depended on the continuation of the social relations of parenting." See *The Reproduction of Mothering*, 34. She contends that

    the family division of labor in which women mother gives socially and historically specific meaning to gender itself. This engendering of men and women with particular personalities, needs, defenses, and capacities creates the condition for and contributes to the reproduction of this same division of labor. The sexual division of labor both produces gender differences and is in turn reproduced by them.

    The Reproduction of Mothering, 38.
3. For Benjamin the intersubjective mode is distinguished from the "mode of representing intrapsychic events, the symbolic use of the body that psychoanalysis discovered, [which] does not distinguish between inside and outside, introjective-projective processes and interaction" (92). Important in her distinction is that this intrapsychic mode "does not distinguish between you as an independently existing subject and you as a fantasy extension of my wishes and desires" (92). Nor, she continues, does it distinguish between the desire to be something for the other (again she refers here to the work of Mitchell, and her assumption that the child's wish to represent the phallus for the mother "constitute[s] desire in its essential aspect" [92]) and being a subject, with a desire of one's own (92). These distinctions, between other as projection of my fantasies or wishes and other as independently existing subject, and between desire for the self and for the other, which she does make in what she calls intersubjectivity, are crucial to the question she explores, that of woman's own desire.
4. Benjamin is interested in a femininity that "has been based not only on lack of male experience but also on access to a different kind of experiences," and experiences that are furthermore "not merely the excluded opposites to male experience, the familiar half of the dualistic equation" (95). Thus with reference to Winnicott, and as already stated above, she argues that the idea of female inner space, and the "idea of *self-discovery* that is associated with having an inside" (95) are part of the experiences that have constituted femininity as now known. She is quick to clarify that this inner space or "the spatial representation of desire can be associated with subjectivity

only when the interior is not merely an object to be discovered or a receptacle in which to put things," but rather "part of a continuum that includes the space between the I and the you, as well as the space within me," and she adds as well that "the space within should be understood as a receptacle only insofar as it refers to the receptivity of the subject" (95). The self-discovery associated with having an inside "points to the side of the self preoccupied not with gender but with whether the drives I feel are really my own, whether they come from within me," and thus this whole issue is about "the *relationship* of the self to desire" (95). The point for her is arriving at the conviction of "owning one's own desire," something that comes from a wide variety of experiences. In fact, her argument is for "simultaneity and equality, not exclusion and the privileging of either male or female sets of experiences, capacities, and relationships" (95).

5. Benjamin concludes her argument by returning to the idea that the "pathway to desire leads through freedom." However, for her, it is not to be found through "the current emphasis on *freedom from*: as autonomy or separation from a powerful other, guaranteed by identification with an opposing power. Rather, we are seeking a relationship to desire in the *freedom to:* freedom to be both with and distinct from the other." Again, she contrasts symbolic structures with the idea of intersubjectivity. While "the phallus as emblem of desire has represented the one-sided individuality of subject meeting object, a complementarity that idealizes one side and devalues the other . . . [t]he discovery of our own desire will proceed, I believe, through the mode of thought that can suspend and reconcile such opposition, the dimension of recognition between self and other" (98).

6. See especially Lynne Huffer, "Inscribing a Gendered *Auctoritas*: Colette's Maternal Model," in *Another Colette: The Question of Gendered Writing*, 15-44.

7. Mireille Gouaux-Coutrix notes as well the appearance already in these early works of themes that Colette would later handle with the depth and assurance characteristic of her mature works. "Leaving aside their artificial aspects," she writes, "the *Claudines* already initiate one of the permanent 'lying' themes of Colette's work: the painful questioning of the flesh, the renunciation of sexuality from the vantage point of a solitary retreat, of a *Retreat from Love*, which allows the heroine to rediscover the world, the richness and variety of which are suddenly returned to her." See "Fiction et autobiographie : le 'mentir vrai' chez Colette," 14. Danielle Deltel presents in her turn a cogent study of the progression in the *Claudine* novels towards this early experimentation with this theme—self-sufficiency or autonomy allowing the heroine a heightened enjoyment of life, posited as the opposite of romantic love. Deltel traces, through the evolution of the enunciative framework for the protagonist's voice in

these works, and through the use of figures such as the mirror, the development of a "Colettian rêverie which is not a loss of self in objects, but rather a movement towards appropriation of the world and of self." See "'Assise en face de moi-même' : Naissance d'une écriture de soi," 66.

8. For another analysis of this issue, see Nancy K. Miller, "Woman of Letters: The Return to Writing in Colette's *La Vagabonde*" in *Subiect to Change,* 229-64. See also Hope Christiansen, "Finding a Room of Her Own in Colette's *La vagabonde,*" 81-96. Christiansen traces the heroine's reconfiguration of space, which allows her the 'room' to write.

9. See especially Jerry Flieger, "'Sido': Imaginary Elegy as Symbolic Play" in *Colette and the Fantom Subject of Autobiography,* 32-66. See also Huffer, "Inscribing a Gendered *Auctoritas*: Colette's Maternal Model," in *Another Colette,* 15-44.

10. One might even say that these semiautobiographical texts do not so much tell the story of 'Minet-Chéri' as that of 'Minet-Chéri' in relation to her mother. According to Lastinger, "more than Minet-Chéri, the 'I' narrator, Sido actually constitutes the central character of the trilogy: without her, none of these novels could exist." See "*La naissance du jour:* la désintégration du 'moi' dans un roman de Colette," 543. See Marie-Françoise Berthu-Courtivron, *Mère et fille : l'enjeu du pouvoir* for an analysis of the power struggle that the daughter's identity formation in relation to the mother involves.

11. The importance of the mother figure in Colette's mature work is underscored in another way, by its absence, in the 1939 novel *Le Toutounier*. In this work, centering on the lives of four sisters, the "four motherless girls" (3: 1270, my translation) create a substitute mother in the womb-like environment they create for themselves in the apartment they share. Ann Philbrick provides an insightful analysis of both the nurturing and the stifling aspects of this substitute mother. See "The Ambiguist Despite Herself: How Space Nurtures and Subverts Identity in Colette's *Le Toutounier,"* 32-39. Yet even the strong negative aspects of the substitute mother in this text argue not so much against the importance of mothering in Colette as for it. For the destructive role played in the young women's lives by the womb-like refuge makes sense in the end as a result of their over-compensation for the absence of this essential relationship. It is the narrator's underscoring of their motherlessness (3: 1270) that precedes the novel's closing scene, in which we witness once again the sisters' collaborative reinforcement and recreation of this closed space and world.

12. See especially Nancy Miller, "The Anamnesis of the Female 'I': In the Margins of Self-Portrayal," in *Colette: The Woman, the Writer,* eds. Erica Eisinger and Mari McCarty, 167; Sylvie Romanowski, "A Typology of Women in Colette's Novels," in

Colette, The Woman, the Writer, 71-73; Michèle Sarde, *Colette, Free and Fettered*, and Joelle Cauville, "L'Archétype de la mère dans l'œuvre de Colette," 92-97.

13. Colette's work undoes the double bind which, Jean Wyatt argues, patriarchal society imposes on the woman artist. Wyatt contends that in patriarchal culture the daughter rejects the mother, and in this way intimacy as well, for autonomy, in order to avoid the degraded status of the mother in the society in which she has grown up. Colette's construction of a feminine selfhood as artist and as daughter of her mother constitutes a more radical and subversive response to patriarchal culture than the "matrophobic" one discussed by Wyatt. This also allows Colette to bring the story of conflict between autonomy and love to a different and more interesting resolution than that of an inevitable split. See Wyatt's *Reconstructing Desire: The Role of the Unconscious in Women's Reading and Writing*, 113.

14. Diana Holmes notes the presence in Colette's work not only of woman's fixed gender role as mask (with negative connotations), but of an exaggerated "femininity" as a consciously assumed mask, which in works such as *La Vagabonde* plays a positive role. See "The Hidden Woman: Disguise and Paradox in Colette's *La Femme Cachée*," 31. See Holmes in its entirety for an excellent analysis of disguise in Colette as means of liberation from conventional gender and its constraints. The exaggerated "femininity" as consciously assumed mask that Holmes discusses can be interpreted in terms of Mulvey's "to-be-looked-at-ness." See Laura Mulvey, "Visual Pleasure and Narrative Cinema," 11.

15. Jessica Benjamin, "A Desire of One's Own," 97.

16. Qtd. in Claude Pichois, Préface to *La naissance du jour*, 7.

17. Marianne Hirsch, *The Mother/Daughter Plot: Narrative, Psychoanalysis, Feminism*, 106.

18. Michel Mercier demonstrated as early as 1984 that the scene of the pink cactus argues for a literary 'Sido' constructed by Colette. See Mercier, "'Homme, mon ami...'. La naissance du jour : l'analyse du texte et les apports de l'histoire du texte," in *Colette, Nouvelles Approches critiques*, ed. Bernard Bray, 59. Lastinger in 1988 again points out that this letter was rewritten, and underlines the importance of this fact for a reading of the Sido of *Break of Day* as textual, rather than conflated with the historical person, and of *Break of Day* as fiction, rather than autobiography. See Valérie Lastinger, "*La naissance du jour*: la désintégration du 'moi' dans un roman de Colette," 545.

19. For an exploration of the father figure in these works, see Jacques Dupont, "Identité et identifications dans l'œuvre de Colette," in *Colette, Nouvelles Approches critiques*, ed. Bernard Bray, 32-33; Flieger, "Colette and the Captain: Daughter as

Ghostwriter," in *Colette and the Fantom Subject of Autobiography*, 67-99; and Huffer, "Writing Double," in *Another Colette*, 45-69.
20. Flieger, *Colette and the Fantom Subject of Autobiography*, 68. Subsequent references to this work are indicated parenthetically in the text.
21. Margaret Callander offers a sensitive and insightful reading of Colette's erotic writing as characterized by a reticent or 'chaste' quality. She sees this, as do I, as a move on the writer's part to distance herself from the "deceitful discourse" and "false eroticism" produced in the *Claudine* series, but warns at the same time that "the reader would be much mistaken if they expected to find a kind of pastoral innocence in Colette's 'chaste' writing just as they would in expecting Colette's Parisian scenarios to stage nothing but jaded, salacious eroticism." See "Colette and the Hidden Woman: Sexuality, Silence and Subversion," in *French Erotic Fiction: Women's Desiring Writing*, eds. Alex Hughes and Kate Ince, 54.
22. See Fraiman for an analysis of "the double aspect of motherhood in Colette." Fraiman argues for a 'Sido' who embodies both aspects of motherhood as described by Adrienne Rich, that is, "not only the original, enabling experience, but also the elaborated, disabling institution" which has been "corrupted by male control." See "The Shadow in the Garden: The Double Aspect of Motherhood in Colette," 46-47.
23. I am indebted to Megan Cameron for the observation that the colors red/pink and blue function as two poles of an opposition in *Break of Day*.

Chapter 4
1. The exceptions are *The Vagabond* already discussed, of 1911, and its sequel, *The Shackle*, published in 1913.
2. Elaine Marks speaks of the drama and heroism, almost invariably demonstrated by women, that characterize, in Colette's fictional world, many a "very small life." See Marks, *Colette*, 183.
3. *The Ripening Seed* presents a relationship of this sort in the making, in the story it relates of the adolescents Vinca and Phil.
4. Helen Southworth presents a cogent analysis of the ways in which space and the relationship to writing function in this novel to figure both Michel's blocked itinerary and Alice's openness to life and to the world. See "Rooms of Their Own: How Colette Uses Physical and Textual Space to Question a Gendered Literary Tradition," 271-73.
5. For example, in *The Last of Chéri* we read:
   > Since childhood he had had it dinned into him that a French woman demeans herself by living with a foreigner, unless, of course, she ex-

ploits him, or he ruins her. And he could reel off a list of outrageous epithets with which a native Parisian courtesan would brand a dissolute foreigner. (58)

[Depuis son enfance [Chéri] savait qu'une Française ne déchoit pas à cohabiter avec un étranger, pourvu qu'elle l'exploite ou qu'il la ruine. Il connaissait par cœur la liste des qualificatifs outrageants dont une courtisane autochtone flétrit, à Paris, l'étrangère dissolue. (3: 212)]

The highly conventional nature of the *demi-monde* is moreover explicitly referred to in this same novel:

His [Chéri's] childhood as a bastard, his long adolescence as a ward, had taught him that his world, though people thought of it as reckless, was governed by a code almost as narrow-minded as middle-class prejudice. (*L of Ch* 107)

[Son enfance [de Chéri] de bâtard, sa longue adolescence en tutelle lui avaient enseigné qu'en un monde qui passe pour effréné règne un code presque aussi étroit qu'un préjugé bourgeois. (3: 247)]

And the main victim of this strict code are relationships of love: "In [this world], Chéri had learned that love is a question of money, infidelity, betrayals, and cowardly resignations" (*L of Ch* 107).

6. I am not arguing for an interpretation of Colette that reads a moral condemnation of these social parasites into her work; in fact, 'parasites' often contribute to productivity, and often at their own expense. For example, Delphy and Leonard offer a brilliant analysis of how housewives' work can simply disappear in the calculation of gross national products, fostering the notion that they contribute nothing to society's productivity, and are therefore 'supported' by their husbands. See "Housework, Household Work and Family Work," in *Familiar Exploitation: A New Analysis of Marriage in Contemporary Western Societies*, 75-104.

7. Elaine Marks even typifies these tales as sentimental for this reason. See Marks, *Colette*, 184.

8. Jessica Benjamin, "A Desire of One's Own: Psychoanalytic Feminism and Intersubjective Space," in *Feminist Studies/Critical Studies*, ed. Teresa de Lauretis, 93.

9. This may in fact be the meaning the author herself would have attributed to it.

10. Even Edmée, though subservient to the older generation, is in a less complicated relationship to it. She does not have the psychological incentive that Chéri has to remain in the child position indefinitely.

11. See Bal, "Inconsciences de Chéri: Chéri existe-t-il?," in *Colette: Nouvelles Approches Critiques*, ed. Bernard Bray, 17.

12. Peter Brooks, *Reading for the Plot*, 104.
13. Towards the end of *The Last of Chéri*, when Chéri has taken refuge in The Pal's apartment in order to remember and relive his days with Léa, we read that The Pal "devoted herself to Chéri with enthusiasm, a revival of her old zeal as a missionary of vice, who, with garrulous and culpable alacrity, would divest and bathe a virgin, cook an opium pellet, and pour out intoxicating spirits or ether" (*L of Ch* 129). On the following page a reference is made to her "aristocratic unpracticalness of a former prostitute."
14. While Edmée's pearl *necklace* participates in the same cluster of meanings as does those of Léa and The Pal, it is interesting to note that Edmée is associated with other pearls, as well, and specifically, a pearl ring. Here, the difference between Léa and Edmée is more marked, for the ring in question contains a *grey* pearl, which has little attraction for Chéri. In fact, this particular pearl appears in a scene in which Chéri imagines Edmée leaving him. He sees the scene thus:

> The image became focused in sharper colour and movement. Chéri could hear the heavy musical note of the iron gate swinging to, and could see beyond it fingers wearing a grey pearl and a white diamond.
> "Farewell," the small hand had said.
> Chéri jumped up, pushing back his chair. "Those are mine, all of them! The woman, the house, the rings... they all belong to me!" (*Chéri* 94)
> [L'image se précisa, gagna en couleurs et en mouvement. Chéri entendit le son grave et harmonieux de la grille et vit, de l'autre côté de la grille, sur une main nue, une perle grise, un diamant blanc...
> "Adieu"... disait la petite main.
> Chéri se leva en repoussant son siège. "C'est à moi, tout ça! La femme, la maison, les bagues, c'est à moi!" (2: 784)]

Chéri is not interested in Edmée, as the cool colors associated with her suggest. At the end of the novel, when he is at last reunited with Léa, Chéri underlines again the distaste he feels for the color Edmée is wearing the night he leaves. The color is white, a "congealed whiteness" (*Chéri* 134), a phrase which in the original French communicates even more clearly the idea of coldness ("blanc tellement gelé" [2: 813]). Yet in spite of the fact that he is not interested in Edmée and does not love her, he views her person *and the pearls she wears* as his property. She is truly viewed as a chattel, thus making even more difficult any genuine relationship of equals between the two.

Chapter 5

1. This work was originally published in 1932 under the title *Ces Plaisirs....* It was retitled *Le Pur et l'impur* in 1941.
2. Lynne Huffer, *Another Colette: The Question of Gendered Writing*, 9.
3. Ann Cothran, "*The Pure and the Impure*: Codes and Constructs," 346.
4. I understand sexuality in Foucault's sense, as a discursive phenomenon. In this view, not only is that which is said about sexuality discursive—linked to power, subject to change—but also sexuality itself. Rather than having an essential nature that is simply viewed differently through different discourses at different moments in history, sexual practices and sexuality itself are created through power and the discursive practices linked to it. See *The History of Sexuality*.
5. Rather than two entirely different types, the "monster" and the "androgynous being" are differentiated only by their success in asserting themselves in the world of gender and sexuality. 'Colette' thus addresses in the following way those whom she calls "monsters":

    > "O monsters, do not leave me alone... I do not confide in you except to tell you about my fear of being alone, you are the most human people I know, the most reassuring in the world." (*PI* 148-49)

    > ["O monstres, ne me laissez pas seule... Je ne vous confie rien, que ma crainte d'être seule, vous êtes ce que je connais de plus humain, de plus rassurant au monde..." (3: 638)]

    Jacob Stockinger points to a similar difference established by the structure of the story "The Patriarch," and notes that what "clearly distinguishes two forms of illegitimacy from each other, the Achille-Hardon girl affair from the Binard incest, making the first one pure and the second impure, is the loss of female equality" and thus, once again, the phenomenon of power. See Stockinger, "Impurity and Sexual Politics in the Provinces: Colette's Anti-Idyll in 'The Patriarch,'" 364.
6. Jessica Benjamin, "A Desire of One's Own: Psychoanalytic Feminism and Intersubjective Space," in *Feminist Studies/Critical Studies*, ed. Teresa de Lauretis, 90.
7. I study Renée Vivien as a construct within Colette's text. For those interested in studying Renée Vivien directly, see Tama Engelking, "Renée Vivien and the Ladies of the Lake," and Karla Jay, *The Amazon and the Page*.
8. Janet Whatley, "Colette's *Le Pur et l'Impur*: On Real and Phony Mysteries," 19.
9. The role of 'Colette' in *The Pure and the Impure* therefore brings to mind the role she plays in the novellas written in the last decades of Colette's life, as Jean Defoix analyses it. He argues that the novellas included in *Chance Acquaintances*, *The Tender Shoot and Other Stories,* and *Gigi and Selected Writings* "belong to that litera-

ture which exists alongside detective fiction" and that "although in them there is neither a police officer nor a professional detective, their interest and their movement are founded on the bringing to light of a hidden truth"; a process in which 'Colette' plays the role of "investigator." Jean Defoix, "Dernières Nouvelles," 20. See Defoix in its entirety for an exposition of the formal elements that are common to the novellas and that lead him to this conclusion.

10. For a further discussion of what she calls the darkness code, see Ann Cothran, "*The Pure and the Impure:* Codes and Constructs," 337-41.

11. See Janet Whatley, "Colette's *Le Pur et l'Impur:* On Real and Phony Mysteries."

12. Thus, while I find her readings of different vignettes very perceptive, I disagree with Elisabeth Ladenson's summing up that in the end this text offers us nothing but "Chinese embroideries made for export, a pattern designed to represent to us our own desire in exotic form." As I have argued above, it is precisely these conventional desires dressed up in exotic form that Colette's text advises us to see through, and that the narrator herself moves beyond. Thus I also disagree with Ladenson's conclusion that Colette, "even when she offers to reveal her desire stands nowhere." I argue that "standing nowhere" is precisely where the narrator wants to be and to bring us, in order to share with us insights on feminine sexuality that do not necessarily come down to 'revealing her desire,' (through either "den[ying] her homoerotic past" or "allow[ing] herself to be outed"), insights she has won through both observation and experience. For Ladenson's argument, See "Colette for Export Only."

13. Janet Whatley, "Colette's *Le Pur et l'Impur:* On Real and Phony Mysteries," 19. Subsequent references to this work are indicated parenthetically in the text.

14. Lillian Faderman notices the same phenomenon. She remarks that "Renée Vivien . . . appears to have inherited many of her views of lesbian life directly from the poets." These are, moreover, male poets, as Faderman remarks in continuing: "[w]hile Vivien apparently chose to devote herself to women at least partly because of her strong feminist consciousness, her poetry shows little of her feminism. . . . Instead she turns to Baudelaire and his followers for both the language and the imagery of lesbianism. Her poetry most often associates lesbian love with vice, artificiality, perfume, and death." Lillian Faderman, *Surpassing the Love of Men: Romantic Friendship and Love between Women from the Renaissance to the Present*, 361-62.

15. Jerry A. Flieger, *Colette and the Fantom Subject of Autobiography*, 130. Subsequent references to this work are indicated parenthetically in the text.

16. See Mary Lydon's discussion of this passage in "Calling Yourself a Woman: Marguerite Yourcenar and Colette."

17. Sherry Dranch, "Reading through the Veiled Text: Colette's *The Pure and the Impure*," 177. See also Jerry A. Flieger, *Colette and the Fantom Subject of Autobiography*, 115.
18. Janet Whatley, "Colette's *The Pure and the Impure*: On Real and Phony Mysteries," 20.
19. D., like the other characters in the world of the dream, has a distinctly androgynous nature. He is described as having a "Herculean force," and at the same time, "the eyes of a young girl" (3: 646, my translation).
20. Julia Kristeva, "Word, Dialogue and Novel," in *Desire in Language*, ed. Leon S. Roudiez, 64-65. I have eliminated the emphasis in the original.
21. The word "abritrary" here recalls the original description of the senses at the beginning, as they are held in check by Charlotte—"intractable and ignorant as the princes of bygone days who learned only what was indispensable: to dissimulate, to hate, to command!" (*PI* 24-25).
22. Colette tells another such tale at length in *The Other One*, the 1929 novel in which the rivals Fanny, the wife, and Jane, the mistress of the well-known playwright Farou, eschew an antagonistic, jealous attitude towards one another for an intimacy which relegates Farou to a position of secondary importance. Once again, however, the text warns the reader against too quickly interpreting this plot according to male paradigms of feminine sexuality. In fact, on an overall level, this text acts out female subversion of male discourse. The play Farou is writing, called *No Woman about the House*, might be the title itself of the traditional patriarchal marriage or relationship between the sexes. However, Colette's novel and its plot subvert this, so that in the end, the house Farou lives in is precisely a "house *of* women." It is the masculine presence as dominant discourse that fades away. In addition to the irony in the title of Farou's play, Fanny's remonstrances with Farou over his plot lines encode another warning to the reader against too facile an interpretation of female sexuality according to received paradigms. Fanny declares that Farou's intention of having his character Denise commit suicide over a lover's betrayal is not true to life, but rather a "man's reaction" (*Other* 38). (The illegitimacy within Farou's literary world of that which is not a "man's reaction" but rather a critical, and feminine, voice, is exemplified not only by Farou's dismissal of Fanny's suggestion, but also by his relegation of Jane to her position of secretary, rather than partner in his craft [*Other* 28].) Another appearance of received notions of sexuality and femininity comes in the form of the gossip resulting from Jane's decision to live within the ménage-à-trois arrangement that includes Fanny and Farou. In speaking of her, the "public" speculates thus:

> "Whose bed does that pretty ash-blonde share? Dark Fanny's, wouldn't you think?"
> "No, no, old boy, Farou's of course, the old goat-foot! He invests her with the title of secretary and foists her on his wife." (*Other* 43)
> ["Avec qui couche cette jolie fille cendrée? Avec Fanny la brune, je pense?
> —Mais non, mon vieux, avec ce chèvre-pied de Farou, qui la décore du titre de secrétaire, et l'impose à sa femme..." (3: 404)]

Thus the public, which through the expression "old boy" is identified as masculine, leaps to the conclusion that Fanny and Jane are lovers. However, the reality that Colette presents us with at the end of the novel, with its characteristic complexity and understatement, belies this assumption. Fanny does muse in this way, contemplating life without Jane: "tomorrow, if she goes away, I shall be like this, alone beside the fire, like a woman who has come to the end of the greater part of love" (*Other* 157) and thus a suggestion of sexual desire between two women is present. However, we are witness to no scene confirming this in unequivocal fashion as the sole, overriding meaning of their relationship. Rather, the companionship and esteem for one another that the two women find they enjoy lends a solidity to their relationship that the relationship of neither with Farou is able to boast. Fanny finds that she loses faith in the "remains of a pure religion" that fighting another woman for Farou would participate in, and instead "she turn[s] again to the help which could spring only from an alliance, even if it were uncertain and slightly disloyal, from a feminine alliance, constantly broken by the man and constantly re-established at the man's expense" (*Other* 158-59). Once again, as in the closing pages of *The Pure and the Impure*, we note that the relationship between two women is described in terms of a dynamic including a third party. Again, while "the man" is clearly of secondary importance, he is nonetheless present and indeed in some sense necessary, as catalyst or mediator, to the relationship between the women. The world of Fanny and Jane, therefore, like that of the women described at the end of *The Pure and the Impur,* does not reproduce the closed, dyadic structure of the world of the Ladies of Llangollen, but participates in a larger, dynamic world where the possibility of change is always present, and where, therefore, the inscription of a lesbian desire, while not rigidly codified, is ever imminent, and at times realized.

23. For another analysis of bisexuality and femininity as resistance to what Felman calls "the phantasmically reified and fetishized *institutions* of masculinity and femininity" (66) in Balzac's *The Girl with the Golden Eyes,* see Shoshana Felman, "Textuality and the Riddle of Bisexuality" in *What Does a Woman Want?: Reading and Sexual Difference*, 41-67.

Works Cited

Works by Colette and Sido
In French:
Colette, *Œuvres*. Bibliothèque de la Pléiade. 3 vols. Ed. Claude Pichois. Paris: Gallimard, 1991.

Sido, *Lettres à sa fille précédé de Lettres inédites de Colette*. Paris: des femmes, 1984.

In English (all by Colette):
Claudine at School. Translated by Antonia White. New York: Farrar, Straus and Cudahy, 1957. Translation of *Claudine à l'école*. Paris: Ollendorff, 1900.

Claudine Married. Translated by Antonia White. New York: Farrar, Straus and Cudahy, 1960. Translation of *Claudine en ménage*. Paris: Mercure de France, 1902.

Retreat from Love. Translated by Margaret Crosland. London: Peter Owen, 1974. Translation of *La Retraite sentimentale*. Paris: Mercure de France, 1907.

The Vagabond. Translated by Enid McLeod. New York: Farrar, Straus and Young, 1955. Translation of *La Vagabonde*. Paris: Ollendorff, 1911.

Music-Hall Sidelights. In *Mitsou* and *Music-Hall Sidelights*. *Mitsou* translated by Raymond Postgate. *Music-Hall Sidelights* translated by Anne-Marie Callimachi. New York: Farrar, Straus and Giroux, 1957. Translation of *L'Envers du music-hall*. Paris: Flammarion, 1913.

Mitsou. In the same edition as *Music-Hall Sidelights*. Translation of *Mitsou ou Comment l'esprit vient aux filles*. Paris: Arthème Fayard, 1919.

Chéri. Translated by Roger Senhouse. London: Secker and Warburg, 1951. Translation of *Chéri*. Paris: Arthème Fayard, 1920.

My Mother's House. In *My Mother's House* and *Sido*. *My Mother's House* translated by Una Vicenzo Troubridge and Enid McLeod. *Sido* translated by Enid McLeod. New York: Farrar, Straus and Young, 1953. Translation of *La Maison de Claudine*. Paris: J. Ferenczi et fils, 1922.

The Ripening Seed. Translated by Roger Senhouse and Hermia Briffault. New York: Farrar, Straus and Giroux, 1978. Translation of *Le Blé en herbe*. Paris: Flammarion, 1923.

The Last of Chéri. Translated by Roger Senhouse. London: Secker and Warburg, 1951. Translation of *La Fin de Chéri*. Paris: Flammarion, 1926.

Break of Day. In *Break of Day* and *The Blue Lantern*. *Break of Day* translated by Enid McLeod. New York: Farrar, Straus and Giroux, 1963. Translation of *La Naissance du jour*. Paris: Flammarion, 1928.

The Other One. Translated by Elizabeth Tait and Roger Senhouse. New York: Farrar, Straus and Cudahy, 1960. Translation of *La Seconde*. Paris: Ferenczi et fils, 1929.

Sido. In the same edition as *My Mother's House*. Translation of *Sido*. Paris: Simon Krâ, 1929.

The Pure and the Impure. Translated by Hermia Briffault. New York: Farrar, Straus and Giroux, 1967. Translation of *Ces Plaisirs....* Paris: Ferenczi et fils, 1932. Title changed to *Le Pur et l'impur*, 1941.

The Cat. Translated by Morris Bentinck. New York: Farrar and Rinehart, 1936. Translation of *La Chatte*. Paris: Bernard Grasset, 1933.

Duo. In *Duo* and *Le Toutounier*. Translated by Margaret Crosland. New York: Dell, 1974. Translation of *Duo*. Paris: Ferenczi et fils, 1934.

My Apprenticeships. Translated by Helen Beauclerk. New York: Farrar, Straus and Giroux, 1957. Translation of *Mes Apprentissages*. Paris: Ferenczi et fils, 1936.

Le Toutounier. In the same edition as *Duo*. Translation of *Le Toutounier*. Paris: Ferenczi et fils, 1939.

Julie de Carneilhan. In *Julie de Carneilhan* and *Chance Acquaintances*. Translated by Patrick Leigh Fermor. London: Secker and Warburg, 1952. Translation of *Julie de Carneilhan*. Paris: Arthème Fayard, 1941.

Other Works:

Adam, Jean-Michel, and Jean-Pierre Goldenstein. "Une poétique du signe: les choses par leur nom?..." Part 1.3 in *Linguistique et discours littéraire: théorie et pratique des textes*. Paris: Larousse, 1976.

Bakhtin, Mikhail. "Discourse in the Novel." In *The Dialogic Imagination*. Edited by Michael Holquist, 259-422. Translated by Caryl Emerson and Michael Holquist. Austin: University of Texas Press, 1981.

———. "Epic and Novel." In *The Dialogic Imagination*. Edited by Michael Holquist, 3-40. Translated by Caryl Emerson and Michael Holquist. Austin: University of Texas Press, 1981.

Bal, Mieke. "Inconsciences de Chéri—Chéri existe-t-il? In *Colette, Nouvelles Approches critiques*. Edited by Bernard Bray, 15-25. Paris: Nizet, 1986.

Barthes, Roland. *The Pleasure of the Text*. Translated by Richard Miller. New York: Farrar, Strauss and Giroux, Hill and Wang: 1975. Translation of *Le Plaisir du texte*. Paris: Seuil, 1973.

Baudelaire, Charles. *Les Fleurs du Mal*. Paris: Gallimard, 1961.

———. *The Flowers of Evil*. Translated by Florence Louie Friedman. Philadelphia: Dufour, 1966.

Baudrillard, Jean. "Simulacra and Simulations." In *Jean Baudrillard: Selected Writings*. Edited by Mark Poster, 166-84. Translated by Jacques Mourrain. Stanford: Stanford University Press, 1988. Originally published in *Simulacres et Simulations*, Paris: Editions Galilée, 1981.

Bauer, Dale M., and Susan Jaret McKinstry, eds. *Feminism, Bakhtin and the Dialogic*. Albany: State University of New York Press, 1991.

Benjamin, Jessica. "A Desire of One's Own: Psychoanalytic Feminism and Intersubjective Space." In *Feminist Studies/Critical Studies*, edited by Teresa de Lauretis, 78-101. Bloomington: Indiana University Press, 1986.

———. "Master and Slave: The Fantasy of Erotic Domination." In *Powers of Desire: The Politics of Sexuality*, edited by Ann Snitow, 280-99. New York: Monthly Review Press, 1983.

Berthu-Courtivron, Marie-Françoise. *Mère et fille: l'enjeu du pouvoir: essais sur les écrits autobiographiques de Colette*. Geneva: Droz, 1993.

Bertrand-Jennings, Chantal. *L'Eros et la Femme chez Zola: De la chute au paradis retrouvé*. Paris: Klincksieck, 1977.

Biolley-Godino, Marcelle. *L'homme-objet chez Colette*. Paris: Klincksieck, 1972.

Bray, Bernard, ed. *Colette, Nouvelles Approches critiques*. Actes du Colloque de Sarrebruck (22-23 Juin 1984). Paris: Nizet, 1986.

———. "La manière épistolaire de Colette: réalité et inventions." *Cahiers Colette* 3-4 (1981): 100-18.

Brooks, Peter. *Reading for the Plot: Design and Intention in Narrative*. New York: Knopf, 1984.

Butler, Judith. *Gender Trouble: Feminism and the Subversion of Identity*. New York: Routledge, 1990.

Callander, Margaret. "Colette and the Hidden Woman: Sexuality, Silence and Subversion." In *French Erotic Fiction: Women's Desiring Writing, 1880-1990*. Edited by Alex Hughes and Kate Ince, 49-68. Oxford and Washington: Berg, 1996.

Cash, Rosanne. "The Summer I Read Collette [sic]." *Ten Song Demo*, compact sound disk. Capitol, 1996.

Cauville, Joelle. "L'Archétype de la mère dans l'œuvre de Colette." *Etudes Francophones* 16, no. 1 (2001): 89-102.

Certeau, Michel de. *The Practice of Everyday Life*. Translated by Steven Rendall. Berkeley, Los Angeles and London: University of California Press, 1988. Translation of *L'Invention du quotidien*. 2 vols. Paris: Gallimard, 1990.

Chambers, Ross. *Story and Situation: Narrative Seduction and the Power of Fiction*. Theory and History of Literature 12. Minneapolis: University of Minnesota Press, 1984.

Chodorow, Nancy. *The Power of Feelings: Personal Meaning in Psychoanalysis, Gender and Culture*. New Haven and London: Yale University Press, 1999.

———. *The Reproduction of Mothering: Psychoanalysis and the Sociology of Gender*. Berkeley: University of California Press, 1978.

Christiansen, Hope. "Finding a Room of Her Own in Colette's *La vagabonde*." *Dalhousie French Studies* 44 (1998): 81-96.

Cohen, Susan D. "An Onomastic Double Bind: Colette's *Gigi* and the Politics of Naming." *PMLA* 100 (1985): 793-809.

Cone, Annabelle. "Misplaced Desire: The Female Urban Experience in Colette and Rohmer." *Literature/Film Quarterly* 24, no. 4 (1996): 423-31.

Corbin, Laurie. *The Mother Mirror: Self-Representation and the Mother-Daughter Relation in Colette, Simone de Beauvoir, and Marguerite Duras*. New York: Peter Lang, 1996.

Cothran, Ann. "*The Pure and the Impure*: Codes and Constructs." *Women's Studies* 8 (1981): 335-57.

Defoix, Jean. "Dernières Nouvelles." *Europe: revue littéraire mensuelle* 631-32 (1981): 20-29.

Delphy, Christine, and Diana Leonard. *Familiar Exploitation: A New Analysis of Marriage in Contemporary Western Societies*. Cambridge, UK: Polity Press, 1992.

Deltel, Danielle. " 'Assise en face de moi-même': Naissance d'une écriture de soi." *Cahiers Colette* 15 (1992): 55-69.

———. "Le meccano du souvenir: les doublets autobiographiques chez Colette." *Cahiers de Sémiotique Textuelle* 12 (1988): 137-51.

Dranch, Sherry A. "Reading through the Veiled Text: Colette's *The Pure and the Impure*." *Contemporary Literature* 24, no. 2 (1983): 176-89.

Dubois, Jacques. *L'Assommoir de Zola: société, discours, idéologie*. Paris: Larousse, 1973.

DuPlessis, Rachel Blau. *Writing beyond the Ending: Narrative Strategies of Twentieth-Century Women Writers*. Bloomington: Indiana University Press, 1985.

Dupont, Jacques. "Identité et identifications dans l'œuvre de Colette." In *Colette, Nouvelles Approches critiques*. Edited by Bernard Bray, 27-36. Paris: Nizet, 1986.

Eakin, Paul John. Foreward to *On Autobiography*, by Philippe Lejeune. Theory and History of Literature 52. Minneapolis: University of Minnesota Press, 1989.

Eisinger, Erica, and Mari McCarty, eds. *Colette: The Woman, the Writer*. University Park: Pennsylvania State University Press, 1981.

Engelking, Tama. "Renée Vivien and the Ladies of the Lake." *Nineteenth Century French Studies* 30, nos. 3-4 (2002): 362-79.

Faderman, Lillian. *Surpassing the Love of Men: Romantic Friendship and Love between Women from the Renaissance to the Present*. New York: William Morrow, 1981.

Felman, Shoshana. *What Does a Woman Want?: Reading and Sexual Difference*. Baltimore and London: Johns Hopkins University Press, 1993.

Fetterley, Judith. *The Resisting Reader: A Feminist Approach to American Fiction*. Bloomington: Indiana University Press, 1978.

Flieger, Jerry Aline. *Colette and the Fantom Subject of Autobiography*. Ithaca and London: Cornell University Press, 1992.

Foucault, Michel. *The History of Sexuality*. Vol. 1, *An Introduction*. Translated by Robert Hurley. New York: Random House, Vintage Books, 1978. Translation of *La Volonté de savoir*. Paris: Gallimard, 1976.

———. "Truth and Power." In *The Foucault Reader*. Edited by Paul Rabinow, 51-75. New York: Pantheon Books, 1984. Originally published as "Intervista a Michel Foucault" in *Microfisica del Potere* by Michel Foucault (Turin, 1977).

———. "What Is an Author?" In *The Foucault Reader*. Edited by Paul Rabinow, 101-20. Translated by Josué V. Harari. New York: Pantheon Books, 1984. Translation of "Qu'est-ce qu'un auteur?" *Bulletin de la Société Française de Philosophie* 63, no. 3 (1969): 73-104.

Fraiman, Susan D. "The Shadow in the Garden: The Double Aspect of Motherhood in Colette." *Perspectives on Contemporary Literature* 11 (1985): 46-53.

Francis, Claude, and Fernande Gontier. *Creating Colette*. 2 vols. South Royalton, VT: Steerforth Press, 1998-99. Originally published in France under the title *Colette* by Librairie Académique Perrin.

Freud, Sigmund. "Instincts and Their Vicissitudes." In *A General Selection from the Works of Sigmund Freud*. Edited by John Rickman, M.D., 70-86. Garden City, NY: Doubleday and Company, Inc., 1957.

Gouaux-Coutrix, Mireille. "Fiction et autobiograhie: le 'mentir vrai' chez Colette." *Europe: revue littéraire mensuelle* 631-32 (1981): 13-20.

Hirsch, Marianne. *The Mother/Daughter Plot: Narrative, Psychoanalysis, Feminism.* Bloomington: Indiana University Press, 1989.

Holmes, Diana. "The Hidden Woman: Disguise and Paradox in Colette's *La Femme Cachée.*" *Essays in French Literature* 23 (1986): 29-37.

Huffer, Lynne R. *Another Colette: The Question of Gendered Writing.* Ann Arbor: University of Michigan Press, 1992.

Hughes, Alex and Kate Ince, eds. *French Erotic Fiction: Women's Desiring Writing, 1880-1990.* Oxford and Washington: Berg, 1996.

Jay, Karla. *The Amazon and the Page: Natalie Clifford Barney and Renée Vivien.* Bloomington: Indiana University Press, 1988.

Jouve, Nicole Ward. *Colette.* Bloomington: Indiana University Press, 1987.

Kristeva, Julia. "Is There a Feminine Genius?" *Critical Inquiry* 30, no. 3 (2004): 493-504.

———. "Word, Dialogue and Novel." In *Desire in Language.* Edited by Leon S. Roudiez, 64-91. Translated by Thomas Gora, Alice Jardine and Leon S. Roudiez. New York: Columbia University Press, 1980. Translation of "Le Mot, le Dialogue, et le Roman." In *Séméiotiké: Recherches pour une sémanalyse.* Paris: Seuil, 1969.

Ladenson, Elisabeth. "Colette for Export Only." *Yale French Studies* 90 (1996): 25-46.

Larnac, Jean. *Colette: sa vie, son œuvre.* Paris: Simon Krâ, 1927.

Lastinger, Valérie C. "*La naissance du jour*: la désintrégation du 'moi' dans un roman de Colette." *The French Review* 61, no. 4 (1988): 542-51.

Lecherbonnier, Bernard, Dominique Rincé, Pierre Brunel and Christine Moatti. *XXe Siècle.* In the collection *Littérature: Textes et Documents.* Paris: Editions Nathan, n.d.

Lejeune, Philippe. "The Autobiographical Pact." In *On Autobiography.* Edited by Paul John Eakin, 3-30. Translated by Katherine Leary. Theory and History of Literature 52. Minneapolis: University of Minnesota Press, 1989. Translation of "Le Pacte Autobiographique." In *Le Pacte Autobiographique* (Paris: Seuil, 1975).

———. *L'Autobiographie en France.* Paris: Armand Colin, 1971.

Lottman, Herbert. *Colette: A Life.* Boston: Little, Brown and Company, 1991.

Lydon, Mary. "Calling Yourself a Woman: Marguerite Yourcenar and Colette." *differences: A Journal of Feminist Cultural Studies* 3, vol. 3 (1991): 26-44.

Marks, Elaine. "Lesbian Intertextuality." In *Homosexualities and French Literature: Cultural Contexts/Critical Texts.* Edited by George Stambolian and Elaine Marks, 353-77. Ithaca and London: Cornell University Press, 1979.

———. *Colette.* New Brunswick, NJ: Rutgers University Press, 1960.

Mercier, Michel. "Homme, mon ami...'. *La Naissance du jour:* l'analyse du texte et les apports de l'histoire du texte." In *Colette, Nouvelles Approches critiques.* Edited by Bernard Bray, 59-65. Paris, Nizet: 1986.

Miller, Nancy K. *Subject to Change: Reading Feminist Writing.* New York: Columbia University Press, 1988.

———. "The Anamnesis of the Female 'I': In the Margins of Self-Portrayal." In *Colette: The Woman, the Writer.* Edited by Erica Eisinger and Mari McCarty, 164-75. University Park: Pennsylvania State University Press, 1981.

Mills, Sara. *Gendering the Reader.* New York and London: Harvester-Wheatsheaf, 1994.

Mulvey, Laura. "Visual Pleasure and Narrative Cinema." *Screen* 16, no. 3 (1975): 6-18.

Norell, Donna M. *Colette: An Annotated Primary and Secondary Bibliography.* New York and London: Garland Publishing Inc., 1993.

———. "Colette and the Burden of a Legend." *Journal of Women's Studies in Literature* 1, vol. 4 (1979): 301-18.

Phelps, Robert. *Earthly Paradise: An Autobiography of Colette Drawn from Her Lifetime Writings.* New York: Farrar, Strauss and Giroux, 1966.

Philbrick, Ann Leone. "The Ambiguist Despite Herself: How Space Nurtures and Subverts Identity in Colette's *Le Toutounier.*" *Modern Language Studies* 11 (1981): 32-39.

Pichois, Claude, and Alain Brunet. *Colette.* Paris: Fallois, 1999.

Pichois, Claude. Préface to *La naissance du jour*, by Colette. Paris: Flammarion, 1984.

Prince, Gerald. "Introduction to the Study of the Narratee." In *Reader-Response Criticism: From Formalism to Poststructuralism.* Edited by Jane Tompkins, 7-25. Baltimore: Johns Hopkins University Press, 1980. Translation of "Introduction à l'étude du narrataire." *Poétique* 14 (1973): 178-96.

Rabinow, Paul. Introduction to *The Foucault Reader,* by Michel Foucault. New York: Pantheon Books, 1984.

Relyea, Suzanne. "The Symbolic in the Family Factory: *My Apprenticeships.*" *Women's Studies* 8 (1981): 273-97.

Rich, Adrienne. *Of Woman Born: Motherhood as Experience and Institution.* New York: W. W. Norton, 1976.

Richardson, Joanna. *Colette.* New York: Franklin Watts, 1984.

Romanowski, Sylvie. "A Typology of Women in Colette's Novels." In *Colette: The Woman, the Writer.* Edited by Erica Eisinger and Mari McCarty, 66-74. University Park: Pennsylvania State University Press, 1981.

Rose, Jacqueline. Introduction—II, to *Feminine Sexuality: Jacques Lacan and the 'école freudienne,'* a collection of essays by Jacques Lacan. Edited by Juliet Mitchell and Jacqueline Rose. Translated by Jacqueline Rose. New York: Norton, 1982.

Said, Edward. *Orientalism*. New York: Pantheon Books, 1978.

Sarde, Michèle. *Colette, Free and Fettered*. Translated by Richard Miller. New York: William Morrow, 1980. Translation of *Colette, libre et entravée*. Paris: Stock, 1978.

Senhouse, Roger. Introduction to *My Mother's House* and *Sido*, by Colette. Translation of *My Mother's House* by Una Vincenzo Troubridge and Enid McLeod. Translation of *Sido* by Enid McLeod. New York: Farrar, Strauss and Young, 1953.

Southworth, Helen. "Rooms of Their Own: How Colette Uses Physical and Textual Space to Question a Gendered Literary Tradition." *Tulsa Studies in Women's Literature* 20, no. 2 (2001): 253-78.

Stewart, Joan Hinde. *Colette*. Boston: Twayne Publishers, 1983, 1996.

———. "The School and the Home." *Women's Studies* 8 (1981): 259-72.

Stockinger, Jacob. "Impurity and Sexual Politics in the Provinces: Colette's Anti-Idyll in 'The Patriarch.'" *Women's Studies* 8 (1981): 359-66.

Strand, Dana. *Colette: A Study of the Short Fiction*. New York: Simon and Schuster Macmillan, Twayne Publishers, 1995.

Taylor, Charles. *Sources of the Self: The Making of the Modern Identity*. Cambridge: Harvard University Press, 1989.

Thoorens, Léon. "Grandeur et misère de Colette." *Revue générale belge* 90 (15 September 1954): 1917-24.

Thurman, Judith. *Secrets of the Flesh*. New York: Alfred A. Knopf, 1999.

Tompkins, Jane, ed. *Reader-Response Criticism: From Formalism to Poststructuralism*. Baltimore: Johns Hopkins University Press, 1980.

Whatley, Janet. "Colette's *Le Pur et l'Impur:* On Real and Phony Mysteries." *Modern Language Studies* 13, no. 3 (1983): 16-26.

Wyatt, Jean. *Reconstructing Desire: The Role of the Unconscious in Women's Reading and Writing*. Chapel Hill: University of North Carolina Press, 1990.

Index

B
Bakhtin, Mikhail, 15, 174, 179
Barthes, Roland, 23-24, 42
Baudelaire, Charles, 189, n. 14, 202, n. 14
Baudrillard, Jean, 56
Benjamin, Jessica, 17, 69-70, 75-80, 83, 85, 88, 94-95, 110, 111-14, 117-18, 131, 152, 194-95, nn. 3-5
Break of Day, 7, 17-18, 21, 79-81, 86-115, 117-120, 121, 147, 198, n. 23
Brooks, Peter, 24, 35

C
Cash, Rosanne, 185, n. 25
The Cat, 122-24
Chambers, Ross, 23-24, 30-31, 187, n. 4
Chéri, 7, 18, 21, 121-145
Claudine novels, 7, 17, 21, 37, 52, 58, 64, 66, 68-71, 73, 80-81, 83, 85, 92, 94-95, 121-24, 192, n. 5, 193, n. 7, 195, n. 7, 198, n. 21
Claudine at School, 20-21, 68
Claudine Married, 71, 80, 92
Cocteau, Jean, 186, n. 40
Colette, Adèle-Eugénie-Sidonie Landoy, 19-21. For the character 'Sido' based on Colette's mother, see also the first three chapters, where she is mentioned on almost every page.
Colette, Jules Joseph, 20. *See also* Father Figure.

D
De Certeau, Michel, 23, 25-27, 38
De Jouvenel, Henry, 9, 21-22
De Jouvenel, Colette-Renée ("Bel-Gazou"), 21-22
Desire, 17, 69, 75-80, 86, 92, 95-97, 103-05, 108-09, 113-19, 131, 165, 190, n. 15
Discourse, theory of, 13-14
Duo, 122-24

F
Father Figure, 16, 45-49, 58-61, 83, 86, 89-90, 111-12
Flieger, Jerry A., 10-12, 111, 158-59, 183, n. 18
Foucault, Michel, 13-15, 46, 201, n. 4
Freud, Sigmund, 69

G
Gauthier-Villars, Henry, 20-21, 61. See also 'Willy'.
Gender, theory of, 26, 75-80, 122-25, 140, 144-45, 147-48, 181, n. 4
Gigi, 33, 38
Giraudoux, Jean, 186, n. 40
Goudeket, Maurice, 22

H
Huffer, Lynne, 12, 17, 79

I
The Innocent Libertine, 23, 190, n. 15

INDEX

J
Julie de Carneilhan, 122-23
'Juliette,' 16, 27-36, 43, 47-48, 50, 86-88, 153, 189, n. 7, 190, n. 15

K
Kristeva, Julia, 15-16, 53, 55, 174, 179

L
Ladies of Llangollen, 157-61, 173, 175, 177
Last of Chéri, 122-23, 126-27, 144, 198, n. 5, 200, n. 13
Lejeune, Philippe, 7-8, 184, nn. 20 and 22

M
Marks, Elaine, 2, 11, 192, n. 5, 198, n. 2, 199, n. 7
Missy (Marquise de Belbeuf), 21
Mitsou, 122-23, 125
Moreno, Marguerite, 164-66, 170
My Apprenticeships, 1, 7, 17, 21, 36, 51-52, 61-68, 92-93, 121, 150
My Mother's House, 7, 16-17, 21, 27-50, 52-58, 72-73, 79-80, 82-84, 86, 91, 174

N
Norell, Donna, 6, 185, n. 31

O
The Other One, 122-24, 203, n. 22

P
Polaire, 37
Postmodernism, 5
Proust, Marcel, 6
Psyche myth, 79, 94
The Pure and the Impure, 7, 18, 21, 147-78, 179-80

R
Rabinow, Paul, 13-14
Reading, theory of, 16, 23-31, 130, 190, n. 15
Retreat from Love, 80, 195, n. 7
The Ripening Seed, 122, 123, 198, n. 3
Romanticism, 4
Rousseau, Jean-Jacques, 3-4

S
Said, Edward, 189, n. 7
Sarde, Michèle, 1, 11, 185, n. 25
Selfhood, theory of, 1-5, 75-80, 85, 90, 93, 95-96, 114, 117, 123, 125, 129-30, 132, 136-38, 140, 142, 144-45, androgynous selfhood, 147-78, masochism as immature selfhood, 63, 69-70, selfhood and writing, 82, 86
Sido, 7, 17, 21, 58-60, 72, 73, 79-80, 82-86, 90-91, 97-98, 100-01, 111, 117

T
Taylor, Charles, 2-6, 79, 82
Tendrils of the Vine, 21, 148, 161
Le Toutounier, 122-23, 196, n. 11

V
The Vagabond, 21, 81-82, 198, n. 1
Valéry, Paul, 186, n. 40
Vivien, Renée, 153-57, 159-60, 173, 201, n. 7, 202, n. 14

W
'Willy,' 17, 37, 58-61 64-65, 81, 95

Z
Zola, Emile, 46-48, 191, n. 22